SPORTS MEDIA RIGHTS IN THE AGE OF STREAMING AND PLATFORMISATION

Against a backdrop of increased online distribution of media, this book provides an in-depth analysis of how the platformisation of television is both shaping and being shaped by the changing sports media market.

Beginning by looking at the business models and strategies of the major stakeholders involved in the 'sports broadcasting value chain', the authors go on to focus on the challenges and opportunities posed by the growth of over-the-top (OTT) delivery for the regulation of sports broadcasting in several key areas, including copyright law and piracy; competition issues linked to the buying, selling, and distribution of premium sports content; and legislation designed to safeguard coverage of certain national and international sporting events for free-to-air television. Key areas of continuity, such as the persistence of national/regional markets; the importance attached to premium sports rights by rival delivery platforms as a source of 'market power'; and the need to update key areas of policy and regulation in order to address challenges posed by the use of OTT delivery, are also discussed. This book makes use of a range of international and regional examples and case studies, not least the Olympic Games and the FIFA World Cup, and identifies different strategies employed in the buying, selling, and distribution of sports rights for all major parties in the sports media value chain, including new-entrant OTT players, traditional pay-tv operators, public service broadcasters, and a range of international sports organisations.

Providing a complete assessment of the relevance and future effectiveness of key areas of policy and regulation in sports media distribution, this book is recommended reading for advanced students and researchers of Sports Media, Sports Management, and Media Industries.

Tom Evens is Associate Professor of Media Industries at Ghent University, Belgium and a senior researcher at imec-mict. He specialises in the political economy of digital media markets. He is the author of *The Political Economy of Television Sports Rights* (Palgrave, 2013, with Petros Iosifidis and Paul Smith) and *Platform Power and Policy in Transforming Television Markets* (Springer, 2018, with Karen Donders).

Paul Smith is Associate Professor of Media and Communication at the Leicester Media School, De Montfort University, Leicester, United Kingdom. He has published widely on sports rights, including a previous book (with Petros Iosifidis and Tom Evens): *The Political Economy of Television Sports Rights* (Palgrave, 2013). He is also author (with Vincent Campbell) of *The British Media Industries: An Introduction* (Routledge, 2023).

SPORTS MEDIA RIGHTS IN THE AGE OF STREAMING AND PLATFORMISATION

Tom Evens and Paul Smith

Routledge
Taylor & Francis Group
LONDON AND NEW YORK

Designed cover image: mel-nik/iStock via Getty images

First published 2025
by Routledge
4 Park Square, Milton Park, Abingdon, Oxon OX14 4RN

and by Routledge
605 Third Avenue, New York, NY 10158

Routledge is an imprint of the Taylor & Francis Group, an informa business

British Library Cataloguing in Publication Data
A catalogue record for this book is available from the British Library

Library of Congress Cataloging-in-Publication Data
A catalog record has been requested for this book

ISBN: 9781032513911 (hbk)
ISBN: 9781032513928 (pbk)
ISBN: 9781003401988 (ebk)

DOI: 10.4324/9781003401988

Typeset in Galliard
by Taylor & Francis Books

CONTENTS

ILLUSTRATIONS

Figure

Tables

Boxes

INTRODUCTION

The Rise of Sports Streaming and the Evolution of the Sports Rights Market

In 2009, a UK government–commissioned independent review of sports broadcasting confidently declared that 'the long predicted market in internet sports rights has not so far materialised' (Davies, 2009, p.11). The same pronouncement could not be made today. In the UK and beyond, a defining feature of the contemporary sports media market is the growing use of the internet to deliver live (and non-live) sports content to viewers online, over-the-top (OTT) (Hutchins et al., 2019; Smith, 2019). Perhaps most notably, the last decade has witnessed a host of new entrants to the sports rights market, such as Amazon and DAZN, who have invested enormous sums to acquire the rights to cover major sports events and attract subscribers to their online platforms. For example, in 2021, in the US, Amazon agreed a ten-year deal with the NFL (American football) to show 'Thursday Night Football' matches at a cost of around $1 billion per year (Bassam, 2021). Just as significantly, if not more, since its launch in 2016, the emergence of the dedicated sports streaming platform, DAZN, has been a 'major disruptive force in the sports rights market' (Ampere Analysis, 2023, p.16). Part of the Access Industries holding company and backed by the billionaire Len Blavatnik, DAZN has acquired premium sports rights in various national markets, including top-tier domestic football rights in Italy and Germany. By 2022, DAZN was estimated to be spending over $2.5 billion per year on rights and, at least partly as a result, it is seen to symbolise the establishment of streaming as a key feature of the sports rights market (Ampere Analysis, 2023, p.17).

The growing use of the internet to deliver sports content is, of course, part of wider technological and economic developments that are reshaping the

DOI: 10.4324/9781003401988-1

nature of the television industry as a whole. Over the last decade, internet-distributed television has effectively abolished the longstanding monopoly over distribution previously enjoyed by traditional (terrestrial, satellite, and/or cable) broadcasters, which, in turn, has facilitated new modes of delivery and business models (Lobato and Lotz, 2021). Most significantly, the television industry is increasingly characterised by 'platformisation', with a range of different delivery platforms (e.g. Netflix, Disney+, BBC iPlayer) playing an ever more active role in the financing, production, aggregation, and/or distribution of audio-visual content (Evens and Donders, 2018). At the same time, however, sport possesses certain characteristics (e.g. unpredictability, the importance of live viewing, highly distinct national/regional markets, and the intense commitment of sports fans) (Smith, 2021), which, taken together, make it a unique form of content. These features have long underpinned the strategic value of sports rights as a source of market power within pay-tv and wider communications markets. Since around the 1990s, pay-tv and/or telecoms operators around the world have used the acquisition of exclusive rights to sports events and competitions as a key means to attract (and retain) subscribers (Smith et al., 2016). Furthermore, established pay-tv broadcasters, such as Sky and ESPN, as well as public service media organisations, like the BBC, remain just as reliant as ever on live sport to retain audiences for their traditional broadcast services, as well as to attract users to their (relatively) new online platforms. For example, in 2022, in the UK, Sky spent around £2 billion on sports rights, making it by far the biggest spender in the UK sports rights market (Ampere Analysis, 2022, p.20).

The growing demand for sports rights over the last few decades has, in turn, led to a rapid escalation in the value of rights, particularly for premium competitions, such as the NFL (US), English Premier League football, and Indian Premier League (IPL) cricket (Evens et al., 2013). Consequently, leading sports organisations have become increasingly reliant on the sale of media rights for a significant proportion of their total income. It is not uncommon, for example, for leading English Premier League football clubs to generate more than half of their total revenue from the sale of media rights (see Box 2.2). In this context, top-level sports organisations increasingly think of themselves as media companies. As put by the Spanish football giant Real Madrid's global head of digital, Rafael de los Santos, 'we're a football club; we dedicate our activity to football, but in reality what we are is a content company' (Joseph, 2017). With this type of mindset, sports organisations have been keen to explore the potential opportunities offered by online delivery. At the very least, many sports organisations have looked to exploit increased competition for their rights and, in some cases, have even introduced new ways of packaging and selling rights specifically designed to appeal to new entrants (e.g. rights for one-off play-off matches in the NFL; 'match of the day' evening sessions for French Open tennis, etc.). Other sports organisations, such as Formula One, have also looked to develop direct relationships with their fans through the launch of direct-to-fan (D2F) video-on-demand (VoD) services, which, in most cases, look to complement, rather than replace, existing rights deals with pay-tv broadcasters by, for example, offering recorded and/or additional supporting content (e.g. behind-the-scenes footage) (see Chapter 5).

This book provides an in-depth analysis of how the rise of streaming and the platformisation of the television industry are shaping the contemporary sports rights market and vice versa. A key theme that runs through the book is that while the sports rights market is certainly changing (e.g. new entrants, potential for increased vertical integration, etc.) this process is best understood as an evolution of the traditional sports broadcasting rights market, rather than a wholesale revolution. More specifically, for some time, it has been the case that the 'traditional term sports broadcasting' no longer reflects a 'market reality' where, as well as a traditional television set, consumers 'increasingly use a range of internet-connected devices to watch sports: via PC, tablet, [smartphones, and smart TVs]' (Asser Institute, 2014, p.62). In this context, it makes more sense to refer to 'sports media rights', a term that 'encompasses the rights to transmit audio-visual material across all transmission techniques' (Asser Institute, 2014, p.62). At the same time, however, the sports media rights market continues to be defined by key aspects from the era of sports broadcasting, including: the concentration of commercial value in live rights; the persistence of national/regional markets; and the importance attached to premium sports rights by rival delivery platforms as a source of market power.

The interplay between elements of continuity and change is also evident in the challenges (and opportunities) posed by the growth of online delivery for the regulation of the sports rights market in several key areas, namely: copyright law and online piracy; competition issues linked to the buying, selling, and distribution of premium sports content; and legislation designed to safeguard coverage of certain national and international sporting events (e.g. the Olympic Games or the FIFA World Cup) for free-to-air television, commonly known as major events or anti-siphoning legislation. Tackling the rise of online sports piracy is obviously a new challenge for policy makers and regulators, but even here there are clear elements of continuity with the traditional sports broadcasting market. For example, patterns of sports piracy largely reflect established national sporting traditions/preferences. Similarly, the fragmentation of rights between different media organisations (and/or viewing platforms) that exacerbates levels of piracy is a trend that can be traced back to the regulation of pay-tv during the 2000s and 2010s (see Chapters 6 and 8). With regard to competition regulation and major events legislation, the underlying objectives remain largely unaltered. Here, the challenge for policy makers and regulators is to update existing legislation and/or regulatory approaches to ensure it remains (or becomes more) effective in a new technological and market context.

Objectives and Structure

In summary, the main objectives of the book are to:

- Highlight key trends (change and continuity) in the sports media rights market and the role of sports content in the wider platformisation of the television industry.
- Analyse the different strategies employed in the buying, selling, and distribution of sports rights by the major players in the sports media value chain, including: new digital entrants (e.g. Amazon); traditional pay-tv broadcasters (e.g. Sky); public service broadcasters (e.g. BBC); and a range of international (e.g. Formula One) and national (e.g. NFL) sports organisations.
- Assess the relevance and effectiveness of key areas of policy and regulation, namely copyright law, competition policy, and major events legislation.
- Illustrate all of the above with a range of different national examples and case studies.

The book is divided into three main parts. Part 1 consists of two chapters that, taken together, provide an overview of some of the key elements of change (Chapter 1) and continuity (Chapter 2) that are shaping the contemporary sports media rights market. Chapter 1 details the platformisation of the television industry and highlights some of the key ways that this trend has impacted the sports rights market, most notably the role of sports content in the so-called 'streaming wars' between competing media organisations/platforms. Chapter 2 details the continued relevance of the underlying economic characteristics of the sports rights market, including the importance of live content and national/regional markets. It also provides a brief historical overview of the development of the sports rights market, with particular reference to changes within the wider television industry.

The three chapters that make up Part 2 of the book focus, in turn, on the different rights strategies of key players in the sports media rights market. Chapter 3 analyses the rights-buying, bundling, and distribution strategies of commercial media organisations, including: digital new entrants (e.g. Amazon, DAZN); traditional pay-tv broadcasters (e.g. Sky, ESPN); and/or commercial free-to-air broadcasters (e.g. Nine). In contrast, Chapter 4 highlights how public service media (PSM) organisations, such as the BBC, Rai (Italy), and SABC (South Africa), continue to regard sport as a key part of their public service remit. Faced with spiralling rights fees and reduced budgets, this chapter examines the different rights-buying strategies adopted by PSM, most notably an increased focus on acquiring the rights for minority and/or traditionally under-represented sports, particularly women's sport. Chapter 5 focuses on the sports media rights market from the perspective of sports organisations. Using a range of international (e.g. Formula One) and national (the English Premier League) sports organisations as examples/case studies, this chapter examines the various approaches being adopted by sports organisations to the sale and distribution of their media rights, including the establishment (or not) of D2F online platforms.

Part 3 of the book focuses on key areas of policy and regulation related to the contemporary sports media rights market. Chapter 6 highlights how in the age of streaming online sports piracy has become ubiquitous. It details the various legal measures that media and/or sports organisations have employed in an attempt to tackle sports piracy, as well as how the growing cost of accessing coverage of live sport, which is at least in part due to the fragmentation of rights across various platforms, is fuelling the problem. Chapter 7 provides an overview of the application of competition law to the buying and selling of sports media rights. Most significantly, this chapter details how competition law remains as important as ever in order to prevent a handful of global media corporations from using control of premium sports rights to dominate national pay-tv markets. The final substantive chapter of the book, Chapter 8, highlights the continued relevance of major events legislation as a means to ensure major sports events/competitions remain available to access via free-to-air television. Focusing on recent government-led reviews in the UK and Australia, this chapter details how in both countries the scope of major events legislation has been extended to prevent streaming services from securing the exclusive live rights to listed events.

Finally, it is worth noting that this book is truly international in its scope and ambition. To understand key developments in the contemporary sports media rights market the book makes use of a range of national and regional examples and/or case studies. Particular attention is given to the largest and/or most valuable national markets, including the US, the UK, Australia, India, and South Africa, as well as other regional markets in Europe (e.g. Nordics) and beyond (e.g. MENA). At least partly as a result, the book also draws on examples linked to a variety of different sports, including premium sports in certain national markets (e.g. football in Europe, cricket in India, etc.), and minority sports across numerous markets (e.g. Formula One, tennis).

References

Ampere Analysis (2022). *Trends and Dynamics in the Sports Broadcasting Sector – Abridged Report for Ofcom.* Available at: https://www.ofcom.org.uk/__data/assets/pdf_file/0019/240553/Ampere-abridged-report.pdf (Accessed: 1 May 2024).

Ampere Analysis (2023). *The Role of Sports in the Global Streaming Wars.* Available at: https://www.ampereanalysis.com/report/the-role-of-sports-in-the-streaming-wars (Accessed: 4 February 2023).

Asser Institute (2014). *Study on Sports Organisers' Rights in the European Union. Final Report for the European Union.* Available at: https://op.europa.eu/en/p

ublication-detail/-/publication/138eb928-2981-11e7-ab65-01aa75ed71a1/langu age-en/format-PDF/source-233927641 (Accessed: 5 September 2023).

Bassam, T. (2021). 'The NFL's new broadcast rights deals: Billions of dollars, evolving contracts and streaming plans', *SportsProMedia*, 23 March. Available at: https://www.sportspromedia.com/insights/analysis/nfl-tv-rights-2021-2032-espn-abc-disney-nbc-cbs-fox-amazon-prime-streaming/ (Accessed: 3 June 2024).

Davies, D. (2009). *Review of Free-to-air Listed Events. Report by the Independent Advisory Panel to the Secretary of State for Culture, Media and Sport.* London: DCMS. Available at: http://webarchive.nationalarchives.gov.uk/+/http:/www.culture.gov.uk/images/consultations/independentpanelreport-to-SoS-Free-to-air-Nov2009.pdf (Accessed: 2 June 2024).

Evens, T. and Donders, K. (2018). *Platform Power and Policy in Transforming Television Markets.* London: Palgrave Macmillan.

Evens, T., Iosifidis, P., and Smith, P. (2013). *The Political Economy of Television Sports Rights.* Basingstoke: Palgrave Macmillan.

Hutchins, B., Li, B., and Rowe, D. (2019). Over-the-top Sport: Live Streaming Services, Changing Coverage Rights Markets and the Growth of Media Sport Portals. *Media, Culture & Society*, 41 (7), pp. 975–994.

Joseph, S. (2017). '"In reality, we are a content company": Football clubs embrace the role of digital publisher', *Digiday*, 12 June. Available at: https://digiday.com/marketing/reality-content-company-football-clubs-embrace-role-digital-publisher/ (Accessed: 1 June 2024).

Lobato, R. and Lotz, A. D. (2021). Beyond Streaming Wars: Rethinking Competition in Video Services. *Media Industries Journal*, 8 (1), pp. 89–108.

Smith, P. (2019). A Whole New Ball Game? The Changing European Sports Rights Marketplace. In: G. Armfield, J. McGuire, and A. Earnheardt (eds.), *ESPN and the Changing Sports Media Marketplace* (pp. 39–56). New York: Peter Lang.

Smith, P. (2021). Sports Rights: Global Content, National Markets, and Regulatory Issues. In: P. McDonald (ed.), *The Routledge Companion to Media Industries* (pp. 413–423). London: Routledge.

Smith, P., Evens, T., and Iosifidis, P. (2016). The Next Big Match: Convergence, Competition and Sports Media Rights. *European Journal of Communication*, 31 (5), pp. 536–550.

PART 1

Change and Continuity in the Sports Media Rights Market

1

THE PLATFORMISATION OF SPORTS MEDIA RIGHTS

The platformisation of the media industries impacts the production, distribution, and consumption of audio-visual content, increasingly including sports programming. Sports media rights have begun to play a decisive role in the competition between streaming platforms. Although pay-tv operators and free-to-air broadcasters remain by far the main buyers of sports rights, internet-distributed television has broken down the almost monopolistic control of premium sports by traditional providers of subscription-funded television services. As a result of this platformisation, the industry is in flux: while pay-tv operators and free-to-air broadcasters are considering how to preserve their status as incumbents, new entrants including dedicated streaming platforms and Big Tech conglomerates are making inroads into the business of live sports. The goal of this chapter is to provide an overall introduction to what is going on in the contemporary sports rights market and to relate these issues with developments in the wider audio-visual industry. What is happening in the sports rights market can thus not be isolated from the macro-trends currently affecting the media industries. First, this chapter introduces platformisation as part of a fundamental transformation of the audio-visual value chain, and elaborates on its potential effects on competition. It then outlines the role of live sports against the background of this wider trend of streamification and platformisation. Specifically, this chapter identifies five different types of sport streaming platforms that are competing in this high-stakes game and examines the incentives of these different players to invest heavily in premium sports. Although the term 'streaming wars' is often used as a catch-all description for competition between all online video services, there is, in reality, much diversity between streaming platforms. Finally, the chapter addresses key challenges platforms face in this streamification of sports. First, the fragmentation of sports rights creates an

DOI: 10.4324/9781003401988-3

overcrowded marketplace, leading to consumer frustration and subscription fatigue. Second, the business model of sports streaming is still to be proven. Third, the streamification of sport increases the prevalence and scope of illegal distribution and online piracy. Fourth, sports streaming faces critical infrastructural problems, such as buffering, bandwidth limitations, and scalability, that impede a real-live experience.

Platformisation of the Audio-Visual Industry

The platformisation of the audio-visual industry is one of the most transformative developments affecting the production, distribution, and consumption of audio-visual content (Evens and Donders, 2018). This development entails the rise of the platform, not only as a digital infrastructure, but also as the dominant business model in the industry (Nieborg and Poell, 2018). The breakthrough of internet-distributed television has enabled the rise of platforms, or portals, as crucial intermediary services that distribute television-like programming via internet protocol technologies (Lotz, 2017). For decades, pay-tv services carried by cable and satellite operators have had the privilege of providing subscription-based access to television programming. Internet-distributed television has, however, broken the traditional audio-visual value chain and eliminated, or at least eroded, the distribution bottleneck. The abundance of broadband capacity has produced incentives for content producers, franchise owners, television broadcasters, and new entrants, such as Netflix and DAZN, to bypass legacy pay-tv services and to develop a direct relationship with viewers. Traditional delivery systems (cable, satellite, terrestrial) are no longer essential to getting programmes distributed to viewers: literally almost every player, from Disney to Red Bull to TikTok and Samsung, potentially becomes an intermediary and service operator able to connect with audiences more directly and monetise its content to viewers.

This form of industrial upgrading enables content producers, aggregators, and brands to establish themselves as new intermediaries, derive greater control of production and distribution, and have greater control over how their brand is presented and commercialised to the audience. Platformisation signals the rise of direct-to-consumer (D2C) business models that allow producers, aggregators, and brands to sell directly to end-customers rather than selling rights through retailers (Wichmann et al., 2022). This form of disintermediation causes disruption in the value chain and puts the privileged position of pay-tv operators under pressure, accelerating, or at least enhancing, the speed of cord-cutting (i.e. cancelling pay-tv subscriptions) among pay-tv consumers. In the US, the share of households without a traditional pay-tv subscription is increasing quickly to about 70 per cent in 2024, leading to a declined audience reach of sports and other premium cable channels. Well-known brands such as ESPN, CNN, or HBO have therefore launched D2C services, often as an extension of their traditional offering – hence the use of Plus and Max in many of the brand names of streaming services – but they may also envisage a replacement of their parent branded services in the not-too-distant future. D2C offerings go together with datafication so that brands can collect valuable data about customers, better understand their drivers and interests, increase audience engagement, possibly provide tailored offerings, and explore opportunities for meaningful new media experiences and monetisation. D2C business models allow media organisations to build a diversified set of revenue streams that may include subscriptions, advertising, sponsorships, merchandising, ticketing, and betting on top of traditional carriage fees generated by linear channels.

Disruption in the value chain may lead to the blurring of distinctions between producers and distributors, and ultimately drive further consolidation in the audio-visual industry. Platformisation brings about a reshuffling of industrial structures and media ownership, leading to new forms of integration, cooperation, and alliances (Evens, 2010). The value chain is in flux with industrial roles being redefined and media organisations bringing multiple roles under the same brand/s. More specifically, the production–service–distribution combination has become a popular model in recent years. Following the success of streaming platforms, pay-tv operators have integrated backwards to secure access to content production, which is needed to differentiate themselves from competing offerings and drive subscriptions in a maturing market. The disintegration between AT&T and Time Warner in 2021, only five years after its $85 billion merger, shows, however, this form of vertical integration is not automatically a match made in heaven. As the number of streaming platforms is growing and consumer growth slowing down, platforms are collaborating with pay-tv operators, who integrate third-party services into their bundles, put them on their set-top box, or add them to mobile and broadband packages. In addition to vertical alliances, platformisation drives players to build the scale needed to compete in an intensely competitive market. Horizontal integration may lead to platforms joining forces, benefiting from synergies, and creating a more powerful position to provide the most attractive offering. Warner Bros. Discovery, for example, was formed after Warner Media and Discovery merged, in 2022, to create an effective competitor to Netflix and Disney+. Platformisation thus accelerates the ongoing concentration of economic power in the hands of a few super-platforms, possibly surrounded by a series of providers of niche and local content services. Scale advantages, fuelled by demand-side network effects, will drive the growth of platform empires that operate on a wide, if not global, level (Chalaby, 2023; Evens and Donders, 2018).

As a result of this 'platform mania', the audio-visual industry has become populated with numerous platform 'wannabes' that are all competing for control and leadership of the audio-visual ecosystem, and to become the go-to platform for viewers. This requires television broadcast and pay-tv companies to build platform capacity to stay ahead in this platform competition.

Evens and Donders (2018, pp.246–254) identified the sources of structural power that help platforms to defend their market position and sustain platform rivalry. First, a high volume of attractive, and preferably exclusive content at a reasonable price is a critical component of a media platform's value proposition and a vital means to differentiate a platform from competing offerings. Second, platforms are seeking to enlarge their scale, increase market share quickly, and attract as many customers as possible. Global platforms, such as Amazon, benefit from network effects when they can pull in their installed base to enter new markets and offer their services at below-cost price to grow market share. Third, platforms depend on providers of connectivity and distribution, who decide on the terms of access to the network. Such gatekeepers include providers of broadband access, but also cloud computing vendors, content delivery networks, app stores, and device manufacturers. Fourth, platform competition is driven by an excessive level of capital intensity and therefore takes the form of a 'balance war': platforms with the deepest pockets are in the best position and can attack or purchase rivals in an attempt to drive them out of the market. Because platform markets tend to show winner-take-most characteristics, many platforms sacrifice long-term financial sustainability for short-term market share and subscriber growth.

Streaming Wars: The Fight for Viewers

As media organisations look to establish themselves in the platform era, competition in the video streaming market has been heating up. This has given rise to the so-called 'streaming wars', a term coined in the late 2010s to discuss a new era of competition between video streaming services. Although this transition to streaming has been termed the 'post-broadcast' (Turner and Tay, 2009), 'post-network' (Lotz, 2014), or 'post-TV' (Strangelove, 2015) era, the notion of streaming wars wrongly suggests the end of television broadcasting, or live television, altogether. Streaming services add to the complexity of today's media-rich, high-choice multiplatform environment in which television broadcasting, pay-tv, and streaming video coexist and complement, rather than replace one another. Following Lotz (2014), streaming technology is not a replacement medium, but has emerged as a new mechanism of distribution. Those that have predicted the death of television overlooked that television is a medium, which is distributed by foundational delivery infrastructure such as terrestrial networks, direct-to-home satellite, cable wires, or internet protocol, via either fixed or cellular networks. Streaming technology, which uses the internet protocol as an underlying infrastructure, is not a medium, but brings about new modes of distribution, more personalised viewing experiences, and revenue models that are uncommon for traditional television broadcasting. But that does not automatically mean that television broadcasters and other legacy media companies, or live television as a medium and business model, are doomed to disappear in the streaming era.

Television broadcasters and pay-tv operators, and media companies from other stages of the audio-visual value chain, have responded – many of them are still in this ongoing process of responding – to the changing market conditions and consumer preferences, and have adjusted to the different 'logics' of video streaming (Herbert et al., 2019; Sundet and Colbjørnsen, 2021). Incumbent pay-tv operators have recognised viewers' demand for greater flexibility when it comes to audio-visual consumption and subscription modes. Mainly as an attempt to preserve their position as the first touchpoint for viewers, pay-tv operators have increasingly integrated online offerings into their portfolios and even launched stand-alone services marketed separately from the lucrative bundle of broadband connectivity, telephony, and data services (e.g. triple and quadruple play). Some of these platforms are provided for free to authenticated subscribers, who can then watch their favourite channels without a traditional TV set. Other services are marketed as skinny bundles of channels complemented by on-demand content, and may win back cord-cutters who left the often costly and large pay-tv bundles that contain channels viewers may not watch but have to pay for. In some cases, pay-tv operators function as a hub providing access to other streaming platforms. Broadcasters, too, have jumped on the streaming bandwagon to offer their programming in live-streaming (simulcast) and/or on-demand (catch-up) mode. Either commercialised with advertising or via subscriptions, broadcasters see an opportunity to tap into a pool of new, often younger, viewers that are hard to reach and also provide more flexibility to existing viewers. The rise of FAST (Free Ad-supported Streaming Television) brings the linear experience into streaming without paying for any subscription. Furthermore, broadcasters are also launching, often as part of joint ventures, subscription-based services, such as BritBox, Videoland, and Streamz, to compete with Netflix. Such a multiscreen strategy allows content distributors to reach a large audience, explore new revenue streams, and become an intermediary, or a platform, themselves (Raats and Evens, 2021; Sundet and Colbjørnsen, 2021).

The streaming era has resulted in a matrix of viewing opportunities, ending up with a massive inventory of choices and platforms that compete for subscribers and/or advertising revenue. The internet offers many legitimate, questionable, and absolutely illegal opportunities to access amateur and professional content, both short-form and long-form productions, via internet protocol distribution infrastructure. Frieden (2014, p.63) distinguishes between three types of alternative sources of television programming enabled by the internet:

1. Access to live television and on-demand programming provided by *incumbent television broadcasters and pay-tv operators* that offer bespoke platforms to viewers via multiple screens and technologies. The

incumbent's involvement may be evident from the platform's brand (BBC iPlayer, ESPN+, HBO Max); other incumbents have launched a fresh brand (e.g. Peacock, Hulu, Stan);

2. Lawful access to live television and on-demand programming provided by *new intermediaries*. Services have emerged from players operating in almost any segment of the value chain, including content producers (Disney+, Lionsgate+), tech giants (YouTube, Amazon Prime Video/ Amazon Channels), social media companies (Facebook, Tencent), and device manufacturers (Apple TV+, Samsung TV+);
3. Illegal, copyright-infringing access to video content via *peer-to-peer file-sharing or remote servers*. BitTorrent is the most common protocol for transferring large files, such as television programmes, series, and movies, and serves as the backbone for illegal streaming platforms that provide access to live television, real-time sports, and streaming catalogues. Piracy websites continue to remain a significant problem for various stakeholders in the audio-visual industry, potentially impacting the value of media and sports franchises (see Chapter 6).

The streaming wars are generally presented as a catch-all term to describe the battle royale between video services. However, Lobato and Lotz (2021, p. 93) rightly argue that 'the category of streaming video is in fact a placeholder for a multiplicity of different services with distinct histories, libraries, and content strategies.' Streaming services differ in terms of the size and variety of their libraries (generalist or specialist). Not all services are automatically interchangeable and compete directly. Streaming services also differ in their revenue source/s, business model, and value to the firm. Separate markets may exist between those services relying on subscriber fees (SVoD, subscription video-on-demand) and those competing for advertising income (AVoD, advertising video-on-demand). Increasingly, services have started to combine different revenue models (HVoD, hybrid video-on-demand). For most firms, streaming services are the core activity or part of a wider set of media activities; for Apple, Amazon, or Alphabet, streaming platforms are only secondary to their larger business objectives. Moreover, some services operate across a large number of countries (multi-territory) whereas other services do not benefit from global scale (national) (Spilker and Colbjørnsen, 2020). Indeed, the industrial logics of the streaming industry are not uniform or coherent (Sanson and Steirer, 2019, p.1218).

Ball (2023) has identified different waves in the streaming wars. Streaming became possible through key innovations in how content was delivered to the audience (access-based competition wave). The streaming wars were initially led by new entrants such as Netflix that took benefit from these innovations to pioneer the business and revolutionise the way video is distributed and commercialised. Gradually, television industry incumbents also entered the streaming business. Because the distribution bottleneck was largely broken, any broadcasting network, movie studio, or content owner was able to launch their service – more often than not, on an international basis. However, ubiquitous distribution resulted in a commodification of access and a competitive environment marked by high rivalry for market share and subscribers. The provision of exclusive, must-have content became a growth driver, with Hulu and Netflix being the pioneers in original series commissioning. Consequently, all streaming services started to commission and produce large slates of original, best-in-class content (series, films, and also sports) to continue to seduce paying customers month after month. This content-based competition wave, however, came with serious costs. The escalation of content spending together with market saturation, growing subscription fatigue, and a high level of customer churn led to a highly unprofitable business model and a margin race to the bottom. The oversupply, and subsequent saturation of content led to a high level of losses and unsustainable business models for many D2C offerings. Hence, during this ongoing wave of platform-based competition, the focus has shifted to profitability and rationalisation, possibly with many platforms exiting the streaming market. Meanwhile, streaming services are building platform capacity, not only to address the complex economics of video streaming, but also to keep on par with the expanding popularity of social media, virtual worlds, and gaming. A rich portfolio of intellectual property and strong brands in video, movies, gaming, and also sports and theme parks may put firms in a unique position to build transmedia entertainment platforms.

The Streamification of Sports

Amidst this platform mania, sports media rights have become a critical aspect of the ongoing 'streamification' of the media industries (Aegidius, 2021; Lindholm, 2019). Streaming platforms are the latest to join the arena for sports rights, with broadcasters and pay-tv operators all contending for viewers. The rivalry between emerging streaming platforms and pre-existing media services has intensified, with each platform vying for top-quality content that helps to differentiate themselves and attract and retain subscribers (Hutchins et al., 2019). As much as television broadcasters and pay-tv operators consider premium sports rights an instrument to grow or maintain their position as significant players in the television industry, streaming services see exclusive sports rights – in addition to original series and movies – as a strategic weapon to win territory in the streaming wars. In the past, sports rights have been used manifoldly to launch new media and entertainment platforms that needed compelling programming to market their services. As DAZN, Amazon Prime Video, ESPN+, and many others have been agreeing expensive sports rights deals, history is showing signs of repeating itself in the streaming era. And, as long as competition continues, the value of sports rights is likely to increase.

Televised sport offers a highly popular form of mass entertainment and has a series of attributes that makes it highly valuable for streaming platforms. Live sport is one of the few genres that consistently attract a large and diverse audience, which allows platforms to charge higher ad rates (Fujak and Frawley, 2016). Since sports create a high level of engagement and emotions with viewers, advertisers are willing to pay higher rates to reach a large, engaged audience. Unlike most other content genres, live sports generally produce real-time engagement from viewers, which creates a sense of community and drives social media engagement and buzz for the platform (Johnson, 2009). Sports are also most often watched in a linear mode, so that viewers are less likely to skip commercials and miss the advertiser's commercial message. In addition to advertising revenue, must-have content, such as premium sports, can help a platform to stand out in a crowded streaming market and drive subscription revenue. Even more, a diversified rights portfolio in terms of type of sports, rather than access to one specific sport, addresses multiple consumer segments and eventually leads to a larger subscriber base. Moreover, sports generate a large volume of content, providing access to regular and recurring events, with seasons and tournaments taking place over several months. This provides platforms with a consistent source of attractive content and revenue over an extended period. Moreover, this 'longevity' of sports content more or less guarantees that subscribers stay loyal to the platform and will not cancel their subscription if they want to keep access to these sporting events. Hence, ownership of sports rights gives streaming platforms a competitive edge.

With the rise of streaming platforms, sports rights owners have additional opportunities to commercialise their product and extract revenue from media rights. An increase in the number of possible buyers does, at least partly, shift value from distribution and aggregation to premium franchises and best-in-class content producers, which drives the overall value of media rights. However, streaming allows rights owners to market their rights in an innovative manner. First, media rights can be split up into different packages, such as in-game or near-live clips, that unlock new market segments and attract buyers that are more price sensitive, or less wealthy. In a similar vein, distinct categories for live rights, such as for broadcasting and digital platforms, and exclusive coverage can be introduced. Second, streaming platforms may provide an avenue to increase international reach and help to grow the popularity of the sport by reaching a global audience. International rights can be attractive for streaming services to acquire content at considerably lower costs than domestic rights and, hence, expand the potential market for sports franchises. Third, streaming delivers sports content to fans without traditional constraints of television, such as limited broadcast times or rigid programme schedules, and needs a huge inventory of content to serve fans all day round. Non-live content, such as documentaries, magazines, historical games, or other behind-the-scenes footage, can be sold too. Fourth, streaming creates chances for sports franchises to launch direct-to-fan (D2F) offerings and build a direct relationship with their fans. In addition to increased advertising and/or subscription revenue, rights owners obtain valuable personal information and behavioural data to understand what consumers want. This data can be used for providing richer fan experiences or monetised via sponsorships (Evans et al., 2019).

Thanks to its relatively low barriers to entry and the opportunistic behaviour of both emerging and incumbent services, the sports streaming landscape has become crowded. As discussed in Part 2 of the book (Chapters 3, 4, and 5), different players may have different incentives to enter the streaming arena and use different tactics to be successful in this industry. Based on these business model differences, Evans et al. (2019) distinguish between five types of sports streaming service operators:

1. For decades, *pay-tv operators and television broadcasters* (both public and private) have been the main buyers of sports rights. In order to address evolving consumer behaviour, incumbents, including beIN, ESPN, and Sky, have launched streaming services, which complement existing pay-tv packages. These services benefit from existing rights deals and scale economics, but need to deal with the danger of possible cannibalisation by lower-priced proprietary or third-party streaming services;
2. Dedicated sports streaming services operated by *pure sports players* provide a full focus on live and/or non-live sports content. Services, such as DAZN and fuboTV, aim to become the 'Netflix of sport' and the prime go-to for sports fans. Although these services can scale up quickly to benefit from international reach, most experience difficulties in building a subscriber base that is large enough to sustain the necessary significant investments in sports rights;
3. Existing *streaming platform operators* have added sports content to diversify their content portfolio, primarily consisting of original series and movies, in an attempt to reach new consumer segments. Netflix and Viaplay have, in varying degrees, acquired a set of rights of live and/or non-live content to complement their existing streaming offerings, but often lack brand association with sports;
4. Big *tech platform companies* have entered the sports rights market, seeing sports content as a means to keep users in their ecosystem and complement their core business. Amazon and Apple are using their streaming services as a flywheel that ultimately generates sales for their core services (e-commerce and devices, respectively). Sports rights acquisition costs are cross-subsidised by revenues from core services;
5. Sports franchises and *rights owners*, such as individual teams, leagues, or associations, are gradually distributing sports content D2F and building a direct relationship with their customers. This allows them to tap into new revenue streams and collect valuable user data. Launching D2F models

may increase a franchise's negotiation power, but can also jeopardise long-standing relationships with traditional buyers of media rights.

Challenges to the Streamification of Sport

The streamification of sports rights is, however, not a straightforward process and comes with a series of serious challenges. First, the fragmentation of rights – especially when packages are sold exclusively to the highest bidder – across a large number of streaming platforms may make it more complicated for fans to get access to coverage of their favourite sport/teams. This situation is not uncommon in several pay-tv markets where different operators were able to secure different packages, and fans were faced with rising expenses because they needed to subscribe to multiple different pay-tv offerings (see Chapter 2). A crowded streaming landscape with different live rights packages dispersed among multiple services leads to a greater hesitancy among consumers to subscribe to additional services (Echauri, 2023). Cost-averse consumers tend to manage costs by cancelling subscriptions, adopting lower-priced tiers, or fleeing to illegal services. Such a myriad of subscriptions brings about complexity and extra costs that may lead to subscription fatigue. Consumers may no longer be able to locate easily the sports content they want to watch and may become frustrated with managing multiple subscriptions. Eventually, this frustration may give rise to cross-service aggregators, or hubs, to help consumers to oversee fragmentation in the market (Peters and Flynn, 2021). Overall, sports rights owners will need to find a difficult balance between developing ways for additional monetisation of their rights and providing a high-class, easily accessible fan experience for consumers.

Second, the long-term business model of sports streaming must still be proven. The streaming wars demand that platforms make substantial investments in must-have content, and these investments often lead to financial losses. In the past, broadcasters and pay-tv operators have struggled with how to make the acquisition of expensive premium sports profitable (see Chapter 2). The same applies to streaming platforms, such as Disney+ and Peacock, even to a greater extent, as these continue to record billions of dollars in annual losses. Diversified platforms, such as Amazon Prime Video and Apple TV+, may be able to cross-subsidise rights expenses with revenue from adjacent businesses, but the viability of dedicated sports streaming services, such as DAZN, remains uncertain. Moreover, it needs to be seen how many subscriptions consumers are willing to hold when streaming services start to increase prices to optimise operating margins (Sun and Zhang, 2021). Because willingness to pay for sports streaming services remains relatively limited, platforms have started to expand ancillary revenue streams from in-game betting, advertising (FAST), and third-party distribution. A healthy sports streaming industry with many possible rights buyers is critical for the further development of the sports rights market.

Third, the streamification of live sports increases the prevalence and scope of illegal distribution of such games (see Chapter 6). Traditional conditional access systems (CAS) and digital rights management (DRM) are simply not effective enough to block digital piracy. Some streams are simply filmed from a computer or television screen using external camera recording or screen recording software, but other streams directly access the original stream, most often pirated from foreign broadcasters based in India, China, Russia, or the US (via High-Definition Multimedia Interface (HDMI) capture devices). The quality of these streams is often low, which makes it difficult to recognise players and follow the game. Moreover, illegal streams are often unreliable and unstable, and may disappear unexpectedly in the middle of a game. Some operators use illegal streaming as an advertising platform, displaying ads via pop-up windows. Others spread malware and enable bot networks, conduct identity theft, or commit credit card fraud. Illegal sports streaming thus comes with costs and risks for users of these services (Hoof, 2016). In addition, digital piracy causes financial damage to all stakeholders involved in sports media, and eventually depresses the economic value of sports rights. Rights owners and media platforms have, therefore, repeatedly teamed up to fight sports streaming piracy.

Fourth, sports streaming services face critical infrastructural problems such as buffering, service interruptions, bandwidth limitations, program crashes, overloaded servers, video compression problems, scalability, and drained batteries (Alexander, 2017; Hutchins et al., 2019). Buffering and latency (at least 30 seconds behind real-time) problems may impede a real-live experience of sports streaming, in contrast to the highly reliable distribution infrastructure of traditional broadcasting that enables fans to enjoy the liveness of sports. Even big tech platforms, such as Amazon and Apple, have experienced outages while offering live sports streams (McCaskill, 2023). Sports streaming services rely on integrated, end-to-end infrastructure, or streaming intermediaries, such as Endeavour and BAMTech, now Disney Streaming – see Box 1.1 – which provide scalable platforms to manage video encoding, interface programming, audience tracking, data analytics, or geolocation services. Streaming services, including D2F models operated by rights owners, highly depend on such intermediaries with the appropriate know-how to build streaming platforms (Secular, 2018).

BOX 1.1 MLB'S FOUNDATIONAL IMPACT ON THE STREAMING INDUSTRY

Major League Baseball (MLB) is generally seen as the first professional sports competition to livestream a regular-season game on the internet. In 2000, club owners founded MLB Advanced Media (MLBAM) to centralise the league's digital rights and ticket sales. The company was capitalised with $120 million, with each of the 30 teams contributing $1 million for four years. MLBAM hired an outside firm to build its digital platforms, but after these failed to work properly, the company decided to self-develop tech capacity and build its own websites. As early as the year 2002, MLB recognised the potential of the internet for livestreaming games via its MLB.tv platform. On 26 August 2002, around 30,000 viewers watched a New York Yankees win over Texas Rangers (10–3) that was broadcast online using RealPlayer, one of the first media players capable of streaming. The video player had the lowest possible resolution (320 × 240 pixels), and struggled with buffering and eventually crashed (Bacharach, 2022). Nevertheless, this first stream would prove to be a significant milestone in the history of media sports. The next year, MLB.tv streamed the entire season: 100,000 subscribers signed up at US$79.95 for a full season package, raising a total revenue of US$80 million. In 2022, MLB.tv celebrated its 20th anniversary with an estimated 3.5 million subscribers, generating $430 million in revenue for MLB (Foster, 2022).

To stress its pioneering role, MLB was the first league to wire its stadiums for high-quality streaming (2005), the first to stream live 720p HD (2009), the first to launch a subscription product to the iPhone (2009) and iPad (2010), the first to stream live games on Roku (2009) and PlayStation 3 (2010), and so on. Meanwhile, MLBAM continued to create a powerful streaming infrastructure that was increasingly solicited by television broadcasters and fellow sports leagues (Bacharach, 2022). In 2006, MLBAM was approached by CBS to stream NCAA March Madness, the annual college basketball tournament, and it would later build streaming infrastructure for, among others, ESPN, HBO, Fox Sports, Eurosport, WWE, PGA Tour, and MLS. This led MLB to spin out its streaming technology business into a separate company, known as BAMTech, with outside investors in 2015. A few months later, NHL announced a six-year deal with BAMTech for the distribution of its streaming service. The deal was worth US$600 million and enabled NHL to acquire a 10 per cent stake in BAMTech. In summer 2016, Disney joined the capital; it increased its ownership to a 75 per cent stake of the company one year later for $1.58 billion. In 2021, Disney purchased the NHL's 10 per cent stake for $350 million and revealed it had acquired the remaining 15 per cent held by MLB for $900 million (Werpin, 2022). BAMTech was renamed Disney Streaming and its infrastructure now underpins the streaming platforms Disney+ and ESPN+. Considering Disney's market leadership and the many streaming services operated by either media companies or sports leagues that are enabled by BAMTech technology, it is fair to conclude that MLBAM has provided a foundational infrastructure for the entire streaming industry, which echoes far beyond the sports industry.

The Elusive Sports Media Consumer

The transition to live sports streaming fits within the wider evolution towards connected viewing, which brings a massive shift in modes of audio-visual consumption. Connected viewing challenges our understanding of how audio-visual media are created, circulated, and consumed (Holt and Sanson, 2014). It relates to a larger trend across the media industries to integrate digital technology and socially networked communication, which directs the flow of entertainment content in new patterns. This produces a viewing experience that provides new forms of user engagement and is more interactive compared with more traditional forms of television. Connected viewing signals a radical move away from the regular TV set: audio-visual content gradually becomes decoupled from a single device, and gets distributed over multiple internet-enabled screens. Because the consumption of audio-visual content is no longer inherently tied to a certain device or platform, media convergence has erased the classic link between a medium, or the channel, and the content that it carries. The common conceptualisation of television consumption, stereotypically consisting of watching a single screen in the living room, surrounded by family members, and confined to a limited number of broadcast networks with scheduled programming, therefore seems out of date for a growing number of media consumers (Evens et al., 2021).

Connected viewing goes together with an increase in the amount of online and mobile viewing, and a decline in live viewing, especially among younger viewing cohorts (Generation Z and Generation Alpha). For many, mobile has become the first screen to use to consume audio-visual content, as well as social media feeds, social videos, games, and text messages. The consumption of streaming video, social media, music, gaming, and other forms of entertainment is becoming highly interconnected. In addition to the rise of streaming services, the change in video viewing behaviour is probably most visible in the decline of traditional pay-tv and the acceleration of cord-cutting. In the ten-year period between 2013 and 2023, the number of pay-tv homes (cable, satellite, and telco) in the US fell from 101 to 67 million. Other regions including Europe and Australia have seen an upsurge in cord-cutting as well. Households are cancelling their pay-tv subscriptions and relying on internet-only television – in most cases, streaming platforms. Other households may wish to keep their basic subscription, but cancel costly channels and packages. Both scenarios have a devastating impact on sports broadcasters, who lose their reach into TV homes, and subsequent income from carriage fees – which are typically the highest for sports channels – and subscription income. These developments led sports channels such as ESPN to launch a D2C version, ESPN+ in this case, to address this loss in pay-tv subscribers. Although ESPN+ has successfully attracted millions of new subscribers, it has not (at least yet) managed to offset ESPN's lost pay-tv revenues (Dixon, 2023).

It goes without saying that these transforming developments affect the sale and distribution of sports media rights. Rights owners have historically placed live games at the core of a sports rights valuation, yet digital platforms create new touchpoints to engage new audiences and expand their reach (Fujak and Frawley, 2022). Live games continue to command by far the highest commercial value, but are increasingly just one component of the sports media consumption mix. Hence, rights owners create incremental value by providing supplementary content rights that address distinct viewing segments or produce new fan experiences (Karg, 2022). Emerging channels and platforms offer plenty of opportunities to monetise embryonic forms of sports media consumption beyond traditional live games, highlights, and near-live clips that include player interviews, analysis, podcasting, fantasy sports, documentaries, and other types of lifestyle and branded content (see Box 1.2). Young media consumers have not lost their interest in sports (e.g. ECA, 2020), but some consider it old-fashioned to watch full-length games on a TV set. They increasingly demand more 'snackable' content that meets changing consumption habits or prefer content genres they are more engaged with. In this context, TikTok and Twitch have become critical channels to appeal to fans that otherwise would have been out of reach for leagues and teams. Social livestreaming services (SLSS), which integrate synchronous two-way communication and real-time video, present an opportunity for sports leagues to reach out to new fans, with both livestreaming and innovative formats (Wymer and Thompson, 2022).

BOX 1.2 REVIVAL OF THE SPORTS DOCUMENTARY

The sports documentary has seen a global revival after streaming services Netflix, Disney+, and Amazon Prime Video brought the genre to a wider audience. Sports documentaries provide fertile ground to present the mythologies, allegories, and narratives of the sports (Rowe, 2004, p.200) and are, therefore, credited with reviving interest in sports that struggle to sell themselves effectively as a media product and lose interest from upcoming generations of sports fans. Sports documentaries distributed via streaming platforms, such as *Drive to Survive* and *The Last Dance*, have proven effective in enlarging the respective sports' fan base and dealing with emerging patterns of video consumption. Documentaries tell engaging stories about the intrigues, rivalries, and friendships behind the scenes, and appeal to the need for lifestyle content among younger audiences and super-fans. Because sports documentaries are often watched by consumers who do not watch live sports, sports franchises have been able to reach a new audience. Even more, documentaries provide an interesting avenue for franchises to commercialise additional rights. For streaming platforms, programming documentaries is much less costly than acquiring rights for live sport. Moreover, sports documentaries prove to be a perfect driver for subscriptions by sports fans.

The sports documentary is, of course, not a new format. The Danish documentary film *A Sunday in Hell* (1976), a chronology of the 1976 Paris–Roubaix bicycle race, is the first well-known case. In 1991, HBO pioneered the genre with *When it Was a Game*, a documentary about the early history of baseball. Over two decades, the premium channel produced all-time classics, ranging from productions about political protests of the 1968 Olympics to the Magic Johnson–Larry Bird rivalry (2010, *Magic & Bird: A Courtship of Rivals*). During that period, two sports documentaries received an Academy Award: *When we Were Kings* (1996, about Muhammad Ali and George Foreman's legendary boxing fight) and *One Day in September* (about terrorist attacks during the 1972 Olympics). In 2009, ESPN challenged HBO's position by launching *30 for 30*, a series of 30 documentaries to celebrate ESPN's 30th anniversary. The series was such a success that they have now featured more than 120 episodes. In addition, ESPN launched a series of *30 for 30 Shorts* that also appeared on the ESPN website. In 2017, ESPN's *O.J.: Made in America*, a five-part documentary series about the life of former NFL star O.J. Simpson, received the Academy Award for Best Documentary Feature (Malitsky, 2014; Smith, 2020).

Sports documentaries received a fresh impetus when streaming platforms started to programme them. In 2016, *All or Nothing: A Season with the Arizona Cardinals* debuted on Amazon Prime Video and won an Emmy Award. The series succeeded with stories about other NFL teams, and later also the New Zealand All Blacks, Manchester City, Arsenal, and Juventus. In 2018, Netflix launched *Sunderland 'Til I Die*, a series documenting the events around English football club Sunderland A.F.C., which received positive reviews from fans (Pratt, 2022). However, sports documentaries did not receive much critical acclaim until *Formula 1: Drive to Survive* came out on Netflix. The series became a global success and had a transformative effect on the F1 viewership and fan base, hence the 'Netflix effect'. The streaming strategy broke F1 away from its older, male audience, and brought a different profile to the sport: younger, affluent, more Hispanic, and white collar. Female viewership has doubled. A substantial share of them started to watch live races after seeing the series. *Drive to Survive* has created another touchpoint for F1 to engage with younger fans, and helps F1 promoter Liberty Media to fuel the sport's popularity in the US. Following growing viewership, the value of the US media rights increased from $5 million (2019–22) to $90 million (2023–26) annually (Brittle, 2022).

Unlike other media generations, the sports media consumption patterns of Generations Z and Alpha are driven by a need for interaction, participation, and personalisation (Nölleke, 2022). Sports organisations have traditionally capitalised on extremely popular franchises including FIFA, Madden, or Fantasy Premier League. More recently, immersive, virtual worlds, such as Fortnite and Roblox, provide additional ways to engage with new audiences, by hosting live games, creating brand awareness, or forging commercial partnerships. Italy's Serie A was the first major soccer league to broadcast a live game in the metaverse, bringing AC Milan's 1–0 victory over Fiorentina to the Nemesis platform in the Middle East and North Africa region (MENA). The region presents fewer obstacles as Serie A has no permanent rights partner there (matches are shown live on YouTube), which allows the league to try and test innovative formats. The league believed that digital platforms were crucial to attract younger demographics in a region where traditional broadcasts have less traction (McCaskill, 2022). The value of the metaverse to sports organisations is still to be determined, and may not yet offer the same immediate opportunities as Twitch or TikTok, but it is certain that immersive technology provides another route to market for rights owners. In the end, the way audiences, especially younger generations, consume media is changing, and sports organisations as well as their media partners need to continue to evolve their commercial strategies.

References

Aegidius, A. L. (2021). The Music Streaming Metaphor and its Underlying Tangle of Transcodes. *Popular Communication*, 19 (1), pp. 42–56.

Alexander, N. (2017). Rage against the Machine: Buffering, Noise, and Perpetual Anxiety in the Age of Connected Viewing. *Cinema Journal*, 56 (2), pp. 1–24.

Bacharach, E. (2022). 'Two decades after MLB.TV pioneered sports streaming, blackout problem persists', *Sports Business Journal*, 29 August. Available at: https://www.sportsbusinessjournal.com/Journal/Issues/2022/08/29/Upfront/Streaming.aspx (Accessed: 4 February 2023).

Ball, M. (2023). *The Streaming Book*. Available at: https://www.thestreamingbook.com/ (Accessed: 4 February 2023).

Brittle, C. (2022). 'Report: F1 signs three-year ESPN US TV rights extension worth up to US$90m a year', *SportsProMedia*, 27 June. Available at: https://www.sportspromedia.com/news/f1-us-tv-rights-deal-espn-disney-comcast-nbc-amazon-netflix-2025/ (Accessed: 27 June 2022).

Chalaby, J. K. (2023). *Television in the Streaming Era: The Global Shift*. Cambridge: Cambridge University Press.

Dixon, C. (2023). 'What ESPN says about the declining traditional TV industry', *nScreenMedia*, 24 January. Available at: https://nscreenmedia.com/espn-declining-pay-tv/ (Accessed: 19 April 2023).

ECA (European Club Association) (2020). *Fan of the Future: Defining Modern Football Fandom*. Available at: https://www.ecaeurope.com/media/4802/eca-fan-of-the-future-defining-modern-football-fandom.pdf (Accessed: 4 February 2023).

Echauri, G. (2023). Digital Subscribers: Between Freedom and Constraint. *Media, Culture & Society*, 45 (6), pp. 1175–1191.

Evans, S., del Valle-Iturriaga, J., Er, B., and Suthagar, R. (2019). *Sports Rights: Not Yet the 'Slam Dunk' for OTTs*. New York: Delta Partners.

Evens, T. (2010). Value Networks and Changing Business Models for the Digital Television Industry. *Journal of Media Business Studies*, 7 (4), pp. 41–58.

Evens, T. and Donders, K. (2018). *Platform Power and Policy in Transforming Television Markets*. London: Palgrave Macmillan.

Evens, T., Henderickx, A., and De Marez, L. (2021). Generation Stream: The Audiovisual Repertoire of Teenagers. *Journal of Broadcasting & Electronic Media*, 65 (2), pp. 185–204.

Foster, J. (2022). 'Fans can have voice in MLB lockout by canceling their MLB.TV subscriptions', *Sporting News*, 2 October. Available at: https://www.sportingnews.com/us/mlb/news/mlb-fans-cancel-mlbtv-subscription-lockout/g4pml31e2nv72gbxzhj5cfeh (Accessed: 3 February 2023).

Frieden, R. (2014). Next Generation Television and the Migration from Channels to Platforms. In: Y.-l. Liu and R. G. Picard (eds.), *Policy and Marketing Strategies for Digital Media* (pp. 60–72). New York: Routledge.

Fujak, H. and Frawley, S. (2016). The Relationship between Television Viewership and Advertising Content in Australian Football Broadcasts. *Communication & Sport*, 4 (1), pp. 82–101.

Fujak, H. and Frawley, S. (2022). Sport Audience Measurement. In: H. Fujak and S. Frawley (eds.), *Sport Broadcasting for Managers* (pp. 20–34). New York: Routledge.

Herbert, D., Lotz, A. D., and Marshall, L. (2019). Approaching Media Industries Comparatively: A Case Study of Streaming. *International Journal of Cultural Studies*, 22 (3), pp. 349–366.

Holt, J. and Sanson, K. (2014). Introduction: Mapping Connections. In: J. Holt and K. Sanson (eds.), *Connected Viewing: Selling, Streaming, & Sharing Media in the Digital Age* (pp. 1–15). New York: Routledge.

Hoof, F. (2016). Live Sports, Piracy and Uncertainty: Understanding Illegal Streaming Aggregation Platforms. In: R. Lobato and J. Meese (eds.), *Geoblocking and Global Video Culture* (pp. 86–93). Amsterdam: Institute of Network Cultures.

Hutchins, B., Li, B., and Rowe, D. (2019). Over-the-top Sport: Live Streaming Services, Changing Coverage Rights Markets and the Growth of Media Sport Portals. *Media, Culture & Society*, 41 (7), pp. 975–994.

Johnson, V. E. (2009). Everything New is Old Again: Sport Television, Innovation, and Tradition for a Multi-Platform Era. In: A. D. Lotz (ed.), *Beyond Prime Time: Television Programming in the Post-Network Era* (pp. 114–137). New York: Routledge.

Karg, A. (2022). Understanding Media Consumers. In: H. Fujak and S. Frawley (eds.), *Sport Broadcasting for Managers* (pp. 118–131). New York: Routledge.

Lindholm, J. (2019). The Netflix-ication of Sports Broadcasting. *The International Sports Law Journal*, 18, pp. 99–101.

Lobato, R. and Lotz, A. D. (2021). Beyond Streaming Wars: Rethinking Competition in Video Services. *Media Industries Journal*, 8 (1), pp. 89–108.

Lotz, A. D. (2014). *The Television Will Be Revolutionized.* New York: New York University Press.

Lotz, A. D. (2017). *Portals: A Treatise on Internet-Distributed Television.* Ann Arbor, MI: Michigan Publishing.

Malitsky, J. (2014). Knowing Sports: The Logic of the Contemporary Sports Documentary. *Journal of Sport History*, 41 (2), pp. 205–214.

McCaskill, S. (2022). 'Serie A broadcasts the first live soccer match in the metaverse', *SportsProMedia*, 3 May. Available at: https://www.sportspromedia.com/technology/emerging-technology/serie-a-live-match-metaverse/ (Accessed: 26 April 2023).

McCaskill, S. (2023). 'Report: Apple TV outage affects MLS coverage as multiview feature enters beta test', *SportsProMedia*, 3 May. Available at: https://www.sportspromedia.com/news/apple-tv-outage-multiview-mls-sport-streaming-tech-canal (Accessed: 18 April 2023).

Nieborg, D. B. and Poell, T. (2018). The Platformization of Cultural Production: Theorizing the Contingent Cultural Commodity. *New Media & Society*, 20 (11), pp. 4275–4292.

Nölleke, D. (2022). Young Audiences' Sports Media Repertoires and Expectations towards Sport Coverage during COVID-19. In: P. Pedersen (ed.), *Research Handbook on Sport and COVID-19* (pp. 99–112). Cheltenham: Edward Elgar.

Peters, J. and Flynn, M. (2021). *Streaming's Next Act: Aggregators to Play a Starring Role in Making Consumers Happier.* Available at: https://www.accenture.com/content/dam/accenture/final/a-com-migration/pdf/pdf-170/accenture-streaming-next-act-report.pdf (Accessed: 4 February 2023).

Pratt, S. (2022). Television Series Review – Sunderland 'Til I Die. *Journal of Tourism Futures*, 8 (1), pp. 138–140.

Raats, T. and Evens, T. (2021). "If you can't beat them, be them". A Critical Analysis of Local Streaming Platform and Netflix Alternative Streamz. *Mediekultur*, 37 (70), pp. 50–65.

Rowe, D. (2004). *Sport, Culture and the Media.* Maidenhead, UK: Open University Press.

Sanson, K. and Steirer, G. (2019). Hulu, Streaming, and the Contemporary Television Ecosystem. *Media, Culture & Society*, 41 (8), pp. 1210–1227.

Secular, S. (2018). Games without Frontiers: Streaming Sports and the Evolution of Digital Intermediaries. *Media Industries Journal*, 5 (2). Available at: https://doi.org/10.3998/mij.15031809.0005.209 (Accessed: 4 February 2023).

Smith, C. (2020). 'Sports documentaries: The real deal', *Sports Business Journal*, 27 April. Available at: https://www.sportsbusinessjournal.com/Journal/Issues/2020/04/27/In-Depth/Sports-docs.aspx (Accessed: 4 February 2023).

Spilker, H. S. and Colbjørnsen, T. (2020). The Dimensions of Streaming: Toward a Typology of an Evolving Concept. *Media, Culture & Society*, 42 (7–8), pp. 1210–1225.

Strangelove, M. (2015). *Post-TV: Piracy, Cord-Cutting, and the Future of Television.* Toronto: University of Toronto Press.

Sun, Y. and Zhang, H. (2021). What Motivates People to Pay for Online Sports Streaming? An Empirical Evaluation of the Revised Technology Acceptance Model. *Frontiers in Psychology*, 12, Article 619314.

Sundet, V. S. and Colbjørnsen, T. (2021). Streaming across Industries: Streaming Logics and Streaming Lore across the Music, Film, Television, and Book Industries. *MediaKultur*, 37 (70), pp. 12–32.

Turner, G. and Tay, J. (2009). *Television Studies after TV: Understanding Television in the Post-Broadcast Era.* New York: Routledge.

Werpin, A. (2022). 'Disney Pays $900M for MLB's Remaining Stake in Streaming Company BAMTech', *Hollywood Reporter*, 29 November. Available at: https://www.hollywoodreporter.com/business/digital/disney-pays-900m-for-bamtech-1235271788/ (Accessed: 4 February 2023).

Wichmann, J. R. K., Wiegand, N., and Reinartz, W. J. (2022). The Platformization of Brands. *Journal of Marketing*, 86 (1), pp. 109–131.

Wymer, S. and Thompson, A.-J. (2022). Broadcast Forms and their Managerial Implications. In: H. Fujak and S. Frawley (eds.), *Sport Broadcasting for Managers* (pp. 103–117). New York: Routledge.

2

THE SPORTS MEDIA RIGHTS MARKET

Economics and History

The commercial value of the contemporary sports media rights market is beyond dispute. In 2022, the total value of the global sports rights market was $55.1 billion and, driven by a host of new deals between streaming services and leading sports organisations, including the NFL (American football, US) and Indian Premier League (IPL; cricket, India), this figure is set to exceed $60 billion by 2024 (SportBusiness, 2022, p.2). The purpose of this chapter is to examine why (free-to-air and pay) television broadcasters and/or streaming services are willing to invest so heavily in the acquisition of sports rights. To this end, the first part of the chapter details the economic characteristics of sports content, namely: the unique value of live sports coverage; the importance of national/regional markets; and the premium value attached to the rights for particularly popular sporting events/competitions (i.e. premium content). The degree to which, if at all, these established characteristics of the sports rights market are being (and are likely to be) challenged by the rise of streaming is also discussed here, as well as in greater depth throughout the rest of the book. Focusing on the buying, selling, and distribution of rights, the second part of the chapter moves on to provide an overview of the functioning of the sports media rights market. This section begins by highlighting how developments in television distribution technology, combined with the 'marketization' of the global media and communications industries (Murdock and Wasko, 2007), have, particularly since around the 1990s, led to increased demand from media organisations for sports rights. However, as is discussed in the final section, the 'double-sided' nature of the sports media rights market means that, paradoxically, increased competition for sports rights does not necessarily benefit consumers. The main argument of this chapter is that the underlying economic characteristics of sports content and the established features of the sports rights market are

DOI: 10.4324/9781003401988-4

as important as ever when it comes to understanding sports media rights in the age of streaming and platformisation.

Key Characteristics of the Sports Media Rights Market

'It's Only Live Once' (Sky Sports, 2021)

The value of the sports rights market is underpinned by the fact that live televised sport offers a highly popular and 'unique form of mass entertainment', due to its explicit telegenic physicality; its innate competitive structure; its nurturing of deep-rooted individual identifications and loyalties; and, perhaps most significantly, its potential for generating visceral excitement created by the uncertainty, real or imagined, surrounding the outcomes of live sporting contests (Andrews, 2003, p.239). Measured in billions, the global television viewing figures for major international sporting competitions, like the Olympic Games and FIFA World Cup football tournaments, are testament to the status of live sport as an enormously popular form of entertainment. According to the International Olympic Committee (IOC), over 3 billion people watched at least some live television coverage of the Tokyo 2020 (postponed to 2021) Summer Olympics (IOC, 2023, p.20). While the final alone of the FIFA (men's) World Cup, Qatar 2022, achieved a global reach of 1.5 billion viewers (FIFA, 2023). In turn, a key defining feature of the sports rights marketplace is that it is the live rights that are by far the most commercially valuable, as distinct from delayed, or highlights coverage. For example, in the UK, the (domestic) live rights for English Premier League football (seasons 2025/26–2028/29) were valued at £6.7 billion, whereas the main highlights package sold for the comparatively low sum of £222 million (Agini and Thomas, 2023).

With the growth of social media, the consumption of highlights and/or short (e.g. 30 seconds) clips has markedly increased over the last decade or so. As put by one commentator, for today's sports fans, 'it has become possible to watch nothing [live], and yet miss nothing' as clips and/or highlights of key moments (e.g. goals, wickets, match points, etc.) are readily available to view for free, and often just minutes after the event, via social media and/or video-sharing platforms (Early, 2016). According to a YouGov survey of 'engaged sports fans' from a host of different countries, around 25 per cent regularly watch 'non-live video content online' and this figure increases to 32 per cent for younger (18–24) fans (YouGov, 2023, p.9). With this trend in mind, some industry analysts have identified clip/highlight rights as a key area of future growth in the sports rights market. For example, sports marketing consultants, *Two Circles*, estimate that, during the mid-2020s, 'in-play clip rights' are set to grow at a rate of 76 per cent and 'short form highlights' by 101 per cent, to reach total global values of $1.7 billion and $3.2 billion, respectively (Advanced Television, 2019). In 2021, similar thinking led

Warner Media's vice president of emerging media and innovation, Peter Scott, to go so far as to predict that 'the evolution of sports rights is going to change' to the point where 'video highlights will be more valuable than live rights' (Dixon, 2020). To date, however, there is little, if any, evidence to support such a dramatic claim. On the contrary, even after some price escalation, the value of highlight and/or clips rights remains dwarfed by live rights, with highlight/clip rights accounting for less than 10 per cent of the total value of the sports rights market. Nevertheless, in the age of streaming highlight/clip rights are still a significant part of the sport rights landscape. This is because, as discussed more in Chapters 3, 4, and 5, for sports and/or media organisations who own live rights, the online distribution of clips and/or highlights via social media and/or video-sharing platforms is often a vital means to promote the visibility of their sport and/or service.

For the television industry, live sport is arguably more important than ever. With television audiences around the world increasingly opting to watch on demand, sport remains one of the few forms of content that most viewers prefer to watch live. Furthermore, watching live sport 'on a [traditional linear] TV channel' is also the most popular way for more than half of sports fans to 'engage with the sports they regularly follow', ahead of watching live via 'a video streaming service' (22 per cent) (YouGov, 2023, p.7). As a result, coverage of live sport continues to provide free-to-air linear television broadcasters throughout the world with a vital means to attract mass audiences. For example, in the US, in 2022, live sport accounted for 94 of the 100 most watched programmes on television, including 99.2 million viewers for NBC's coverage of NFL Super Bowl LVI (Crupi, 2023). In turn, live sport provides a vital source of advertising revenue for commercially funded free-to-air broadcasters. In the US, in 2022, the average cost of a 30-second advertising spot during NFL matches was nearly $600,000 and, across the (2021–22) season as a whole, a total of $4.33 billion was earned by broadcasters from the sale of advertising time during their live coverage of NFL matches (Crupi, 2023).

For traditional (i.e. cable and/or satellite) pay-tv services live sport is equally important. As discussed more below, exclusive live sport has long been the cornerstone of 'bundled' pay-tv services across the world, whereby sport channels are packaged and sold together with other entertainment channels, or services (e.g. broadband access), in order to maximise consumer revenues for both the pay-tv operator and individual channel owners. However, the last decade or so has witnessed growing numbers of consumers opting to cancel their traditional pay-tv bundle in favour of (relatively cheaper) subscriptions to one, or more, subscription video-on-demand (SVoD) providers. This trend is widely referred to within the television industry as 'cord-cutting'. While there is some evidence of cord-cutting in Europe, it has been most prominent in the US, where, during the 2010s, the number of households subscribing to a pay-tv bundle declined from nearly nine in ten to just over half (The Economist, 2021). Over around the same period, the US's largest specialist pay-tv sports channel, ESPN, suffered a similarly dramatic decline in subscribers, from around 100 million in 2011 to 74 million by 2023 (McCaskill, 2023a). Given the enormous investment in original scripted content by SVoDs during the 2010s, it is arguably only the provision of exclusive live sport that has prevented an even steeper decline in pay-tv subscriptions. On this basis, live sport is often seen, in the US largely but to at least some degree in other countries too, as 'the glue' holding the pay-tv bundle together (McCaskill, 2023a). Or even, with the importance of sport for free-to-air broadcasting in mind too, live sport, alongside news, has been described as 'the last defence for linear TV' (Advanced Television, 2023). Whether live sport is able to continue to protect linear television in the US and beyond during the age of streaming will no doubt depend on the buying, selling, and distribution strategies of all the key players in the sports rights market, as is discussed throughout much of the remainder of the book.

Cultural Discount and the Importance of National Markets

To a greater or lesser degree, the international trade in media products, such as films and television programmes, is shaped by 'cultural discount', whereby a product 'rooted in one culture' will often be less appealing elsewhere (Hoskins and Mirus, 1988, p.500). The global sports rights market is no exception. While a number of international sporting mega-events (e.g. the Summer Olympics) have widespread global appeal, for the most part, it is local and/or national teams, athletes, and competitions that are most popular with television audiences. This leads to a second key feature of the contemporary sports rights market, namely that for most, if not quite all, sports organisations the vast majority of revenue raised from the sale of media rights comes from domestic (i.e. national) markets. For example, in the case of European football, only the English Premier League (UK) and Spain's La Liga have sufficient cross-border appeal to generate a major share of their total broadcast revenues from the sale of international rights: 53 and 48 per cent, respectively (UEFA, 2023, p.98). Of the remaining 'big five' European leagues (France, Germany, and Italy), over 80 per cent of their total revenue originates from domestic markets (UEFA, 2023, p.98). For mid-size European leagues, the reliance on domestic rights sales is even greater. The Dutch Eredivisie, for example, raises just 12 per cent of its total rights revenue from international markets. While for many of Europe's smaller leagues, such as the Belgian Pro League, international rights are of such limited value that they are included as part of domestic rights deals, rather than sold separately (UEFA, 2023, p.97). Some sports/competitions, perhaps most notably Grand Slam tennis tournaments and Formula One motor racing, benefit from a degree of popularity across a number of different countries/regions, but even here the value of rights tends to reflect the importance of a small number of key markets where the sport (i.e. Germany, Brazil, Italy, and the UK for Formula One), or a specific competition (e.g. France for the French Open tennis tournament), is particularly popular. In this sense, the global sports rights market is, in fact, a host of different nationally, or regionally, focused markets, reflecting particular national/regional sporting traditions and preferences.

The national/regional focus of the global sports rights market means that the most valuable rights are for those sports/competitions that are popular in the largest and/or richest national television markets, perhaps most notably the NFL in the US. The NFL is by some distance the most valuable sports rights property in the world, with, in 2022, an annual rights value of $8.4 billion, accounting for 15 per cent of all global sports media rights spending, and more than double the value of the second most valuable property, the English Premier League (SportBusiness, 2022, pp.5–6). The leading position of the NFL is largely a product of command over its domestic market, which is by far the richest national sports rights market in the world, accounting for, in 2022, $24.8 billion of global sports rights sales, around five times the size of the next most valuable market, the UK. In 2022, the NFL generated 97 per cent of its total media rights revenue from the rich US domestic market (SportBusiness, 2022, pp.5–6). Paradoxically, the commercial significance of the US market is also illustrated by its importance to non-US-based sports organisations. For example, the English Premier League and Spain's La Liga each generate the lion's share of their international rights revenue from long-term billion-dollar rights deals with US broadcasters, NBC and ESPN, respectively (Germano and Ahmed, 2021; Coster and Pingue, 2021). In much the same way, other large (and rapidly growing) national television markets, such as China and India (see Box 2.1), are also increasingly targeted by a host of different sports organisations looking to grow their international rights revenues. However, a combination of entrenched local sporting preferences and/or wider political factors can make generating significant revenues from these markets a challenge for many, if not quite all, international sports organisations. For example, the status of basketball as China's most popular sport has, since 2015, enabled the NBA to agree successive lucrative rights deals with China's leading sports streaming platform, Tencent (Moore, 2023). However, in 2019, just months after agreeing a record $1.5 billion contract, comments from the general manager of the NBA's Houston Rockets, Daryl Morey, supporting political protests in Hong Kong, led Tencent to temporarily suspend match coverage, as well as attracting widespread criticism of the league in both China (for being critical of the Chinese government) and the US (for prioritising commercial interests over freedom of speech) (Shephered et al., 2019).

There is an inherent tension between the established national/regional contours of the global sports rights market and the globally orientated business models of the (relatively) recently established digital media giants, sometimes known collectively as FAANG (i.e. Meta, formerly Facebook; Amazon; Apple; Netflix; and Alphabet, formerly Google). Since around the early 2000s, the rapid growth of FAANG has been built on utilising the 'economies of scale' and 'network effects' of digital markets, whereby the marginal cost of providing a service to an extra consumer is close to zero and the value of the network to consumers increases as others join (Barwise and Watkins, 2018, pp.24–7). As is discussed in more detail in Chapters 3 and 5, one of the key areas of uncertainty for the sports rights market in the age of streaming is the degree to which, if at all, either FAANG or other media/sports organisations will seek to adopt a global rights deals strategy. To date, there has been little evidence of a concerted shift away from national sports rights contracts, but a handful of rights agreements have adopted a global approach. Most notably, in 2022, Apple agreed a landmark $250 million (minimum) a year, 10-year, global partnership with US-based Major League Soccer (MLS), to show all matches across the world via the Apple TV+ streaming platform (Silvermann and Ourand, 2022). For the most part, however, sports rights contracts remain focused on national/regional markets.

Not All Sports are Equal

Also linked to the national/regional popularity of particular sports and competitions, a third clearly discernible feature of the sports rights market is the disproportionately high value attached to the rights for one sport and/or competition, or at most a handful of them, often referred to as premium content. For example, in most, if not quite all, of Europe and South America, football is by far the most popular sport and accounts for the vast majority of sports rights spending. In the UK, for instance, the two biggest football competitions – the English Premier League and the UEFA Champions League – account for nearly 80 per cent of the total UK sports rights spending (Ampere Analysis, 2022, p.20). In some other countries, such as Australia, sporting preferences are spread a little more evenly between a handful of different sports, which results in slightly less concentrated spending on rights. In Australia, the AFL (Australian Rules Football League), NRL (National Rugby League), and Cricket Australia are each able to command a sizeable share of the domestic sports rights market, with annual rights valued at just over AUS$643 million, AUS$400 million, and AUS$197 million, respectively, although the value of these premium rights still far exceeds those of numerous other sports (Jones, 2021; Dixon, 2022, 2023).

The ability to offer exclusive live coverage of premium sports events/competitions is a highly prized asset within the contemporary television industry. This stems from the fact that for many viewers there are few, if any, acceptable substitutes for being able to watch live coverage of a particular sporting event, team, or competition. For this reason, commercially funded free-to-air television broadcasters, such as Channel Nine (Australia), ITV

(UK), TF1 (France), Globo (Brazil), NBC and Fox (US), and e.TV (South Africa), have long utilised exclusive coverage of live sport to generate mass audiences and attract advertisers (Evens et al., 2013). Just as, if not more, significantly, since around the 1990s, pay-tv broadcasters across the world have, in Rupert Murdoch's much-quoted phrase, used exclusive live sports rights as a 'battering ram' to open up national pay-tv markets (see more below). In the age of streaming, media organisations continue to utilise premium sports rights in order to either attract/retain subscribers and/or maximise revenue from other bundled services (e.g. home shopping, gambling, etc.) (see Chapter 3). Premium sports rights are therefore a key source of market power within national pay-tv and/or wider communications markets.

While most media attention (and academic research) understandably focuses on premium sports rights, the value of other, albeit less popular and commercially valuable, rights properties should not be overlooked. Sometimes referred to as secondary, minority, niche, or lower-tier rights, by definition, such sports and/or competitions have fewer followers, but these fans are often just as, if not more, committed to their sport and as such can be an attractive potential audience for broadcasters and/or streaming services. For example, for public service media organisations, such as the BBC, coverage of relatively niche sports (in the UK), such as swimming and athletics, is an important part of the Corporation's commitment to serve a wide range of audience interests (see Chapter 4). Certain niche sports may also prove valuable to commercially funded television broadcasters due to their ability to attract a particular audience demographic. In Europe, for example, coverage of international rugby by commercial broadcasters, such as TF1 (France) and ITV (UK), tends to increase advertising revenue because of the sport's relatively wealthy fan base (Barker, 2019). For pay-tv services, acquiring rights for various niche sports can be an important part of an overall rights strategy, not least because subscription services require large volumes of content to attract/retain subscribers. Pay-tv services will often look to attract/retain subscribers by providing niche sports alongside premium content, or even aggregating coverage of various niche sports/competitions. For niche sports organisations themselves, demand for their rights can lead to a significant dilemma, namely: revenue versus audience reach (see Chapter 5). A niche sport organisation may well be able to maximise rights revenue by selling to a pay-tv service, but at the expense of wider exposure for both the sport and its commercial sponsors, to audiences that are not already fans of the sport via free-to-air television coverage. In the UK, for example, since the early 2000s, the sale of England cricket rights to pay-tv has prompted ongoing political and public debate (Modha, 2023). With the growth of streaming an additional dimension is added to the established reach versus revenue dilemma, namely how to combine streaming (either via a media organisation, or independently) with traditional (pay and/or free-to-air) television coverage to best optimise revenue/reach.

BOX 2.1 THE INDIAN SPORTS MEDIA RIGHTS MARKET: A GROWING MARKET

For several decades, the Indian television market has been defined by seemingly never-ending growth (Kohli-Khandekar, 2010, p.56). By the early 2020s, the number of television-owning households had increased to over 210 million (around two-thirds of all households), with around 900 million individual viewers, making India the second-largest television market in the world, behind China (BARC, 2020). Facilitated by government deregulation, during the 1990s and 2000s, the growth of the Indian television industry was driven by cable and satellite services, offering access to hundreds of different channels (Athique, 2012). The television market in India continues to grow, but the engine behind most recent growth is online (digital) distribution, particularly via smartphones. In 2022, there were already 750 million smartphone users in India and this number is predicted to reach 1 billion by 2026 (Business Today, 2022). Alongside its sheer scale, a distinct feature of the Indian television market is that, unlike in Western countries, both traditional and online television distribution are still growing and appear some way from saturation point.

India's population of around 1.4 billion people (about 20 per cent of the world's population) is incredibly culturally diverse. However, one of the few things able to unite India is a shared love of cricket. Cricket is by far the most popular sport in India and this is reflected in the country's sports rights market. In 2020, the total annual value of the Indian sports media rights market was estimated to be $1.1 billion, with cricket accounting for 87 per cent of that total (Tewari, 2020). Premium cricket rights have long been a key strategic asset in the Indian television market, with rival broadcasters using exclusive coverage to attract subscribers and/or generate advertising revenue (Evens et al., 2013, pp.152–6). In the era of streaming, rival media organisations, most notably Hot Star (Disney) and Viacom18 (JioCinema/Reliance Industries), continue to rely on the popularity of cricket to underpin their services (see Chapter 3, Box 3.1). A related notable feature of the Indian television market is that revenues are divided fairly equally between subscriptions and advertising, with, in 2021–22, revenues split 57:43 per cent, respectively (TRAI, 2022, p.6). This is partly because average revenue per user (ARPU) for pay-tv is relatively low by international standards, but also because the enormous scale of the Indian market makes free-to-air television particularly attractive for advertisers. In the early 2020s, between 85 and 95 of the 100 most watched broadcasts in India each year were live cricket matches (Bassam, 2021). Furthermore, cricket offers countless natural short breaks in play (new overs, wickets, etc.), which provide perfect opportunities for advertising; not least because the breaks are so short that viewers tend to keep watching. In 2020, the cost of a 10-second advertising spot during IPL cricket coverage was $14,000 (Badale and Hughes, 2020, p.64).

First played in 2008, the IPL has quickly become the premium cricket sports rights property in India. Owned and organised by the Board of Control for

Cricket in India (BCCI), the national governing body of all cricket in India, the IPL is an annual competition using a shortened (20-over) form of the game. The tournament is played between ten teams/franchises (in 2023), which are based in different Indian cities, and features star players from around the world, as well as India itself. In 2023, the IPL consisted of around 70 matches, spread evenly across weekday evenings and weekends between March and May. The tournament reached a record television audience of around 500 million (domestic) viewers and the most popular matches were viewed by audiences of up to 90 million, with around 60 million watching via linear television (Disney+ Hotstar) and 30 million online (JioCinema) (Financial Express, 2023). Given this level of popularity, it is perhaps unsurprising that the value of IPL rights far exceeds that of all other sports properties in India, including other cricket rights. In 2022, the BCCI agreed a record new five-year deal worth $6.2 billion for IPL rights. By contrast, a year later, the BCCI sold the rights for the (home) matches of India's national team(s) for the next five years for the relatively modest sum of $720 million, albeit for far fewer matches (McCaskill, 2023b). Outside India, however, interest in the IPL is very limited, even in other cricket-playing countries, such as England and Australia. As a result, the IPL derives only a tiny fraction of its total rights revenue from international rights sales, with, in 2022, the sale of television and digital rights for the rest of the world accounting for just $135.5 million of the $6.2 billion total rights revenue (Gollapudi, 2022).

Two other sports/competitions register significant levels of interest in India: kabaddi and football. Traditionally played mostly in rural India, kabaddi is a 'tag and tackle'-style sport and has grown in popularity since the IPL inspired the establishment of the Pro Kabaddi League (PKL) in 2014. The PKL is the second most watched league on television in India, after the IPL, with, in 2022, an estimated reach of nearly 400 million viewers (The Economist, 2022). With particularly strong interest in West Bengal, the eight north-eastern states, Kerala, and Goa, football is the third most popular sport in India (Ghosal, 2022). In 2021, television coverage of India's domestic football league, the Indian Super League (ISL), reached around 120 million viewers. However, the rights for the PKL and ISL raise only a tiny fraction of the sums paid for IPL and other leading cricket rights. The most recent television (linear and digital) rights deals for the PKL (2021–25) and the ISL (2023/24–2024/25) generated US$120.5 million and US$33.6 million, respectively (King, 2021; Rest, 2023).

International sports events/competitions have struggled to attract significant television audiences (and rights fees) in India. English Premier League football has built a degree of popularity in certain regions, but even major international events, such as the Olympic Games, have not proved particularly attractive to Indian viewers. At least in part, this explains the decision of the IOC, in 2023, to add cricket to the 2028 Los Angeles Summer Olympics. Without cricket, the television rights to the Olympic Games in India have previously sold for 'a handful of millions', but, with cricket included, the IOC is expecting to raise around $150 million (Ingle, 2023). In this sense, India is a perfect illustration of the primacy of national sporting preferences and, in turn, the importance of domestic rights markets.

The Buying, Selling, and Distribution of Sports Media Rights

The Growing Demand for Sports Rights

Sports media rights markets are typically characterised by supply-side monopolies. For example, the UEFA Champions League and NBA basketball are each unique products with no perfect substitutes (for media companies or viewers). By contrast, on the demand side, since around the 1980s, a defining feature of almost all national/regional sports rights markets has been the growing number of interested buyers, particularly for premium rights. Facilitated by new distribution technologies and the widespread, if not quite universal, liberalisation and deregulation of global media and communication markets, rights owners have benefited from (and in some cases orchestrated) competition between rival media organisations, which has produced a rapid escalation in the value of media rights (Solberg and Gaustad, 2022). In this way, the growing value of the global sports rights market has been intrinsically linked to the wider historical development of the television industry. To date, albeit with some national/regional variations, the sports media rights market has been shaped by three broad phases in the history of television distribution: (i) television broadcasting; (ii) pay television; and (iii) internet-protocol television, with the current rise of streaming platforms constituting a new emergent fourth phase (Evens, 2024).

(i) Television broadcasting

From around the 1950s until the 1980s, during the 'television broadcasting' phase, national television services across the world were limited to a single channel, or a handful of channels, which provided relatively little sports coverage. This was partly due to the limited amount of time available to dedicate to sport alongside other forms of programming, but it was also a result of the widely held belief amongst many sporting organisations that television coverage would lead to reduced attendance at live events and thus reduced revenue (Forrest et al., 2004). Live coverage of sport was therefore restricted to a small number of major events. For example, in the UK, the BBC broadcast live coverage of the football FA Cup Final, Test Match Cricket, and Wimbledon tennis. As a result, these events quickly became 'national events' enjoyed by millions of viewers, including many that were not regular followers of the respective sports (Scannell, 1992, p.323). The BBC, as well as other public broadcasters in Western Europe, Australia, Canada, and a host of Latin American and Asian nations, benefited from an association with sport as it helped them to establish both their popularity with audiences and their status as part of the 'national estate' (Scherer and Rowe, 2014, pp.4–5). In the US, while television broadcasting was commercially driven from its inception, national broadcasters (NBC, CBS, and ABC) similarly benefited from offering access to a limited amount of 'major league sport', such as World Series baseball matches (Wenner et al., 2014, p.81). For sports organisations, the benefits of television coverage during this period were largely limited to increased public exposure, rather than significant revenue from the sale of rights. With often only a single broadcaster, or, at best, a handful of broadcasters, interested in providing television coverage there was little, or no, competition for rights. In this context, even the most popular sports struggled to command little more than token rights fees (see, e.g. Box 2.2).

(ii) Pay television

During the late 1980s and 1990s, the global sports rights market was transformed by the widespread introduction and growth of pay-tv services. Utilising new satellite and cable broadcasting distribution technologies, pay-tv broadcasters used exclusive live sports rights to attract and retain subscribers. Perhaps most notably, Rupert Murdoch's News Corporation used this approach to establish numerous national pay-tv services, most conspicuously Sky (formerly BSkyB) (UK, Germany, Italy), Foxtel (Australia), and Star Sports (India). The same strategy was also employed by a host of other pay-tv broadcasters, such as Canal Plus (France), Mediaset (Italy), DStv (South Africa), and DirecTV (US). The emergence of pay-tv led to a significant increase in the amount of sports content available on television. For example, in Europe, between 1989 and 1995, 'sports coverage increased from 24,000 hours to some 58,000 hours' per year (Maguire, 1999, p.144). For Murdoch (and some others), the subscription revenues generated from exclusive premium sports coverage enabled even greater spending on rights and thus the establishment of a 'virtuous circle of profitability' that rivals found almost impossible to challenge (Maguire, 1999). During the early 2000s, a host of new entrant European pay-tv broadcasters overpaid for sports rights and faced the 'winner's curse' of heavy losses and/or bankruptcy, including ITV Digital and Setanta (UK), Premiere (Germany), Telepìu and Stream (Italy) (which merged to form Sky Italia), Alpha Digital Synthesis (Greece), and Quiero TV (Spain). By the early 2000s, national/regional pay-tv markets had become 'winner-takes-all-markets', largely dependent on the exclusive ownership of premium sports rights (Cudd, 2007).

(iii) Internet-protocol television

Since around 2005, the convergence of telephony, television, and internet networks facilitated by digitalisation of communications infrastructure has paved the way for many established, often formerly state-owned, telecommunications operators to play a significant role within the sports rights market. Most significantly, telecommunications companies across Europe have attempted to use sports rights, in particular the rights to their respective national football competitions, to promote new pay-tv services delivered over the internet. For example, in 2005, Belgian operator, Belgacom (now Proximus), became the first European telecommunications operator to purchase live sports rights, with a record €36 million per annum deal designed to promote the take-up of its new internet-protocol television (IPTV) service, Belgacom TV (Evens and Lefever, 2013). During the 2010s, telecommunications companies, including BT (UK), Deutsche Telekom (Germany), Orange/France Telecom (France), and Telefonica (Spain), as well as Verizon (US) and Optus (Australia), adopted a similar approach, investing heavily in premium sports rights within their respective national markets as part of 'triple play' strategies, which bundle together broadband, pay-tv, and telephony services, in an attempt to ensure a competitive position in increasingly converged pay-tv and broadband markets (Smith et al., 2016).

The strategic importance attached to sports rights by pay-tv operators has led to a major escalation in the value of rights since the 1990s. For example, between 1992 and 2020, the global value of television rights for the summer Olympic Games increased from $638 million to over $3.1 billion (IOC, 2023, p.22). In Europe, the exclusive live rights for domestic football have experienced some of the biggest increases in value, most notably the English Premier League (Burn-Murdoch, 2023) (see Table 2.1). Just as starkly, in the US, the cost of rights for the most popular sports leagues – the NFL, NBA, and MLB – increased by 60, 180, and 100 per cent, respectively, during the 2010s (Mance et al., 2015).

In turn, the escalation in the value of rights has meant that major sports organisations have become increasingly reliant on the sale of media rights for a significant proportion of their total income. For example, between 2017 and 2021, the IOC generated 61 per cent of its total income from the sale of media rights (IOC, 2023, p.6). Similarly, for clubs in Europe's 'big five' football leagues, in 2021, the sale of media rights (domestic leagues and UEFA Champions League combined) accounted for an average of 61.4 per cent of total revenue, with English, Spanish, and Italian clubs each relying on media rights for around two-thirds of total revenue (UEFA, 2023, p.83). Furthermore, while far from a new trend (Rowe, 2004, pp.32–3), the growing dependence of sports organisations on media rights revenue has also accentuated the tendency for sports organisations to cater for the preferences of their television paymasters. For example, between 2009 and 2020, the US,

TABLE 2.1 The Value of Live English Premier League Football Rights

Years	*Domestic Rights (£m) (matches per season)*	*Overseas Rights (£m) (all matches)*
1992–97	191 (60 matches)	40
1997–2001	670 (60 matches)	98
2001–04	1,200 (106 matches)	178
2004–07	1,024 (138 matches)	325
2007–10	1,706 (138 matches)	625
2010–13	1,773 (138 matches)	1,440
2013–16	3,018 (154 matches)	2,230
2016–19	5,136 (200 matches)	3,100
2019–22	4,815 (200 matches)	4,000
2022–25	5,100 (200 matches)	5,050
2025–29	6,700 (270 matches)	–

Source: Mackey (2023); Garrick and Slater (2023).

French, and Wimbledon Grand Slam tennis tournaments each invested in the construction of retractable roofs for their main show court/s, at least in part to satisfy the desire of broadcasters to avoid delays due to poor weather and/or provide live coverage during peak evening viewing hours.

BOX 2.2 THE TELEVISION RIGHTS FOR ENGLISH FOOTBALL

During the 1950s and 1960s, the growth of television was viewed with suspicion by England's leading football clubs. The English Football League feared that television coverage would reduce match attendance and, in 1955, the 92 league teams agreed a total ban on televised league football (Horrie, 2002, p.7). However, around a decade later, the BBC managed to secure an agreement with the League to offer edited highlights of matches. In 1964, the BBC launched *Match of the Day*, to offer 20 minutes of highlights from a single match, the identity of which was a closely guarded secret. The programme was an instant success and once it became clear that there was no significant impact on live attendances, the Corporation was permitted to add (10-minute) highlights from a handful of other matches and increase the length of the programme to 50 minutes (Horrie, 2002, p.22). Nevertheless, until the early 1980s, live domestic football remained a rarity on British television. Live matches were limited to the English and Scottish FA Cup Finals (carried by both the BBC and ITV) and the European Cup Final, which alternated between the BBC and ITV each year.

Initially, the BBC paid the League around £3,000 a year – shared equally between all 92 clubs – for the rights to produce *Match of the Day*. To see off competition from its new commercially funded rival, ITV, in 1966, the BBC agreed to increase the amount it paid the Football League to £60,000 per season. Undeterred, in 1968, ITV introduced its own regional highlights programme, *The Big Match*, and between 1968 and 1979 the cost of securing highlight rights to English league football rose from £120,000 a season to £534,000 (Boyle and Haynes, 2004, p.17). It was not long, however, before the BBC and ITV realised that by working together they could secure football rights at a relatively low cost. During the 1980s, the BBC and ITV effectively operated a buying cartel and kept the value of football rights to around £2 million per annum, even after a groundbreaking agreement to offer live coverage of around ten matches per season on a Sunday afternoon (when no other games were played) (Cowie and Williams, 1997, p.622).

The BBC/ITV cartel was broken by the introduction of pay-tv. By the early 1990s, England's leading football clubs had become increasingly frustrated with having to divide television revenue between all 92 League clubs, when it was primarily their matches that were televised. Their solution, in 1992, was the formation of a breakaway league – the English Premier League (EPL), which would sell its television rights separately from the rest of football (Conn, 1998, pp.11–28). The launch of the EPL coincided with the establishment of BSkyB, Rupert Murdoch's satellite pay-tv service, and the new broadcaster quickly set its sights on obtaining the exclusive live rights to broadcast Premier League football. In 1992, BSkyB teamed up with the BBC and outbid ITV for the rights to televise the EPL, with BSkyB paying £260 million for the live rights and the BBC £44 million for the highlights (Conn, 1998, p.20). Securing the rights to the EPL transformed the fortunes of BSkyB. With a rapidly increasing subscriber base, BSkyB was able to acquire further expensive live rights to other sports events, such as England home football internationals, international one-day cricket, World Championship boxing matches, and Ryder Cup golf (Smith, 2010). By 1995, BSkyB had 4 million subscribers and annual profits of over £150 million (Horsman, 1997, p.xiii).

As the leading, if not sole, provider of live Premier League football, BSkyB's success continued into the 2000s and, by the mid-2010s, it (by now renamed 'Sky') had grown its subscriber base to around 10 million, with annual profits of over £1 billion (Goldblatt, 2014, p.18). During the 2000s, UK/EU competition authorities attempted to tackle Sky's domination of the UK pay-tv market by instigating changes to how EPL rights were sold, most notably preventing a single broadcaster from acquiring the rights to all EPL matches (Smith, 2010). However, this regulatory intervention had only a limited impact on Sky's domination of the UK sports rights market. Faced with competition from Sky and the resulting high cost of securing EPL and/or other rights, some rival media organisations were pushed close to bankruptcy (e.g. ITV Digital, 2002; NTL, 2002; Setanta, 2009), while others have opted to withdraw from the UK sports rights market (e.g. ESPN/Disney, 2013; BT, 2022; Amazon, 2024).

The strategic importance of the Premier League to Sky's continued commercial success, together with albeit limited (domestic) competition between media organisations, has led to three decades of virtually uninterrupted growth in the value of Premier League rights (see Table 2.1). Premier League teams have benefited fairly equally from the league's growing media rights revenue, with rights sold collectively by the league. Premier League domestic rights revenues are (and have always been) shared: 50 per cent equally, 25 per cent according to league position, and 25 per cent based on the number of television appearances. Initially not expected to raise a significant sum, until fairly recently, revenues from the sale of international media rights were simply shared equally between all teams. However, particularly during the 2010s, increasingly competitive global pay-tv markets, combined with the growing popularity of the Premier League, have led to burgeoning international rights revenues (see Table 2.1). In 2018, on the basis that it is their matches that attract by far the most interest from international fans (and media organisations), the Premier League's biggest teams instigated a new arrangement for the distribution of international rights revenues, whereby any revenues from international rights above the existing level (around £3.3 billion) would be distributed according to league position (Conn, 2018). On average, EPL clubs generate 59 per cent of their total revenue from the sale of media rights (UEFA, 2023, p.95), and for smaller teams, such as Newcastle United, this figure rises to around 70 per cent (Deloitte, 2023).

Fuelled largely by the growing value of media rights, total annual revenues for Premier League teams have grown enormously since the league's inception. In 1992, the combined annual revenue of all clubs amounted to £170 million (Goldblatt, 2014, p.17). By 2022, this figure had reached over £6 billion (Harraghy, 2023). Yet, albeit with much variation between teams, for most seasons the Premier League has collectively managed to generate only a small, if any, profit (Harraghy, 2023). For the most part, this is due to increased spending on player transfers and wages. In 1992, the average wage of a Premier League player was £75,000 per year; by 2019, it had increased to over £3 million (Goldblatt, 2014, p.24; Sporting Intelligence, 2019, p.26). Players have therefore arguably been the chief beneficiaries of the escalation in the value of Premier League media rights. Whether UK pay-tv subscribers have also benefited is more debatable. Over the last couple of decades in particular, increased spending on Premier League rights has been underpinned by spiralling UK pay-tv subscription fees and paradoxically this trend has been exacerbated by the attempts of EU/UK regulators to enable greater competition for rights. The multi-sided character of the sports rights market (see below), increased competition for EPL rights (upstream), and the ending of Sky's Premier League (live) rights monopoly led to a significant jump, by as much as 50 per cent, in the cost paid by consumers (downstream) to access all available matches, as well as the inconvenience of subscribing to multiple services (Butler and Massey, 2019, p.620).

A Market of Two Halves

At the heart of classical economics is the idea that competition between rival suppliers leads to reduced prices (and improved service) for consumers. However, over the last couple of decades, this has not been the experience for pay-tv viewers, and in particular subscribers to sports channels. Paradoxically, in various national pay-tv markets in Europe and beyond, increased competition between rival media organisations has led to price rises for consumers (Budzinski et al., 2019; see also Box 2.2). To some degree, this trend can be explained by the growing amount of sports content made available by pay-tv services, but, at best, this is a partial explanation. A full explanation requires an understanding of the fact that the sports media rights market consists of two separate (albeit interconnected) halves: an upstream and a downstream market (Szymanski, 2006) (see Figure 2.1). The downstream market is the primary market for sports content, where media organisations compete for viewers, advertisers, and/or subscribers. Whereas, the actual sale of sports rights takes place in the upstream market, in which sports organisations (or agencies acting for rights owners) and media organisations negotiate rights deals. Media organisations are at the heart of the sports media rights market as they often (although not always) operate in both upstream and downstream markets. In the upstream market, media organisations function as rights buyers. These rights are then packaged into programming schedules/online portals that are monetised through advertising and/or subscriptions in the downstream market. However, while conceptually separate, upstream and downstream markets should not be seen as wholly distinct. On the contrary, there are constant interactions between the two markets. For example, pay-tv services around the world, such as DAZN, continue to attempt to replicate the success of News Corporation during the 1990s by building an audience with popular sports programming (downstream) and then using the revenues generated to invest in even more sports rights (upstream). Equally, for sports organisations, the 'revenue versus exposure' dilemma discussed above means that while rights are sold (upstream) the distribution strategy of the media organisation (downstream) is always a key concern, or at least it should be. In this sense, the sports media rights market is an example of what economists refer to as a 'multi-sided market' (Budzinski and Satzer, 2011).

As regards the sale of sports rights, the selling of rights to team sports is arguably the most controversial issue (Evens et al., 2013), with debate focused on whether media rights should be controlled by individual teams (e.g. Real Madrid) or by a league (e.g. La Liga), usually acting as a joint venture between the teams or occasionally as the rights owner itself (e.g. the UEFA Champions League). For most major sports leagues, including in the US and Europe, the sale of rights collectively by leagues has become the dominant approach. Not least because collective selling enables a league to control/

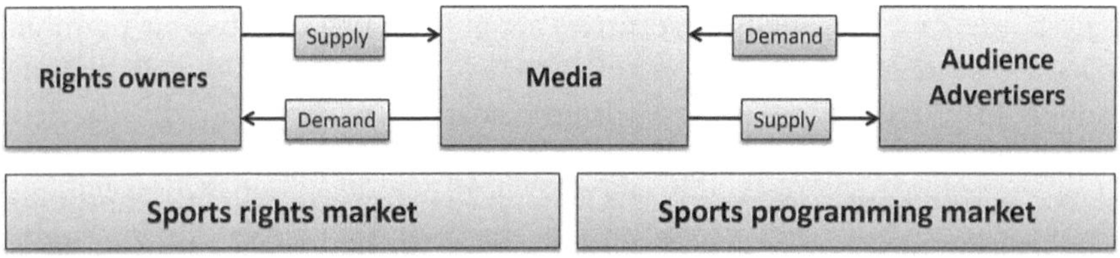

FIGURE 2.1 The Sports Rights Market: A Market of Two Halves (adapted from Evens et al., 2013)

limit the number and/or geographic availability of matches and thus maximise total revenue. Another major advantage often claimed for collective selling is that it facilitates the sharing of rights revenue between teams with differing levels of support and can thus improve competitive balance within leagues. For example, in 40 of Europe's domestic football leagues, including the 'big five', rights are sold collectively, with revenues distributed between clubs on the basis of three main criteria: equal distribution, sporting merit, and other factors (e.g. number of times broadcast; size of fan base; investment in youth facilities, etc.). In 2021, the high to median ratio for the distribution of media rights revenues between teams in these leagues averaged 2.3 (i.e. the team that received the most revenue from the sale of rights received 2.3 times the sum received by the median team). By contrast, in 2021, in Portugal, the largest of a handful of leagues in Europe where rights are sold by individual teams, the high to median ratio for rights revenues distribution was 12.8 (UEFA, 2023, pp.99–100). However, in Europe at least, support for collective selling arrangements is being tested by the rise of online distribution, which, particularly for larger teams, such as Manchester United and Barcelona, offers the enticing prospect of potentially securing a significant increase in rights revenues from selling directly to a global fan base (see Chapter 5). Against this backdrop, the early 2020s witnessed a couple of notable examples of Europe's biggest football teams pressing for more leeway to market rights individually, or at least for a greater share of the revenues sold collectively, namely, first, 'Project Big Picture' advocated by England's biggest Premier League teams and, second, the ill-fated launch of a European Super League by teams from Italy, Spain, and England (Evens and Smith, 2022).

Albeit for different reasons, the collective selling of media rights has also been seen as problematic by numerous national/regional government competition authorities (Smith et al., 2015). In summary, from the perspective of competition regulators, leagues that sell media rights collectively on behalf of individual teams are effectively acting as cartels, which dictate the price of rights by restricting/controlling supply and thus inflating prices for both media organisations and consumers. As a result, collective selling is also seen by some to undermine competition in national pay-tv markets, as only the biggest and/or established broadcasters are able to afford to bid for premium rights. Nevertheless, competition authorities in most, if not quite all, national markets have tended to allow collective selling on the grounds that it is required to facilitate revenue distribution and preserve/promote competitive balance within sports leagues (see Chapter 7). However, certain conditions have been imposed by competition authorities on how rights are sold in an effort to curb the anti-competitive tendencies of collective selling. Perhaps most notably, in the European Union, following a landmark case in 2003 on the selling of media rights to the UEFA Champions League, the rights to domestic football leagues in Europe's leading markets were to be sold for a limited duration (typically three or four years) and in a number of separate packages, with no single broadcaster able to secure all the available packages (Asser Institute, 2014, p.78). Together with the changes to television distribution technology detailed above, during the 2010s, these regulations facilitated increased competition for premium football rights in Europe's biggest markets and ended several national pay-tv monopolies (Smith et al., 2016). In doing so, however, the new regulations also contributed to a rapid escalation in the price paid by media organisations for premium football rights, which, to at least some degree, was then passed on to consumers (downstream) in the sports programming market. Furthermore, the obligation imposed on Europe's main domestic national football leagues to sell rights to at least two different buyers also led to the fragmentation of rights between different media organisations and thus additional subscription costs for consumers who want to be able to view all the available matches from a particular league (Budzinski et al., 2019). The introduction of new streaming services threatens to fragment live sports coverage across even more media organisations. As is discussed throughout the rest of the book, a key challenge for sports and media organisations in the age of streaming, therefore, is to provide consumers with sports content that is easily accessible at a reasonable cost. A failure to do so could risk (further) incentivising sports content piracy and undermining the value of the global sports media rights market (see Chapter 6). At the same time, for competition regulators, a greater focus on the regulation of the (downstream) sports content programming market is long overdue (Smith et al., 2016). The growth of streaming services provides a window of opportunity to ensure that the application of competition law to the buying, selling, and distribution of sports media rights benefits consumers, as well as sports organisations (see Chapter 7).

References

Advanced Television (2019). 'Forecast: 'Sport highlight value to grow faster than live', 18 October. Available at: https://advanced-television.com/2019/10/18/forecast-sports-highlights-value-to-grow-faster-than-live/ (Accessed: 4 August 2023).

Advanced Television (2023). 'Report: Sports remain the last defence for linear TV in US', 14 February. Available at: https://advanced-television.com/2023/02/14/report-sports-remain-last-line-of-defence-for-linear-tv-in-us/ (Accessed: 7 September 2023).

Agini, S. and Thomas, D. (2023). 'Sky snaps up most Premier League matches in £6.7bn broadcast deal', *Financial Times*, 4 December. Available at: https://www.ft.com/content/f4b40127-74c6-48f7-a8b9-b2d9c9194e07 (Accessed: 4 December 2022).

Ampere Analysis (2022). *Trends and Dynamics in the Sports Broadcasting Sector – Abridged Report for Ofcom*. Available at: https://www.ofcom.org.uk/__data/assets/pdf_file/0019/240553/Ampere-abridged-report.pdf (Accessed: 1 May 2024).

Andrews, D. (2003). Sport and the Transnationalizing Media Corporation. *Journal of Media Economics*, 16 (4), pp. 235–251.

Asser Institute (2014). *Study on Sports Organisers' Rights in the European Union. Final Report for the European Union*. Available at: https://op.europa.eu/en/publication-detail/ /publication/138eb928-2981-11e7-ab65-01aa75ed71a1/language-en/format-PDF/source-233927641 (Accessed: 5 September 2023).

Athique, A. (2012). *Indian Media: Global Approaches*. Cambridge: Polity Press.

Badale, M. and Hughes, S. (2020). *A New Innings: How the IPL's Reinvention of Cricket Provides Lessons for the Business of Sport*. London: Clink Street Publishing.

BARC (Broadcast Audience Research Council India) (2020). 'TV universe estimates 2020'. Available at: https://barcindia.co.in/whitepaper/barc-india-tv-universe-estimates-2020.pdf (Accessed: 5 November 2023).

Barker, A. (2019). 'Rugby World Cup boosts ITV's advertising revenue', *Financial Times*, 12 November. Available at: https://www.ft.com/content/36867322-0526-11ea-9afa-d9e2401fa7ca (Accessed: 12 September 2023).

Barwise, P. and Watkins, L. (2018). The Evolution of Digital Dominance: How and Why we Got to GAFA. In: M. Moore and D. Tambini (eds.), *Digital Dominance: The Power of Google, Amazon, Facebook, and Apple* (pp. 22–49). Oxford: Oxford University Press.

Bassam, T. (2021). 'An expert's guide to the Indian sports media market with Star's Sanjog Gupta', *SportsProMedia*, 6 July. Available at: https://www.sportspromedia.com/insights/interviews/india-sports-tv-rights-streaming-star-disney-sanjog-gupta-ipl-isl-kabbadi/ (Accessed: 7 November 2023).

Boyle, R. and Haynes, R. (2004). *Football in the New Media Age*. London: Routledge.

Budzinski, O., Gaenssle, S., and Kunz-Kaltenhäuser, P. (2019). How Does Online Streaming Affect Antitrust Remedies to Centralized Marketing? The Case of European Football Broadcasting Rights. *International Journal of Sport Finance*, 14 (3), pp. 147–157.

Budzinski, O. and Satzer, J. (2011). Sports Business and Multisided Markets: Towards a New Analytical Framework? *Sports, Business, Management: An International Journal*, 1 (2), pp. 124–137.

Burn-Murdoch, J. (2023). 'Football's broadcast revenue boom is over — what happens now?', *Financial Times*, 29 December. Available at: https://www.ft.com/content/a0430c7a-c8b8-4ca4-b86f-803b369a3f46 (Accessed: 29 December 2023).

Business Today (2022). 'India to have 1 bn smartphone users by 2026: Deloitte study', 22 February. Available at: https://www.businesstoday.in/technology/story/india-to-have-1-bn-smartphone-users-by-2026-deloitte-study-323519-2022-02-22 (Accessed: 10 November 2023).

Butler, R. and Massey, P. (2019). Has Competition in the Market for Subscription Sports Broadcasting Benefited Consumers? The Case of the English Premier League. *Journal of Sports Economics*, 20 (4), pp. 603–624.

Conn, D. (1998). *The Football Business: Fair Game in the '90s?* Edinburgh and London: Mainstream.

Conn, D. (2018). 'Premier League's top six win battle for larger share of overseas TV rights', *The Guardian*, 7 June. Available at: https://www.theguardian.com/football/2018/jun/07/premier-league-big-six-win-battle-overseas-television-rights (Accessed: 2 December 2023).

Coster, H. and Pingue, F. (2021). 'Premier League reaches six-year U.S. TV deal with NBC Sports', *Reuters*, 19 November. Available at: https://www.reuters.com/markets/europe/premier-league-reaches-six-year-us-tv-deal-with-nbc-sports-2021-11-18/ (Accessed: 31 October 2023).

Cowie, C. and Williams, M. (1997). The Economics of Sports Rights. *Telecommunications Policy*, 21 (7), pp. 619–634.

Crupi, A. (2023). '2022 TV recap: It's the NFL's world; the rest of us just live in it', *Sportico*, 6 January. Available at: https://www.sportico.com/business/media/2023/nfl-games-account-for-82-of-100-top-tv-broadcasts-1234700381/ (Accessed: 4 September 2023).

Cudd, A. E. (2007). Sporting Metaphors: Competition and the Ethos of Capitalism. *Journal of the Philosophy of Sport*, 34 (1), pp. 52–67.

Deloitte (2023). 'Football Money League'. Available at: https://www2.deloitte.com/uk/en/pages/sports-business-group/articles/deloitte-football-money-league.html (Accessed: 3 December 2023).

Dixon, E. (2020). 'Video highlights will be more valuable than live rights,' says WarnerMedia VP', *SportsProMedia*, 21 August. Available at: https://www.sportspromedia.com/news/sports-video-highlights-live-tv-rights-value-warnermedia-peter-scott/ (Accessed: 3 August 2023).

Dixon, E. (2022). 'AFL inks record AUS$4.5bn broadcast rights deal with Foxtel, Seven and Telstra', *SportsProMedia*, 6 September. Available at: https://www.sportspromedia.com/news/afl-tv-broadcast-rights-2025-2031-foxtel-seven-telstra-gillon-mclachlan/ (Accessed: 13 October 2023).

Dixon, E. (2023). 'Cricket Australia confirms AUS$1.5bn broadcast rights extension with Foxtel and Seven', *SportsProMedia*, 3 January. Available at: https://www.sportspromedia.com/news/cricket-australia-tv-broadcast-rights-foxtel-seven-big-bash-2024-2031/ (Accessed: 13 October 2023).

Early, K. (2016). 'You can watch nothing and yet miss nothing', *The Irish Times*, 17 October. Available at: https://www.irishtimes.com/sport/soccer/english-soccer/ken-early-you-can-watch-nothing-and-yet-miss-nothing-1.2832070 (Accessed: 2 August 2023).

Evens, T. (2024). Global Sports Media Rights Market. In: U. Rohn, M. B. von Rimscha, and T. Raats (eds.), *De Gruyter Handbook of Media Economics* (pp. 267–278). Berlin: De Gruyter.

Evens, T., Iosifidis, P., and Smith, P. (2013). *The Political Economy of Television Sports Rights*. Basingstoke: Palgrave Macmillan.

Evens, T. and Lefever, K. (2013). The Struggle for Platform Leadership in the European Sports Broadcasting Market. In: B. Hutchins and D. Rowe (eds.), *Digital Media Sport: Technology, Power and Identity in the Network Society* (pp. 66–80). New York: Routledge.

Evens, T. and Smith, P. (2022). Regulating the Digital Sports Broadcasting Market: New Players, Old Problems. In: H. Fujak and S. Frawley (eds.), *Sport Broadcasting for Managers* (pp. 6–19). New York: Routledge.

FIFA (2023). *The FIFA World Cup Qatar 2022 in Numbers*. Available at: https://digitalhub.fifa.com/m/546158158e52f1c9/original/The-FIFA-World-Cup-Qatar-2022-in-numbers.pdf (Accessed: 2 August 2023).

Financial Express (2023). 'Total TV viewership of IPL playoffs at 496 million: Disney Star', 2 June. Available at: https://www.financialexpress.com/business/brandwagon-total-tv-viewership-of-ipl-playoffs-at-496-million-disney-star-3110966 (Accessed: 4 November 2023).

Forrest, D., Simmons, R., and Szymanski, S. (2004). Broadcasting, Attendance and the Inefficiency of Cartels. *Review of Industrial Organization*, 24 (3), pp. 243–265.

Garrick, O. and Slater, M. (2023). 'Explained: The record £6.7bn TV rights deal and what it means for Premier League football', *The Athletic*, 4 December. Available at: https://theathletic.com/5111541/2023/12/04/premier-league-television-rights-deal (Accessed: 5 December 2023).

Germano, S. and Ahmed, M. (2021). 'ESPN wins US broadcast rights to Spain's La Liga', *Financial Times*, 14 May. Available at: https://www.ft.com/content/a53e83ef-9088-4130-8918-a9eb5b9f3a52 (Accessed: 2 October 2023).

Ghosal, R. (2022). 'The curious case of Indian sports consumers', *The Other Eye*, 5 April. Available at: https://theothereye.substack.com/p/the-curious-case-of-indian-sports?s=r (Accessed: 3 November 2023).

Goldblatt, D. (2014). *The Game of Our Lives: The Meaning and Making of English Football.* London: Viking.

Gollapudi, N. (2022). 'Disney Star and Viacom 18 share the spoils in 6 billion-dollar-plus IPL rights deal', *ESPN Cricinfo*, 14 June. Available at: https://www.espncricinfo.com/story/disney-star-and-viacom-18-share-the-spoils-in-6-billion-dollar-plus-ipl-rights-deal-1319863 (Accessed: 5 November 2022).

Harraghy, D. (2023). 'Premier League clubs generate record revenues, but losses reach £2bn in four years', Ampere Analysis. Available at: https://www.ampereanalysis.com/insight/premier-league-clubs-generate-record-revenues-but-losses-reach-2bn-in-four-years (Accessed: 12 December 2023).

Horrie, C. (2002). *Premiership: Lifting the Lid on a National Obsession.* London: Simon & Schuster.

Horsman, M. (1997). *Sky High: The Inside Story of BSkyB.* London: Orion Business Books.

Hoskins, C. and Mirus, R. (1988). Reasons for the US Dominance of the International Trade in Television Programmes. *Media, Culture and Society*, 10 (4), pp. 499–515.

Ingle, S. (2023). 'Feuds, truces and dollar signs: How five sports made cut for 2028 Games', *The Guardian*, 10 October. Available at: https://www.theguardian.com/sport/2023/oct/10/olympics-la-2028-cricket-flag-football-breakdance (Accessed: 2 November 2023).

IOC (2023). *Olympic Marketing Fact File: 2023 Edition.* Available at: https://library.olympics.com/Default/doc/SYRACUSE/3023162/olympic-marketing-fact-file-2023-edition-international-olympic-committee?_lg=en-GB (Accessed: 15 August 2023).

Jones, R. (2021). 'NRL extends Nine FTA broadcast pact in "AUS$575m" deal', *SportsProMedia*, 20 December. Available at: https://www.sportspromedia.com/broadcast-ott/media-rights/nrl-nine-fta-tv-rights-state-of-origin-grand-final-arlc (Accessed: 2 October 2023).

King, T. (2021). 'Star India retains Pro Kabbadi League media rights for five years', *SportsProMedia*, 19 April. Available at: https://www.sportspromedia.com/news/star-india-pro-kabbadi-league-media-rights/ (Accessed: 3 November 2023).

Kohli-Khandekar, V. (2010). *The Indian Media Business.* London: Sage.

Mackey, E. (2023). 'How Premier League TV rights work and how they impact your costs and subscriptions', *The Athletic*, 25 August. Available at: https://theathletic.

com/4240951/2023/08/25/premier-league-tv-rights-how-work-cost (Accessed: 2 December 2023).

Maguire, J. (1999). *Global Sport: Identities, Societies, Civilizations.* Cambridge: Polity.

Mance, H., Garrahan, M., and Blitz, R. (2015). 'TV sports rights: Show them the money", *Financial Times*, 13 February. Available at: https://www.ft.com/content/91570e92-b369-11e4-9449-00144feab7de (Accessed: 2 December 2023).

McCaskill, S. (2023a). 'ESPN linear services will shift to DTC eventually says chairman', *SportsProMedia*, 4 May. Available at: https://www.sportspromedia.com/news/espn-plus-jimmy-pitaro-streaming-dtc-when/ (Accessed: 30 September 2023).

McCaskill, S. (2023b). 'Viacom18 lands global broadcast rights for Indian cricket in US $720m deal', *SportsProMedia*, 1 September. Available at: https://www.sportspromedia.com/news/viacom-18-tv-deal-india-bbci-cricket-streaming-global/ (Accessed: 12 November 2023).

Modha, M. (2023). 'The Ashes has delivered but here's why Test cricket needs more free-to-air coverage to survive', *SportsProMedia*, 26 July. Available at: https://www.sportspromedia.com/insights/opinions/the-ashes-2023-england-australia-test-cricket-free-to-air-broadcast/ (Accessed: 2 December 2023).

Moore, D. (2023). 'Basketball nets the highest sports rights in China', Ampere Analysis. Available at: https://www.ampereanalysis.com/insight/basketball-nets-the-highest-sports-rights-in-china (Accessed: 7 October 2023).

Murdock, G. and Wasko, J. (eds.) (2007). *Media in the Age of Marketization.* Cresskill, NJ: Hampton Press.

Rest, J. (2023). 'Viacom18 acquires exclusive rights to ISL, India national team', *Sport Business*, 7 September. Available at: https://www.sportbusiness.com/news/viacom18-acquires-exclusive-rights-to-isl-india-national-team/ (Accessed: 7 November 2023).

Rowe, D. (2004). *Sport, Culture and the Media: The Unruly Trinity.* Maidenhead, UK: Open University Press.

Scannell, P. (1992). Public Service Broadcasting and Modern Public Life. In: P. Scannell, P. Schlesinger, and C. Sparks (eds), *Culture and Power: A Media, Culture & Society Reader* (pp. 317–348). London: Sage.

Scherer, J. and Rowe, D. (2014). Sport, Public Service Media, and Cultural Citizenship. In: J. Scherer and D. Rowe (eds.), *Sport, Public Broadcasting, and Cultural Citizenship: Signal Lost?* (pp. 1–29). London: Routledge.

Shephered, C., Fei Ju, S., and Mitchell, T. (2019). 'China state broadcaster and Tencent stop airing pre-season NBA games', *Financial Times*, 8 October. Available at: https://www.ft.com/content/7e45008a-e98c-11e9-a240-3b065ef5fc55 (Accessed: 3 October 2023).

Silvermann, A. and Ourand, J. (2022). 'MLS goes with Apple in landmark 10-year global media rights deal', *Sports Business Journal*, 14 June. Available at: https://www.sportsbusinessjournal.com/Daily/Issues/2022/06/14/Media/MLS-TV-rights.aspx (Accessed: 3 October 2023).

Sky Sports (2021). 'It's only live once'. Available at: https://www.skysports.com/watch/video/sports/f1/12243857/its-only-live-once-watch-sky-sports-f1s-promo-for-the-2021-season (Accessed: 5 September 2023).

Smith, P. (2010). The Politics of Sports Rights: The Regulation of Television Sports Rights in the UK. *Convergence*, 16 (3), pp. 316–333.

Smith, P., Evens, T., and Iosifidis, P. (2015). The Regulation of Television Sports Broadcasting: A Comparative Analysis. *Media, Culture & Society*, 37 (5), pp. 720–736.

Smith, P., Evens, T., and Iosifidis, P. (2016). The Next Big Match: Convergence, Competition and Sports Media Rights. *European Journal of Communication*, 31 (5), pp. 536–550.

Solberg, H. and Gaustad, T. (2022). International Sport Broadcasting. In: H. Fujak and S. Frawley (eds.), *Sports Broadcasting for Managers* (pp. 84–102). New York: Routledge.

SportBusiness (2022). *Global Media Report.* Available at: https://www.sportbusiness.com/global-media-report-2022 (Accessed: 22 August 2023).

Sporting Intelligence (2019). *Global Sports Salaries Survey 2019.* Available at: https://www.globalsportssalaries.com/GSSS%202019.pdf (Accessed: 2 September 2023).

Szymanski, S. (2006). The Economic Evolution of Sport and Broadcasting. *The Australian Economic Review*, 39 (4), pp. 428–434.

Tewari, S. (2020). 'Sports rights in India expected to touch $1.3bn by 2024', *Mint*, 6 March. Available at: https://www.livemint.com/industry/advertising/sports-rights-in-india-expected-to-touch-1-3-bn-by-2024-11583490221074.html (Accessed: 3 November 2023).

The Economist (2021). 'As Americans cut the cord, Europeans sign up for more pay-TV', 11 September. Available at: https://www.economist.com/business/2021/09/11/as-americans-cut-the-cord-europeans-sign-up-for-more-pay-tv (Accessed: 23 September 2023).

The Economist (2022). 'The rise and rise of kabaddi, an ancient Indian sport', 6 October. Available at: https://www.economist.com/culture/2022/10/06/the-rise-and-rise-of-kabaddi-an-ancient-indian-sport (Accessed: 1 November 2023).

TRAI (Telecom Regulatory Authority of India) (2022). *Annual Report: 2021–2022.* Available at: https://trai.gov.in/sites/default/files/Annaul_Report_23022023_0.pdf (Accessed: 7 November 2023).

UEFA (2023). *The European Club Footballing Landscape.* Available at: https://www.uefa.com/insideuefa/news/027e-1747598eeb3b-436611261ff3-1000–new-european-club-landscape-report (Accessed: 8 September 2023).

Wenner, L., Bellamy, R., and Walker, J. (2014). Selling out: The Gaming of the Living Room Seat for the US Sports Fan. In: J. Scherer and D. Rowe (eds.), *Sport, Public Broadcasting, and Cultural Citizenship: Signal Lost?* (pp. 74–95). London: Routledge.

YouGov (2023). *2023 Sports Report: The Global Sports Media Landscape.* Available at: https://business.yougov.com/content/8845-2023-sports-report (Accessed: 8 September 2023).

PART 2

The Platformisation of Sports Rights

3

COMMERCIAL MEDIA ORGANISATIONS

Live sport is no longer the privilege of traditional television broadcasters and pay-tv operators: new modes of distribution, most notably online streaming, have ended the monopoly of legacy broadcasters in the sports programming market. Increasingly, media platforms run by pure streaming players, tech giants, social media companies, and device manufacturers have entered the sports rights arena. The fact that live sports programming, even when on-demand viewing begins to be established as the default mode of video consumption among a large proportion of viewers, remains highly attractive to win and retain subscribers and advertisers, explains the enduring appetite for premium sports rights among traditional players as well as new entrants. Nevertheless, despite the rising prominence of tech giants including Amazon, Netflix, and Apple in the sports streaming market, traditional providers of live sports, notably free-to-air broadcasters and pay-tv operators, continue to dominate the sports programming market. In a similar vein, as put forward in this chapter, there is no such thing as a standard sports streaming platform: different players have their own economic logic and unique value proposition. Therefore, this chapter discusses the different business strategies of different types of players in terms of sports rights portfolio, business model, and geographic scale. Furthermore, the chapter discusses the long-term viability of sports streaming platforms, which, following developments in the wider streaming market, struggle to become profitable at all. This may remind us of the fact that sports broadcasters have traditionally found difficulties turning the expensive acquisition of premium sports rights into a profitable activity. The situation in the post-network era is, in this regard, little different than the situation in the broadcasting era. Finally, this chapter debunks the high expectations held in the industry that big tech platforms will inevitably become the main investor in the sports rights market. Instead, it is argued

DOI: 10.4324/9781003401988-6

here that, to date at least, big tech has largely adopted a pragmatic and opportunistic approach to the sports rights market, with sports programming bundled with hardware or with e-commerce services, and that this approach is likely to continue for at least the foreseeable future.

The Last Bastion of Broadcasting

While many still regard live sports as the last bastion of television broadcasting (see Chapter 2), the platformisation of the media industries has allowed non-traditional media organisations to make a significant push into the sports streaming market and intensify competition for premium sports rights (Duncan, 2020). Facebook and Twitter (now X) were among the first social media platforms to offer a selection of live games, and soon got company from Amazon, Yahoo, Tencent, YouTube, and other tech platforms that made inroads into the delivery of live sports. While their offerings are, at least in most instances, complementary to the supply of traditional sports broadcasters, the streaming platform DAZN competes head-to-head with legacy sports broadcasters to acquire premium rights. In response to the increase in cord-cutting, the decline in linear viewing, and the popularity of streaming, legacy broadcasters and pay-tv operators in numerous different national markets complemented their traditional sports coverage with streaming options to deal with changing consumer habits and preferences. For example, this led to the launch of ESPN+ (US), Kayo (Australia), Movistar Plus (Spain), and other streaming equivalents that carry live sports, to win back viewers that lost interest in the traditional pay-tv offer, or, even better, to prevent the loss of viewers and/or attract new viewers happy with the more flexible way of watching sport content online. In the streaming era, players from all stages of the audio-visual value chain – sports properties, broadcasters, pay-tv operators, telecom providers, social media platforms, tech platforms, device manufacturers, and others – are exploring how sports content can be incorporated into their existing or new business models. Hence, sports media rights have become a quintessential part of the ongoing streaming wars. Despite inflated rights fees and often limited prospects of return on investment, media platforms remain extremely interested in building a sports rights portfolio. The almost endless list of sports rights deals illustrates that media platforms have two important incentives to continue to spend huge sums of money to acquire sports rights: market *penetration* and market *control*.

First, live sports draws high audience ratings and can reach a variety of consumer profiles that go beyond the archetype of male, older, and higher-educated sports viewers typically associated with pay-tv (Gantz and Wenner, 1991). Over time, there has been a significant rise in the proportion of female viewers, as well as growing media coverage of and ratings for women's sports. The FIFA Women's World Cup 2023, for example, broke viewership records, becoming the biggest streaming event in many countries (Noakes,

2023). Streaming is able to attract unique, hard-to-reach audiences that would otherwise have been entirely missed when offering no sports on the platform (Xu et al., 2023). Live sports continues to provide consistent viewership and is able to hold viewers' attention for long periods of time as sports events regularly last for at least one hour, if not more, and championships often run throughout large periods of the year (Fortunato, 2001). This is crucial for streaming services, who suffer from subscribers dipping in and out frequently, and have to deal with increasing churn. Moreover, live sports drives overall audience reach, increases branding power, and adds to the prestige of a platform. These factors determine the rates commercial media platforms can charge advertisers for their commercial breaks or digital advertising (Fujak and Frawley, 2016). Platforms expect spillover effects and presume that viewers who tune in to the platform for sports may stay on that platform to consume other content. Lastly, sports creates opportunities for valuable exposure to new programmes through promotional spots by means of in-stream ads, screen overlays, sponsored cards, or other digital advertising formats (Mondello and Fortunato, 2022).

Second, live sports has long been proven to be an effective means for positioning a newly entering platform in the market and for putting it firmly on the map. For example, Fox's purchase of the NFL rights, in 1993, was critical to break the dominance of the traditional network triumvirate in the US and gain credibility as a major network. The broadcaster took a financial loss, but also increased its national coverage substantially, which brought in additional revenue from affiliation fees (Evens et al., 2013). In the past, incumbent television broadcasters, pay-tv operators, and telecom providers were keen on exclusive live rights to position themselves in the market and to create a competitive advantage over their rivals. Streaming platforms are copying this strategy to build a significant position in the market. As mentioned in Chapter 2, sports rights can be considered a source of market power. First-moving pay-tv operators have claimed exclusive rights as a unique selling proposition and were able to foreclose the market, which eventually evolved into monopolistic market structures. As such, competition *in* the market was replaced by competition *for* the market (Nicita and Ramello, 2005). Accepted as a widespread practice in the media industries and in itself not breaching the principles of free and fair competition, exclusive dealing is an essential component of pre-emption strategies deployed by first movers raising rivals' costs, creating entry barriers, deterring market entry, and preserving market power (see Chapter 7). Previously, incumbents were able to buy all rights available in the market, even for distribution platforms in which they had no interest, and were able to reduce the availability of media rights for newcomers effectively (Evens et al., 2011). Some rights owners have decoupled the supply of broadcasting and digital rights so as to create new dynamics in the market, allowing newcomers to bid for individual rights packages and challenge historical market leaders (see Box 3.1).

BOX 3.1 DISNEY+ HOTSTAR'S SPORTS SUPREMACY CONTESTED

Disney Star, a subsidiary of the Walt Disney Company, has become a one-stop destination for sports fans in India and South Asia. Pay-tv channel Star Sports, originally Prime Sports, launched in 1991 as a joint venture between Star and American cable company Tele-Communications, Inc. (TCI). It later merged with its main competitor ESPN, forming ESPN Star Sports. In 2012, News Corporation acquired ESPN's stake in the company. After Disney's acquisition of Star's parent company, 21st Century Fox, in 2019, Star became part of the world's largest media and entertainment conglomerate. By the early 2020s, Star Sports was the major broadcaster of cricket in South Asia, controlling the pay-tv rights to, among others, the Indian national team, the Indian Premier League (IPL), and International Cricket Council (ICC) tournaments, in addition to the Pro Kabaddi League (kabaddi), Hero Indian Super League (soccer), English Premier League (soccer), and Wimbledon (tennis).

In 2015, Star launched the streaming service Hotstar after it had acquired both the pay-tv and the streaming rights for the 2015 Cricket World Cup and the upcoming 2015 IPL season. The ad-supported service generated record views of these tournaments, and also featured live coverage of football and kabaddi. Star's impressive sports rights portfolio, in addition to a new deal with HBO, helped to position Hotstar as the leading digital subscription-based platform, overcoming competition from global streamers such as Amazon Prime Video and Netflix. Following Disney's acquisition of 21st Century Fox, the service was relaunched as Disney+ Hotstar and benefited from Disney's extensive content library to grow further. Hotstar also benefited from economies of scale, which lowered costs and allowed for more competitive pricing. As part of its penetration pricing strategy, Hotstar provided its service at a lower cost compared to other platforms to aggressively get subscribers in and gain market share (Singh and Kumar, 2023).

The IPL, the most popular sports property in the country, has repeatedly broken viewing records and was crucial to Hotstar becoming the dominant streaming platform. In 2017, Star acquired the global IPL rights under a five-year contract valued at US$2.55 billion, the most expensive broadcast rights deal in the history of cricket at the time. Although Sony made the highest bid for domestic broadcasting and Facebook for domestic digital rights, Star was the only bidder for all packages and was therefore awarded the rights. This led to concerns that Star would have a monopoly on major cricket rights in the country. For the 2023–27 cycle, the Board of Control for Cricket in India (BCCI) created four rights packages to benefit from more competition in the market. Ultimately, three different bidders were awarded rights packages, almost tripling the value of the deal to US$6.2 billion. Star acquired the domestic broadcasting rights (US$3.02 billion), but had to leave the domestic digital rights (US$3.06 billion) to Viacom18, a newly formed broadcasting and streaming giant owned by Reliance Industries. Viacom18 showed the IPL for free via its JioCinema platform in order to generate a higher volume of advertising sales (Dixon, 2022). Viacom18's acquisition of the IPL rights put an end to Star's monopoly on cricket, and, at least in the first instance, intensified competition in the Indian sports rights market. Although highly overpriced, the acquisition of digital rights boosted Viacom18's ambition to penetrate the market, aiming for a dazzling number of 550 million viewers, and provided a tempting alternative for advertisers, especially keen on younger viewers. The loss of IPL rights seriously impacted Hotstar's ability to attract new subscribers and eventually led to a merger between Disney Star and Reliance in 2024. The joint venture integrates both JioCinema and Disney+ Hotstar and leads to a new streaming behemoth that caters to all segments of viewers (Sim, 2024a).

Despite internet-distributed television having lowered barriers for entrants entirely new to the audio-visual industries, at least to date legacy broadcasters and pay-tv operators continue to dominate the sports rights market. Except for DAZN and possibly a few smaller-scale platforms, such as Fubo (in the US and Canada), entering the market, the sports streaming business remains mainly concentrated in the hands of a few platforms that have their roots in television broadcasting. Linear viewing, and consequently advertising revenues and subscriptions, are in decline, but the broadcasting business model is still highly profitable, which is in stark contrast to the volatile and highly unprofitable business model of streaming platforms (see below). Thanks to this profitability and relative stability, broadcasters and pay-tv operators can afford to take considerable financial risks and bid for expensive premium rights. Their financial means, corporate scale, production expertise, and operational back-office give legacy sports broadcasters the opportunity to subsidise the acquisition of live rights and, possibly, turn them into a profitable activity. Despite the significant impact of digital infrastructure on the modes of television distribution and viewing patterns, the rather techno-optimistic vision, often spread by industry consultants and trade magazines, reasoning that video streaming would bring about a dramatic revolution in the sports broadcasting industry tends to neglect the persistency of structural power in the audio-visual industries (Evens and Donders, 2018). Online delivery is undoubtedly transforming industrial, audience, and regulatory practices, but this ongoing transformation is accelerated or decelerated by pre-existing power relationships, market structures, and institutions: the television industry itself, not technology, reinvents television (Lotz, 2021). This institutionalist approach hinges upon Williams (2003), who claims that television, like any other technology, develops within a complex set of socio-cultural definitions and institutions, and therefore tends to sustain prevailing power structures and relationships. Hence, the power structures of traditional sports broadcasting could well be reproduced in the streaming era, albeit enabled by different modes of distribution, business models, audience practices, and regulatory institutions.

The persistency of pre-existing power structures does not, as Lotz (2021) argues, rule out the possibility of disrupting platforms entering the market and aiming for market control. In the past, the sports broadcasting industry has, however, seen several new entrants that joined rights auctions in such an aggressive manner that they overestimated consumer demand, largely over-paid for these rights, and finally went bankrupt. Winners of sports rights auctions may be hit by the winner's curse when they spend much more than the actual value of a rights package and ultimately become insolvent and run out of business (Andreff, 2014). The cursed broadcasters were often not incumbent broadcasters or pay-tv operators, but new entrants eager to win rights packages (see Chapter 2). Mediapro's fiasco, in 2020, is the latest case of a winner's curse in the sports rights market. After losing out on the domestic La Liga rights in its core market of Spain, Mediapro acquired the rights to the French Ligue 1 and Ligue 2 for €780 million per year, leading to a 62 per cent increase in rights fees. Due to failed negotiations with existing pay-tv operators to sub-license the rights, Mediapro was forced to start its own channel Téléfoot from scratch. An unrealistic business plan and the COVID-19 pandemic accelerated the meltdown of the broadcaster, which missed two rights payments and exited the contract (Feuillet and Scelles, 2022; Feuillet et al., 2023). Streaming platforms, too, may face the winner's curse when spending too much on premium sports rights. Combined with slowing uptake and revenue, ambitious international expansion strategies and growth at all costs may eventually drive some streaming platforms into financial trouble – Viaplay is a notable example of this (see Box 3.4).

A Mix of Platforms

As much as the streaming wars are presented as a catch-all for competition between video services (see Lobato and Lotz, 2021), there is simply no such thing as a standard sports streaming platform. Services are operated by different types of players, originating from different stages of the audio-visual value chain and each having their own value proposition and economic logic. The sports streaming landscape populates a mix of platforms with varying sports rights portfolios, business models, and geographic scale (see Box 3.2).

BOX 3.2 AUSTRALIA'S SPORTS STREAMING WARS

Few media landscapes have embraced streaming live sports as quickly as Australia, whose sports rights market has long been dominated by pay-tv operator Foxtel and free-to-air networks, like Channel Nine. This development is remarkable, given that subscription-based streaming was not available until

2015, when Netflix first entered the market and was followed soon by Stan, owned by Nine. In 2016, Foxtel lost the English Premier League to Optus Sport, ending a partnership of nearly 20 years. This was the first time a top-tier sports property moved from exclusive broadcast coverage to a streaming service in the country. Optus Sport, which comes free with many of Optus' telecom services, continued to focus on soccer and purchased the exclusive rights to broadcast 39 live matches of the 2018 FIFA World Cup. However, its coverage of the international tournament was marred by technical difficulties, and it was ultimately forced to relinquish its rights to the public service channel SBS. At that time, the technical issues supported the arguments of opponents of streaming that the technology was premature (Carp, 2021a).

Today, streaming live sports has become mainstream, marking a generational shift within Australia's media landscape. Over the years, a series of sports streaming platforms have emerged, revitalising a sports rights market that was previously controlled by dominant pay-tv operator Foxtel. Late in 2018, Foxtel launched Kayo as a cheaper offer to appeal to customers unwilling to pay higher prices for pay-tv. Kayo, which is often described as the 'Netflix of sport', has an unmatched position in terms of the breadth of its rights portfolio (Knox, 2018). Being part of the Foxtel group, Kayo streams any sport that is broadcast on Fox Sports, ESPN, and beIN Sports, and covers over 50 sports, probably the widest range of any dedicated sports streaming service in the world. The offer includes Formula One, NBA, NFL, MotoGP, international cricket, the four men's golf majors, and WTA/ATP tennis tournaments. An agreement with Telstra, part-owner of Foxtel, gave Kayo access to the Australian Football League (AFL) and National Rugby League (NRL), the country's two most valuable and popular sports properties. In 2021, Kayo Freebies was launched, a free tier with non-live content and limited live offering, which may generate advertising revenues and eventually convert non-paying viewers into subscribers.

With also Stan Sport (rugby union, owned by Nine), Paramount+ (domestic soccer and national team soccer, owned by Ten), Amazon Prime Video (swimming), DAZN, 7Plus (hockey, owned by Seven), and SBS On Demand (owned by SBS) as the most significant sports services, the Australian market for streaming live sports has become a crowded space. This creates new opportunities for media rights owners, especially second-tier properties, who can finally let the market play, gain negotiation power, and choose how to distribute their rights. The National Basketball League (NBL), for example, was able to sign the most lucrative deal in its history when it sold its domestic rights to pay-tv channel ESPN/Foxtel, free-to-air channel Ten, and streaming platform Kayo (2022–24). For the first time since its inaugural season in 1979, the NBL was able to bargain a rights fee, reportedly totalling AUS$45 million (Carp, 2021b). In a similar vein, the newly founded soccer league Australian Professional League (APL) closed a landmark partnership (AUS$200 million for the 2022–27 period) with, among others, Paramount+, which allowed the streaming platform to launch in Australia.

However, incumbent pay-tv operator Foxtel and free-to-air networks Nine and Ten have been active to take the lead in the battle for live sports supremacy, and showed perseverance when top-tier rights were to be renewed in late 2022. Despite significant bids from Stan and Paramount+, Seven and Foxtel (with Kayo) were able to extend their AFL partnership following an unprecedented AUS$4.5 billion contract (until 2031). Similarly, Nine and Foxtel/Telstra extended their NRL partnership as part of an AUS$1.8 billion deal (until 2027). The new contracts illustrate how a hybrid rights model may possibly work in future, in which free-to-air coverage is quintessential for building a sport's reach and popularity, and streaming can help to renew and rejuvenate the audience. Overall, Australia is an interesting case suggesting how traditional players respond to new developments, how different business models co-exist, and how this expanding landscape unlocks opportunities for rights owners.

Sports Rights Portfolio

The global sports streaming landscape is defined by a wide variation in the sports programming that is offered. No two sports streaming platforms are alike. Platforms generally seek to differentiate themselves from competitors in an attempt to provide a unique offering of sports competitions and events. Exclusive rights are therefore instrumental in building a distinct portfolio of live sports. Sports rights are defined by heterogeneity of demand and command very limited overlap in audiences. Most Formula One fans are unlikely to view Formula E as a substitute; the English Premier League does not constitute an alternative to the Spanish La Liga. Sports events and competitions, even in the same sports discipline, are differentiated products that are not interchangeable (Noll, 2007). As a result, sports streaming services are not readily substitutable because of the extent of breadth and depth in rights portfolios and the particular mix of sports they provide.

In general, there are different types of streaming platforms in terms of the variety of programming they offer. A distinction in strategy can be made between those platforms that almost exclusively focus on sports (*specialists*) and those that provide sports programming as part of a wider catalogue of movies, series, documentaries, and other shows (*generalists*). First, specialists such as Kayo, DAZN, and ESPN+ build a large portfolio of sports rights (live, magazine shows, documentaries) and promote themselves as the prime destination for sports fans. For these platforms, the acquisition of premium rights is a must-have if they want to build a wide audience base and develop a sustainable business model. These platforms are susceptible to subscriber loss when they lose the rights to popular competitions. They also face challenges in keeping subscribers loyal during the off-season (Ampere Analysis, 2023). Second, generalists such as JioCinema, Amazon, and Discovery+ provide a wider mix of content genres, and are usually less aggressive in pursuing premium rights. For them, sports programming is an important part of the value proposition (often, but not always, packages on separate tiers), but generally not as crucial as original series and blockbuster movies. In addition, they benefit from scale economies, due to their higher market penetration.

Moreover, sports streaming platforms may differ in terms of the breadth in their sports rights portfolios and the number of different sports they provide. A distinction in strategy can be made between those platforms that provide access to one particular sport (*single-sport*) and those that carry multiple sports in their portfolio (*multi-sports*). Single-sport streaming platforms are dedicated to one particular sport and often have a deep catalogue of rights providing coverage of multiple events and competitions of that sport. In Australia, Paramount+ and Optus Sport are the home of football, providing coverage of national and international soccer competitions. Single-sports platforms generally compete against direct-to-fan platforms operated by sports properties (see Chapter 5) and attract super-fans that are interested in one particular sport, team, or athlete. Multi-sports streaming platforms, in contrast, provide coverage of a wide array of different sports. By securing such a large number of rights deals, multi-sports platforms may risk falling into the trap of pay-tv services, which carry generally too many sports competitions at too high a cost for consumers. In response, a growing proportion of consumers may cancel their subscription because they feel they pay for sports they do not watch. Alternatively, carrying a variety of sports may help platforms to retain subscribers during off-season periods for certain sports.

Business Model

Sports streaming platforms differ in their business model and the way they create and appropriate value to the firm. Similarly to legacy media organisations, streaming platforms adopt different strategies and rely on a wide variety of revenue sources (hybrid business models). In addition to the differentiated nature of sports competitions (see above), this multitude of business logics makes it hard to assess the competitive dynamics in the wider audio-visual market. Streaming platforms that generate revenue from subscriber payments do not automatically compete against traditional pay-tv services (e.g. observe the differences between ESPN and ESPN+). Similarly, Amazon Prime Video may not be a direct contender for more sports-dedicated streaming services, such as DAZN, because the Prime Video service aims at increasing retail spend with Amazon rather than raising subscription revenue. Hence, competition for viewers between sports streaming services is not automatically a zero-sum game.

In general, payments from subscribers form the main revenue source for most sports streaming platforms. Viewers are willing to pay for high-quality content, such as live coverage of premium sports. However, increased prices to recover inflated content costs may slow new subscriber sign-ups. Platforms need exclusive, preferably live, sports rights to provide a unique, differentiated programming portfolio and to maximise the number of paying consumers. For subscription video-on-demand (SVoD) platforms, the number of subscribers is the crucial metric of success. New subscription plans give access to different sports content tiers, multiple devices access, and even pay-per-view options. Segmented subscription plans may address different types of sports fans and enlarge the base of subscribers. DAZN was a first-moving sports streaming platform, but more recently generalist platforms, such as Peacock and Viaplay, have started to invest in sports rights as a differentiator in an increasingly overcrowded streaming market. The commercial strategy of subscription-funded platforms resembles that of pay-tv broadcasters, such as Sky and Canal+, which have been using live sports as a 'battering ram' to open up national television markets and increase average revenue per user (ARPU) since the 1990s (see Chapter 2). The use of sport by pay-tv broadcasters has been a significant part of a mutually reinforcing trend towards the marketisation of the television and sports industries, and ultimately led to inflated rights fees (Rowe, 2004). At least partly, intense competition for key sports rights, in many parts of the world, has also resulted in monopolistic pay-tv market structures (Leandros and Tsourvakas, 2005). In contrast to traditional pay-tv markets, the sports streaming landscape has not turned into a 'winner-takes-all' market (yet), probably due to the lower entry barriers in this industry and the availability of original drama series and movies as another key differentiator among streaming competitors.

Following a general trend in the streaming industry, the share of advertising income has gained importance in the sports streaming landscape. Whereas sports streaming platforms originally emphasised subscriptions as the main revenue source, subscription-funded platforms are rapidly turning to advertising as a complementary revenue stream. DAZN, for example, shows brief commercials in short breaks during live games and schedules ads in non-live content at specific intervals. Like other platforms, DAZN uses ad technology to pool unsold ad inventory and makes it available to advertisers who might not have the financial means to advertise around premium sports content (Joseph, 2023). Advertisers are discovering sports streaming platforms to reach new audiences and cultivate a new generation of sports fans that are hard to reach otherwise. Not only does streaming attract a significantly younger, more affluent, and more female audience than traditional broadcasts, streaming audiences show higher engagement (in terms of number of viewing minutes) and are more likely to search for brands and products during the game (Carney, 2023). Additionally, subscription-funded platforms are launching free or lower-priced advertising-supported plans: ad-supported video is becoming the preferred streaming option for the majority of consumers. The bulk of new sign-ups are ad-supported, accounting for up to 60 per cent for Peacock and Hulu, 40 per cent for Discovery+, one-third for Disney+ and Paramount+, and one-fifth for Netflix and HBO Max (Yuen, 2023). Consumers may pay for their favourite sports competition, but rely on free ad-supported plans to access other sports. Increased subscription prices may also lead to churn with paying consumers fleeing to cheaper content tiers. Free ad-supported television (FAST) represents another huge development in the streaming landscape, and is the fastest-growing segment in the streaming industry. FAST positions itself at the crossroads of traditional linear television and curated streaming services, and aggregates linear channels carrying almost all types of content genres. Sports-dedicated channels represent about 9 per cent of the total number of FAST channels, in both the US and Europe. The FAST landscape is dominated by device manufacturers (such as Amazon's Freevee, Roku, and Samsung TV Plus) and major media companies (such as Paramount's Pluto TV, Fox's Tubi, and ITV's ITVX). Samsung TV Plus, for example, has over 200 channels including Red Bull Media House, the PGA Tour, FIFA+, DAZN Ringside, and DAZN Women's Football (Bassam, 2023). Pluto TV and Tubi have the advantage of being able to tap into the extensive content libraries held by their respective parent companies. With a few exceptions, however, FAST sports channels focus on archive footage and highlights rather than on live coverage. FAST channels are most similar to linear, commercial broadcasters: sports programming is used to enlarge audiences and maximise advertising revenues. For these platforms, the revenue generated from advertisements is the crucial metric for success.

Other streaming platforms see sports rights as an instrument to sell other, more profitable services or hardware. Apple and Amazon cross-subsidise their streaming platforms, Apple TV+ and Amazon Prime Video, respectively, with revenues/profits from interconnected businesses, leverage the power of their installed base, and lock in this existing customer base by tying video with access to other software and/or hardware – a business strategy commonly referred to as the 'flywheel effect' (Collins, 2001). Despite generating substantial revenue streams and attracting millions of subscribers, the value of Apple TV+ and Amazon Prime Video is only secondary to the larger business objectives of their parent companies. Amazon's sports rights investments, securing exclusive rights to NFL's Thursday Night Football, the NBA, and top-flight European soccer leagues, are designed to support its core retail business by driving Prime memberships. As Klatt (2022, p.1544) suggests, Amazon Studios and Amazon Prime Video is a key spoke in the company's flywheel, which explains why winning a Golden Globe generates more shoe sales and parcel deliveries. Of course, these commercial tactics are not entirely new and are highly similar to the bundling strategies perfected by telecommunication and internet service providers. Since the mid-2000s, telecom operators have attempted to acquire premium sports rights to introduce and promote new pay-tv services delivered over the internet (Smith et al., 2016) (see Chapter 2). Bundling is considered an effective retention strategy because it raises financial and psychological costs for consumers who want to switch platforms (McGrail and Roberts, 2005). It facilitates the 'locking in' of subscribers (i.e. a lower 'churn rate'), by raising the cost (and inconvenience) of switching to other providers: customers cannot cancel pay-tv without cancelling connectivity – which they can probably least afford to lose – consumers' strings are literally attached to the bundle. Perhaps most importantly, bundling allows for cross-subsidisation: operators reduce subscription prices for a less price-elastic service such as pay-tv and compensate with higher prices for connectivity.

As with the introduction of advertising, sports streaming platforms tend to follow a general trend observable in the wider streaming market: re-bundling. Whereas the early development of the streaming industry was marked by a rather extreme form of unbundling strategy – streaming platforms explicitly presented themselves as a more 'skinny' alternative to the 'fat' pay-tv bundle – the latest developments in the sports streaming industry tend to suggest that bundling is back on the agenda after never actually going away. For example, in an attempt to remain the go-to destination for online television, traditional pay-tv operators such as Sky have reached distribution agreements with streaming platforms, who, in turn, benefit from increased exposure and, in some instances, distribution income. But also other parties are playing the bundling card leading to innovative business models (also see Box 3.3). Amazon bundles its video service, including sports programming, with its Prime membership; the purchase of an Apple iPhone or Mac comes together with free access to Apple TV+; and so on. Device manufacturers such as Samsung, Roku, and Amazon are also leading the FAST hype, acting as a hub of hundreds of FAST channels. Lastly, betting operators such as bet365, bwin, Betfred, and Unibet provide live sports streaming allowing fans to watch the game while placing bets on events, with odds changing as the game progresses. Even DAZN has made betting a cornerstone of its business model.

BOX 3.3 GOALS AND HIGHLIGHTS IN A BANKING APP

A few years ago, no one would have expected that a bank would be interested in buying sports media rights. However, this is exactly what happened when Belgian bank, KBC, entered into an agreement with rights holder, Eleven Sports, to become the first bank in the world to provide sports programming. In 2020, KBC acquired the exclusive rights to offer digital near-live clips (until 30 minutes after the final whistle) and non-exclusive rights to digital highlights of the Jupiler Pro League, Belgium's top football league (for an annual fee estimated at around €2 million). All goals and highlights were be pushed to the KBC Mobile app, which is available for customers and non-customers. For customers of a premium banking account, the Goal Alert service was free; other customers as well as non-customers could get the service for €0.99 per month. Goal Alert was part of KBC's vision to develop an all-in-one application where customers can do almost everything – take out insurance, buy a bus ticket, pay for fuel, watch sports and entertainment, etc. This is just one example of how innovative bundling strategies are bringing together sports content with other, seemingly unrelated services.

Geographic Scale

In terms of the territorial structure of the streaming industries, a key differentiation must be made between platforms that operate in one single country (*single-territory*) and platforms that operate across a number of countries (*multi-territory*). First, single-territory platforms, such as JioCinema, ESPN+, and Kayo, are often affiliated with legacy sports broadcasters operating in the same national market and can therefore benefit from the programming catalogue of the parent company. They have profound knowledge of the market and the sports programming preferences of the target audience. In addition, they may have developed close relationships with domestic sports leagues and associations to become/remain their preferred broadcasting partner. Single-territory platforms independent of incumbent broadcasters may not be able to match the bidding power of incumbent sports broadcasters. For that reason, single-territory online platforms generally tend to focus on the sports rights that incumbent platforms do not want to exploit (such as highlights or near-live clips), or live rights of second-tier sports.

Second, multi-territory streaming platforms such as DAZN, Viaplay, and Amazon Prime Video generally benefit from economies of scale, due to the low marginal costs associated with internet-distributed television (Lobato and Lotz, 2021). Platforms seek for the widest possible audience so that they can recoup their investment in original drama productions. In this regard, cross-border distribution, at least in theory, provides the most efficient cost structure for streaming platforms. However, the economics of sports rights are markedly different than those of original drama productions. Whereas platforms can spread the costs of original drama over their entire audience across all countries where they operate, the costs of sports rights mount up with every country that is added. Rights owners typically negotiate their rights, especially for the biggest markets, on a territory-by-territory basis to maximise income from rights sales. Moreover, the value of premium live rights is usually skewed towards one or two markets – generally the home market of the league (see Chapter 2). Taken together it may simply be too costly for multi-territory sports streaming platforms to cover the same sports on a global level. Because there are few truly global sports properties, platforms may wish to localise their offerings and secure the most popular sports for each territory that is served.

To address the geographical fragmentation of rights – for sports events and competitions, but also for other media and entertainment products –

streaming platforms have been pushing to enter into multi-territory agreements with rights owners. Instead of following a market-by-market approach, multi-territory platforms have embraced pan-regional deals to substantially decrease transaction costs. Viaplay applies such a pan-regional strategy while taking pan-Baltic and pan-Nordic rights to international soccer; Discovery+ secured the rights to the Tour de France and La Vuelta across 38 markets, the French Open/Roland Garros across 50 markets, and Wimbledon in 11 markets. Or another example: Apple's innovative revenue-sharing deal with Major League Soccer (MLS) secures the hardware company the worldwide rights to the emerging soccer league and the opportunity to introduce the MLS Season Pass in more than 100 countries. Leaving the most lucrative territories out of some of these rights agreements, rights owners welcome the simplicity of dealing with one rights buyer that exploits the rights over a multitude of countries. This also secures coverage of the sports in difficult-to-approach markets, where the sports can grow in popularity, and thus the coverage eventually becomes more valuable (EBU, 2021). This strategy is, of course, not new: EBU, the alliance of public service media organisations in Europe, has long secured broadcasting rights, among others for the Olympics, for its member organisations. Similarly, beIN Sports usually acquires the rights to broadcast sports competitions in the Middle East and North African region (MENA).

Boom or Bust

The rise of streaming technology may upend, or at least challenges, the business model for sports broadcasting. Historically, dedicated sports broadcasters, especially in smaller and/or less developed markets, have struggled to reach profitability: the pool of financial resources derived from audiences and advertisers was barely enough to sustain the business model. Advertising and subscription revenues barely offset high expenditures on sports rights, but sports channels such as ESPN and TNT were able to tap into supplementary revenue sources such as retransmission/carriage fees to develop a viable business case (Corrigan, 2015). In essence, the pay-tv model raised high entry barriers and proved extremely lucrative for the abovementioned sports channels that provided must-have programming for television distributors. However, the rising popularity of streaming technology and the decline in linear viewership have started to erode the subscriber base (cord-cutting), which ultimately affects the level of retransmission/carriage fees. Towards the end of 2023, Charter's Spectrum and Disney were locked in a ten-day-long carriage dispute leading Disney to pull ESPN, ABC, and other cable channels off Spectrum in the middle of US Open tennis coverage and the college football season. The dispute was mainly over ESPN's carriage fees and Disney + that cannibalises Charter's business. The issue was settled with Spectrum subscribers gaining access to Disney+ and ESPN+ as part of different packages. The deal suggests that cable television is anything but dead, but also that finding a balance between an endangered legacy business and an all-streaming future is tricky (McCaskill, 2023b).

However, the economic foundation of this all-streaming future has been anything but bright. Unlike their highly profitable broadcasting and cable counterparts, streaming platforms continue to bear financial losses and struggle with profitability. Most streaming services face huge financial losses, negative cash flows, and low ARPU: expensive marketing and technology costs, inflationary expenditures on programming, and flattening subscriber growth are destabilising streaming as a business model. After strong market growth marked by a multitude of players trying their luck as a platform, the streaming industry is going through a shake-out period eventually leading to higher industry consolidation. As the market matures, platforms seek to create scale and build empires (see Ball, 2023). Cost-cutting, less investment, and higher prices are all part of the road to profitability: Warner Bros. Discovery has reconsidered licensing titles to rival platforms, Disney has saved substantially on content investments, Peacock has raised subscription prices, and so on. Against all odds, subscription-funded platforms including Netflix have even introduced advertising as an extra revenue source to reach break-even (or better). The television industry is in the midst of a migration from an oligopolistic cash-flowing broadcasting business to a streaming business marked by hyper-competition, low entry barriers, and – if present at all – thin operational margins. The negative operational results of almost all global streamers, except for Netflix, are illustrative of the fact that, to date, the streaming business has been structurally less profitable than the broadcasting industry because of lower pricing and higher churn.

Amidst this industry transformation, sports streaming platforms too are seeking their way to profitability. Sports streaming platforms are faced with a high cost structure, limited possibilities for scale economies (due to territory-by-territory rights agreements), and relatively limited willingness to pay. Pioneers such as Viaplay (see Box 3.4) and DAZN have been pursuing rapid short-term growth and expansion at any price, and now need to pivot towards long-term profitability. DAZN has invested heavily in top-tier sports rights to accelerate subscription growth at an early stage. However, the stand-alone platform has lost multiple billions since its launch in 2016, highlighting the difficulty in selling enough subscriptions to offset huge investments in attractive premium sports like La Liga, Bundesliga, and Serie A (Genovese, 2023). Early in 2022, DAZN was close to buying BT Sport, which would have given it access to sought-after rights to the English Premier League and UEFA Champions League. Following the failed bid, the company had to reduce the number of staff at its London headquarters. Nevertheless, it was able to take over sports broadcaster Eleven Sports, which fits DAZN's strategy of international expansion and revenue diversification. The company has been developing ancillary revenue streams such as (programmatic) advertising, carriage fees from third-party distribution platforms such as Movistar Plus and Amazon Channels, betting, merchandise, ticketing, and non-fungible token (NFT) marketplaces. Although the company strives for profitability from 2024 onwards, time will tell whether DAZN can build a sustainable business model.

BOX 3.4 VIAPLAY'S THREE-PILLARED SPORTS PORTFOLIO

Headquartered in Stockholm, Viaplay Group (previously Nordic Entertainment Group, NENT) is a leading media and entertainment group, presenting itself as an international streaming challenger for global streaming platforms. Originally launched in the Nordics (Denmark, Finland, Iceland, Norway, and Sweden), in 2018, the subscription streaming service expanded rapidly inside and outside Europe and had rolled out its service to over a dozen countries, including the US and Canada. Viaplay's mission was to be the European streaming champion: the target was to serve 12 million paying subscribers by the end of 2025 (equally divided between the Nordics and internationally). However, this international expansion strategy proved overly ambitious.

In addition to an extensive movie and series catalogue – including numerous Viaplay Originals – Viaplay's unparalleled and long-term live sports portfolio is vital to penetrate new markets and grow its number of subscribers. This portfolio was built using a three-pillared approach. First, Viaplay centres on football, especially the English Premier League, which comes week in, week out: this seasonality is key for building a long-term subscriber base. Second, motorsports such as Formula One form a driver for Viaplay's subscription base, not least because motorsports fans are different from football fans. Third, Viaplay adds locally relevant rights, such as winter sports or darts, to each market, catering to local tastes of each territory (Bassam, 2021).

Viaplay's strong position in the Nordics is partly based on its extended broadcast partnership with the English Premier League, which draws higher audiences than the domestic football leagues in most Nordic countries (Denmark's Superliga is the only exception). In 2020, Viaplay was able to secure the rights to the English Premier League for the Nordic area under a landmark six-year deal until 2028 for a reported £2 billion. The company clearly benefited from the three-year sports rights cycle to grasp an impressive rights portfolio and launch in new markets. International football competitions such as the UEFA Champions League, English Premier League, and national team tournaments were also instrumental in its expansion to the Baltics. Moreover, Viaplay's exclusive coverage of the NHL was key, because ice hockey is one of the most popular sports in the region. Similarly, Viaplay's access to Germany's Bundesliga, which has a long history of Polish players, until 2029 in nine European markets was crucial to launch in Poland and consolidated the platform's position in its other markets. Surprisingly at the time, early 2022, Viaplay trumped leading Dutch pay-tv operator, Ziggo, who had been broadcasting Formula One for nine years. Viaplay's bid was rumoured to be around three times the figure that Ziggo had been paying before and secured the platform's access until 2024. Formula One was the element underpinning Viaplay's successful launch in the Netherlands. The service capitalised on the popularity of the Dutch driver Max Verstappen. Viaplay was able to renew its licence until 2029.

In July 2022, Viaplay acquired UK-based pay-tv channel and sports streamer Premier Sports for a reported fee of £30 million. The acquisition accelerated Viaplay's development in the UK and Ireland, and followed a four-year partnership with UEFA agreed earlier to show at least 40 live matches of the Scottish, Welsh, and Northern Irish men's national football teams in the European Qualifiers for the FIFA World Cup 2026, UEFA Euro 2028, and in the UEFA Nations League 2024/25 and 2026/27. Premier Sports' portfolio of sports rights complemented the rights secured earlier by Viaplay. Similar to its position in other markets, Viaplay had no access to top-tier domestic football rights, but focused on a diversified portfolio of lower-tier non-domestic football and other sports. Viaplay's five-year deal (2023–27) with the Professional Darts Corporation (PDC) European Tour in ten markets was a boost for the service's offering in the UK, which is the biggest darts market (the Netherlands is also a key market for darts). Moreover, Viaplay was available across the UK through long-term pay-tv distribution agreements, which allowed Viaplay to generate extra revenue from carriage deals with these distribution partners.

The deal with the PDC highlights how Viaplay unlike smaller streaming platforms benefited from its pan-European network. The company's ability to combine multiple territories with its expanded footprint was attractive to rights owners to bet on thriving platforms and provided Viaplay with a competitive advantage when bidding for rights. This ability to secure a similar set of sports rights across its markets had not only made Viaplay one of the biggest sports broadcasters in Europe, but allegedly also created scale advantages where production facilities were concerned. Its presence across multiple territories allowed Viaplay to invest in facilities at sporting events and produce lots of content that could be used in all local broadcasts it provided (Bassam, 2021).

However, the bubble burst in early 2023, when Viaplay confirmed its plans to focus on its core markets in the Nordics and the Netherlands and exit the UK and US, less than one year after it had acquired Premier Sports to become a challenger in the market (McCaskill, 2023d). The company struggled with the escalating costs of its rapid international expansion and content portfolio and faced the pressure of a difficult macroeconomic environment, including a weak advertising market, declines in subscription uptake, adverse currency effects, and high interest rates. There is no chance that Viaplay's international strategy would have led to profitability so early, but the streaming market had dramatically changed. In contrast to investors' initial focus on subscriber growth at all costs, profitability and operating margin had become the main metrics for a platform's success. With rising interest rates, investors started to demand immediate financial returns instead of risky international expansion.

No Big Tech Sports Bonanza

As discussed in Chapter 2, the value of sports rights is largely determined by the level of competition and the number of possible buyers in a market. Rights sellers have benefited greatly as competition for sports rights grew over the years, and believe that the entry of streaming platforms will spike the future value of rights. After Viaplay's decision to withdraw from its non-core markets (the UK and the US), however, DAZN remains the only serious streaming challenger to chase premium rights, at least in Western markets. Many rights owners now hope that the big tech companies constituting the notorious FAANG – an acronym to describe some of the most prominent Western platform companies including Facebook, Apple, Amazon, Netflix, and Google – and BAT – an acronym covering the leading Chinese platforms Baidu, Alibaba, and Tencent – will show appetite for sports rights and, consequently, spend billions to acquire these rights. Over the last decade, we have seen a growing presence of these platform companies in the sports industry and some of them have been quite active in purchasing live rights indeed (Fakataulavelua et al., 2023). These companies have significant financial resources and have repeatedly outbid major media organisations in the battle for premium rights. Some industry watchers, therefore, believe that big tech will be a game-changer for the sports industry, leading to yet another inflationary push into the sports rights market and yielding significantly higher media rights income for sports leagues. However, a less dramatic vision for the development of the market, especially in Europe, seems more likely: an evolution of the sports media rights market, rather than a revolution. According to Maes (2019), the big 'bonanza' of sports rights will shortly come to an end. While providers of pay-tv and telecom services, including Canal+, Sky Italy, and TNT Sports, are increasingly reluctant to pay excessive fees for sports rights, streaming services, such as DAZN and Viaplay, are having difficulties in recouping their aggressive rights bids to claim a sustainable position in the market. Just as importantly, big tech companies have tended to apply a selective approach to sports rights acquisition as sports programming is only of secondary value to their platforms: sports programming drives traffic to other services within their ecosystem, and gives access to detailed data on fan behaviour and sports consumption. Moreover, they tend to limit their investments to a limited number of high-profile rights in large markets, or pick up cheaper rights in smaller markets.

Each of these platforms has possible strategic reasons to bid for live sports, yet, more often than not, acquires rights on a more opportunistic basis.

Take Amazon for example, probably the most active tech platform in the sports rights market. The retail giant has built a media empire around Amazon Prime Video, which drives traffic to its online marketplace. In 2018, Amazon became the first tech company to secure live rights to one of Europe's top five soccer leagues. It broke up the duopoly of Sky Sports and BT Sport by purchasing an exclusive live package of 20 English Premier League matches per season from one bank holiday and one midweek matchday (for an estimated annual fee of £30 million). The video service, which also provides access to a wide range of series, movies, and (sports) documentaries, is used as a loss-leader to boost the Prime membership. Subscribers to Amazon Prime's membership, which includes perks such as free product delivery and access to free music and games, are hugely valuable to the company, because they tend to spend twice as much with Amazon as non-subscribers (Sweney, 2018). The company capitalised on the financial impact of COVID-19 on traditional broadcasters, and was able to pick up Bundesliga rights following Eurosport's withdrawal, bought the majority of France's Ligue 1 for a reduced fee, and sub-licensed English Premier League rights from Viaplay in some Nordic countries. Amazon's biggest deal is its exclusive 11-year media rights deal with NFL's Thursday Night Football, for which it pays $1 billion per year (2023–33). It is the first time a streaming service is carrying a full package of NFL games exclusively. Amazon's NFL coverage is scoring all-time audience records, which once again underscores the strategic importance of live sports – and NFL in the US – for the platform (Petski, 2023). Furthermore, Amazon has agreed an 11-year deal to become one of the main media partners of the NBA. This move represents the most significant investment of Amazon into live sports so far (Sim, 2024b).

Although Apple was repeatedly rumoured to be a potential buyer of English Premier League rights, it has never entered a territory-per-territory rights auction so far. The company claims it has no interest in partial rights for a specific market and eyes all-encompassing deals on a global scale (McCaskill, 2023a). In 2022, Apple acquired MLS's media rights for a reported $2.5 billion as part of a ten-year partnership. Apple won the worldwide rights, so that soccer fans from all over the world can watch games via the MLS Season Pass on Apple TV+. Under the deal, Apple also shares an undisclosed cut of the subscription revenue with MLS, bringing the league's total media rights revenue close to $300 million per year. The deal is also said to have an opt-out clause, leaving Apple the possibility to walk away from the agreement if the league does not drive a large enough number of subscribers. Although the production value of the MLS Season Pass was initially criticised, the signing of global superstar Lionel Messi by Inter Miami helped Apple to double the number of subscribers in less than one month (McCaskill, 2023c). Apple's MLS deal tends to suggest that the platform is looking for more affordable sports that still have ample room for commercial growth rather than joining an expensive bidding race for premium rights. At the time of writing, Apple is reported to be close to securing a global streaming deal for the expanded FIFA Club World Cup, a new worldwide club competition due to be held in the US in 2025, for a US$1 billion fee. Coverage of this month-long competition would complement MLS coverage and benefit from the worldwide appeal of soccer (McCaskill, 2024).

Unlike Amazon's and Apple's subscription models, Google (YouTube) and Meta (Facebook) have adopted partnership models. Instead of purchasing live rights in an aggressive fashion, both companies encourage rights owners and broadcasters to provide free content in exchange for a share of advertising revenues. These mainly involve secondary rights with the aim to grow the audience and enlarge the global fanbase (Fakataulavelua et al., 2023). Facebook initially took a traditional approach when it acquired international soccer rights in Asia and Latin America, but scaled back those ambitions at the start of 2020. YouTube, on the other hand, recently won the live rights to the popular NFL's Sunday Ticket, which had been held by DirecTV since 1994. Google paid around $14 billion for this seven-year deal (2023–30) and will broadcast Sunday games on its subscription service YouTube TV, available only in the US. It needs to be seen whether Google will expand its interest in sports rights beyond the NFL – a must-have to address the US audience – and enlarge its footprint to international markets.

Netflix has until now been a notable outlier amidst the streaming landscape in that it believes live sports rights are too expensive and geographically fragmented compared to the other forms of entertainment content it provides at a global scale. Netflix has repeatedly said that it does not see a clear path towards profitability with live sports: chief content officer Ted Sandaros was quoted as saying, 'Netflix is not anti-sports, but just pro-profit' (McCaskill, 2022). The value of live sports was often considered too temporal for a platform that is building a catalogue of content to be consumed at any time. Instead of purchasing live rights, Netflix created a unique approach to sports programming by producing critically acclaimed docuseries like *Drive to Survive, The Last Dance*, and *Beckham* that appealed to an engaged, youthful audience. However, with the introduction of an advertising tier, at the end of 2022, offering live sports programming started to make sense. In November 2023, Netflix presented *The Netflix Cup*, a one-off live golf event bringing together stars from Netflix's popular sports series *Drive to Survive* and *Full Swing*. The event was followed by *The Netflix Slam*, in 2024, a one-off exhibition tennis match between the Spanish star duo, Rafael Nadal and Carlos Alcaraz. Furthermore, in 2024, Netflix featured a live boxing event between Jake Paul and Mike Tyson and added *Monday Night Raw* wrestling to its platform as part of a five-year deal worth US$500 million per year. Although one can hardly deny these are all sporting events, they also exhibit elements of scripted entertainment, which differentiate them from premium live sports. In May 2024, however, Netflix surprised industry observers by agreeing a global deal with the NFL to show two games on Christmas Day until 2026, for an estimated fee of $150 million per year. It is too early to tell whether this deal signals Netflix's intention to become a major player in the sports media rights market (in the US and/or beyond), but it is certainly the case that sports content is an increasingly significant part of its commercial strategy.

References

Ampere Analysis (2023). *The Role of Sports in the Streaming Wars.* Available at: https://www.ampereanalysis.com/report/the-role-of-sports-in-the-streaming-wars (Accessed: 19 February 2023).

Andreff, W. (2014). The Winner's Curse in Sports Economics. In: O. Budzinski and A. Federsen (eds.), *Contemporary Research in Sports Economics* (pp. 177–205). Frankfurt am Main: Peter Lang.

Ball, M. (2023). *The Streaming Book.* Available at: https://www.thestreamingbook.com (Accessed: 3 February 2023).

Bassam, T. (2021). 'That's Nent-ertainment: How Viaplay is using sport as a springboard for its expansion', *SportsProMedia*, 29 October. Available at: https://www.sportspromedia.com/from-the-magazine/nent-viaplay-sports-rights-strategy-peter-norrelund-interview-anders-jensen/ (Accessed: 19 February 2023).

Bassam, T. (2023). 'DAZN, PGA Tour and Red Bull Media House bringing FAST channels to Samsung TV Plus', *SportsProMedia*, 14 September. Available at: https://www.sportspromedia.com/news/dazn-pga-tour-red-bull-media-fast-channels-samsung-tv-plus-streaming/ (Accessed: 19 February 2023).

Carney, D. (2023). 'The future of live sports: Why streaming is a touchdown for advertisers', *AdAge*, 22 June. Available at: https://adage.com/article/media/future-live-sports-why-streaming-touchdown-advertisers/2500591 (Accessed: 19 September 2023).

Carp, S. (2021a). 'How Australia's streaming wars have created "a competitive alternative" in its sports rights market', *SportsProMedia*, 26 November. Available at: https://www.sportspromedia.com/from-the-magazine/australia-sports-streaming-platforms-kayo-optus-nbl-paramount-stan/ (Accessed: 23 February 2023).

Carp, S. (2021b). '"It's a turning point for our code": NBL commissioner Jeremy Loeliger reveals all about the league's new TV deal', *SportsProMedia*, 23 November. Available at: https://www.sportspromedia.com/interviews/nbl-commissioner-jeremy-loeliger-interview-tv-rights-foxtel-espn-kayo/ (Accessed: 23 February 2023).

Collins, J. (2001). *Good to Great: Why Some Companies Make the Leap … and Others Don't.* New York, NY: HarperCollins.

Corrigan, T. F. (2015). Digging the Moat: The Political Economy of ESPN's Cable Carriage Fees. In: J. McGuire, G. G. Armfield, and A. Earnheardt (eds.), *The ESPN Effect: Exploring the Worldwide Leader in Sports* (pp. 37–52). New York, NY: Peter Lang.

Dixon, E. (2022). 'The IPL's new media rights deals: Analysing Indian cricket's multi-billion dollar auction', *SportsProMedia*, 1 July. Available at: https://www.sportspromedia.com/analysis/ipl-t20-cricket-india-tv-media-rights-disney-star-viacom18-times-internet-bcci/ (Accessed: 25 February 2023).

Duncan, S. (2020). *The Digital World of Sport: The Impact of Emerging Media on Sports News, Information and Journalism.* London: Anthem Press.

EBU (2021). *Sport on European TV: Maximising Commercial Value.* Geneva: EBU Media Intelligence Service.

Evens, T. and Donders, K. (2018). *Platform Power and Policy in Transforming Television Markets.* London: Palgrave Macmillan.

Evens, T., Iosifidis, P., and Smith, P. (2013). *The Political Economy of Television Sports Rights.* Basingstoke: Palgrave Macmillan.

Evens, T., Lefever, K., Valcke, P., Schuurman, D., and De Marez, L. (2011). Access to Premium Content on Mobile Television Platforms: The Case of Mobile Sports. *Telematics and Informatics*, 28 (1), pp. 32–39.

Fakataulavelua, A., Lang, M., and Moulard, J. (2023). Streaming the Beautiful Game: Exploring Big Tech's Growing Presence in the Soccer Industry. *Frontiers in Sports and Active Living*, 5, Article 1156601. Available at: https://www.frontiersin.org/articles/10.3389/fspor.2023.1156601/full (Accessed: 19 February 2023).

Feuillet, A., Alem, A., Durand, C., Terrien, M., and Scelles, N. (2023). What Can be Learnt from Failures in the Sports Media Business? A Case Study of the Mediapro Crash in Football Media Rights in France. *Journal of Media Business Studies*, 21 (1), pp. 1–22.

Feuillet, A. and Scelles, N. (2022). Valuation and Negotiation of Sport Broadcast Rights. In: H. Fujak and S. Frawley (eds.), *Sport Broadcasting for Managers* (pp. 70–83). New York: Routledge.

Fortunato, J. (2001). *The Ultimate Assist: The Relationship and Broadcast Strategies of the NBA and Television Networks.* Creskill, NJ: Hampton Press.

Fujak, H. and Frawley, S. (2016). The Relationship between Television Viewership and Advertising Content in Australian Football Broadcasts. *Communication & Sport*, 4 (1), pp. 82–101.

Gantz, W. and Wenner, L. A. (1991). Men, Women, and Sports: Audience Experiences and Effects. *Journal of Broadcasting & Electronic Media*, 35 (2), pp. 233–243.

Genovese, J. (2023). 'DAZN's path to profitability', Ampere Analysis. Available at: https://www.ampereanalysis.com/insight/dazns-path-to-profitability (Accessed: 2 April 2023).

Joseph, S. (2023). "'Start making more from the inventory we can't sell": DAZN is quietly ramping up its programmatic ads business', *Digiday*, 8 September. Available at: https://digiday.com/media/start-making-more-from-the-inventory-we-cant-sell-dazn-is-quietly-ramping-up-its-programmatic-ads-business/ (Accessed: 19 September 2023).

Klatt, T. (2022). The Streaming Industry and the Great Disruption: How Winning a Golden Globe Helps Amazon Sell More Shoes. *Media, Culture & Society*, 44 (8), pp. 1541–1558.

Knox, D. (2018). 'Kayo Sports is a game-changer', *TV Tonight*, 9 November. Available at: https://tvtonight.com.au/2018/11/kayo-sports-is-a-game-changer.html (Accessed: 23 February 2023).

Leandros, N. and Tsourvakas, G. (2005). Intensive Competition and Company Failures in Subscription Television: Some European Experiences. *International Journal on Media Management*, 7 (1–2), pp. 24–38.

Lobato, R. and Lotz, A. D. (2021). Beyond Streaming Wars: Rethinking Competition in Video Services. *Media Industries Journal*, 8 (1), pp. 89–108.

Lotz, A. D. (2021). *Media Disrupted.* Cambridge, MA: MIT Press.

Maes, P. (2019). *Le Business des droits du Foot.* Limoges: FYP Editions.

McCaskill, S. (2022). '"Pro-profit" Netflix has no plans to invest in live sport, says co-CEO', *SportsProMedia*, 7 December. Available at: https://www.sportspromedia.com/news/netflix-live-sport-streaming-f1-wsl/ (Accessed: 29 September 2022).

McCaskill, S. (2023a). 'Apple unlikely to bid for Premier League domestic rights as it eyes global deals', *SportsProMedia*, 24 July. Available at: https://www.sportspromedia.com/news/premier-league-apple-tv-rights-broadcast-us-viaplay/ (Accessed: 28 September 2023).

McCaskill, S. (2023b). 'The Charter dispute shows cable isn't dead but ESPN isn't the master of the bundle's fate', *SportsProMedia*, 14 September. Available at: https://www.sportspromedia.com/insights/opinions/sportspro-blog/charter-disney-dispute-espn-spectrum-cable-streaming-dtc-everpass/ (Accessed: 25 September 2023).

McCaskill, S. (2023c). 'Report: Apple secures 1m MLS Season Pass subscribers as Messi sets TV record', *SportsProMedia*, 26 July. Available at: https://www.sportspromedia.com/broadcast-ott/lionel-messi-mls-apple-tv-ratings-subscribers/ (Accessed: 27 September 2023).

McCaskill, S. (2023d). 'Viaplay exiting UK sports broadcasting market to focus on Nordics and Netherlands', *SportsProMedia*, 20 July. Available at: https://www.sportspromedia.com/news/viaplay-uk-exit-sale-scotland-nordics-streaming/ (Accessed: 12 September 2023).

McCaskill, S. (2024). 'Apple TV nears "US$1bn" global Fifa Club World streaming deal', *SportsProMedia*, 23 April. Available at: https://www.sportspromedia.com/news/apple-tv-fifa-club-world-cup-global-streaming-rights-deal/ (Accessed: 26 September 2023).

McGrail, M. and Roberts, B. (2005). Strategies in the Broadband Cable TV Industry: The Challenges for Management and Technology Innovation. *Info: The Journal of Policy, Regulation and Strategy for Telecommunications, Information and Media*, 7 (1), pp. 53–65.

Mondello, M. and Fortunato, J. (2022). Economics of Sport Broadcasting. In: H. Fujak and S. Frawley (eds.), *Sport Broadcasting for Managers* (pp. 55–69). New York: Routledge.

Nicita, A. and Ramello, G. B. (2005). Exclusivity and Antitrust in Media Markets: The Case of Pay-TV in Europe. *International Journal of the Economics of Business*, 12 (3), pp. 371–387.

Noakes, C. (2023). 'Matildas smash records to become biggest TV sports program in a decade', *7News*, 13 August. Available at: https://7news.com.au/sport/fifa-womens-world-cup/matildas-smash-records-to-become-biggest-tv-sports-program-in-a-decade-c-11573024 (Accessed: 31 August 2023).

Noll, R. G. (2007). Broadcasting and Team Sports. *Scottish Journal of Political Economy*, 54 (3), pp. 400–421.

Petski, D. (2023). '"Thursday Night Football" scores record high for Prime Video in season debut', *Deadline*, 15 September. Available at: https://deadline.com/2023/09/thursday-night-football-record-high-prime-video-season-debut-ratings-1235548375/ (Accessed: 27 September 2023).

Rowe, D. (2004). *Sport, Culture and the Media*. Maidenhead, UK: Open University Press.

Sim, J. (2024a). 'The Disney-Reliance merger, pay-TV's future, and IPL supremacy: Analysing the Indian sports broadcast market in 2024', *SportsProMedia*, 27 March. Available at: https://www.sportspromedia.com/insights/features/india-sports-broadcast-market-2024-ipl-disney-reliance-pay-tv-mobile-streaming/ (Accessed: 1 June 2024).

Sim, J. (2024b). 'NBA agrees "framework" for rights deals with Amazon and ESPN', *SportsProMedia*, 29 April. Available at: https://www.sportspromedia.com/news/nba-amazon-prime-video-espn-disney-broadcast-rights/ (Accessed: 3 June 2024).

Singh, M. and Kumar, A. (2023). A Critical Political Economy Perspective on Indian Television: STAR, Hotstar, and Live Sports Streaming. *tripleC: Communication, Capitalism & Critique*, 21 (1), pp. 18–32.

Smith, P., Evens, T., and Iosifidis, P. (2016). The Next Big Match: Convergence, Competition and Sports Media Rights. *European Journal of Communication*, 31 (5), pp. 536–550.

Sweney, M. (2018). 'Amazon breaks Premier League hold of Sky and BT with Prime streaming deal', *The Guardian*, 7 June. Available at: https://www.theguardian.com/media/2018/jun/07/amazon-breaks-premier-league-hold-of-sky-and-bt-with-streaming-deal (Accessed: 7 June 2018).

Williams, R. (2003). *Television: Technology and Cultural Form*. New York, NY: Routledge.

Xu, M., Li, B., Scott, O. K. M., and Wang, J. J. (2023). New Platform and New Excitement? Exploring Young Educated Sport Customers' Perceptions of Watching Live Sports on OTT Services. *International Journal of Sports Marketing and Sponsorship*, 24 (4), pp. 682–699.

Yuen, M. (2023). 'Peacock and Hulu subscribers opt for ad-supported plans', *Insider Intelligence*, 2 August. Available at: https://www.insiderintelligence.com/content/peacock-hulu-subscribers-opt-ad-supported-plans (Accessed: 19 September 2023).

4

PUBLIC SERVICE MEDIA ORGANISATIONS

Given the enormous sums spent on acquiring premium sports rights, it is perhaps unsurprising that recent debate within the media/sports industries has focused predominately on the rights buying, selling, and distribution strategies of commercial media organisations (see Chapter 3). Yet, in many countries, particularly, though not exclusively, in Western Europe, public service media organisations (PSM) (formerly, and sometimes still, referred to as public service broadcasters), such as the BBC (UK), Rai (Italy), and France Télévisions (France), continue to play a significant role in the sports media rights market. For example, in 2022, PSM spent approximately €3.8 billion on the production and distribution of sports content across the European Union (and UK) (Oxford Economics, 2024, p.16). With this investment, 44 different PSM across Europe broadcast over 134,000 hours of sport on free-to-air television, providing audiences with access to a host of major sporting events and competitions, including the European Championships (multi-sport), the World Athletics Championships, the Olympic Winter Games, and the FIFA World Cup (Oxford Economics, 2024, p.10). Using a range of different national examples, but particularly focusing on the BBC, by some way the world's largest and most well-funded PSM, the underlying objective of this chapter is to examine the position of PSM in the contemporary sports media rights market and in doing so also highlight the social/cultural value of PSM sports coverage.

In Europe and beyond, (live and recorded) coverage of major and/or minority sporting events and competitions has long been a highly valued part of the programming mix offered by public service broadcasters (see Chapter 2). For today's PSM, sport provides a way to bring communities and/or the nation together, as well as to reach audiences that are otherwise often underserved by PSM, such as lower-income audiences. However, over the last decade or so, the ability of PSM to utilise sports programming to

DOI: 10.4324/9781003401988-7

enhance 'cultural citizenship' in such ways has increasingly come under threat from a combination of the escalating cost of sports rights and a squeeze on their own finances (Scherer and Rowe, 2014; Smith, 2017). With these developments in mind, this chapter is divided into two main parts. The first part sets out in more detail why sport remains such a key genre for PSM and their viewers. The second part of the chapter then highlights the extent of the financial challenge faced by PSM and considers three of the main (inter-related) strategies that PSM have adopted in response, namely: first, increased coverage and promotion of women's sport; second, a renewed focus on minority sports, often involving partnerships with commercial media organisations; and third, a growing use of online platforms to enhance the attractiveness of PSM for both viewers and sports organisations.

Cultural Citizenship, PSM, and Sport

Broadly speaking, citizenship can be conceptualised as consisting of three 'overlapping zones': the political (the right to reside and vote), the economic (the right to work and prosper), and the cultural (the right to know and speak) (Miller, 2014). As outlined in Chapter 2, the marketisation of the relationship between sport and television throughout much of the world over the last couple of decades is symptomatic of the growing primacy of the economic zone, namely the conceptualisation of the citizen as a consumer. This has undoubtedly served the commercial interests of some (mainly the biggest) sporting and media organisations, but whether citizens have benefited is more debatable. Sports fans certainly have access to more content than ever before, but much of it depends on the ability/willingness to pay, including at least some events which were previously available free-to-air via public service broadcasters (see Chapter 8). In this context, universally available sports coverage (i.e. free at the point of use) offered via PSM represents a means to dilute the predominance of the economic zone in the realm of sports media and embodies an alternative, or at least complementary approach, based on the values of cultural citizenship.

By providing coverage of a mix of national and international sports events, PSM can fulfil their public service remits and enhance cultural citizenship in a number of interrelated ways. First, in an era of increasingly fragmented audiences, live television coverage of major sporting events remains one of the few forms of content able to bring the nation together for a shared viewing experience. For example, in Italy, in 2021, Rai's coverage of Italy's victory in the UEFA European Championship was watched by an average audience of 18.2 million, a 73.7 per cent market share, and peaked at more than 18.5 million (Carp, 2021). Similarly, in 2022, in the UK, England's quarter-final match against France at the 2022 FIFA World Cup, broadcast live on the commercially funded public service broadcaster, ITV, attracted a peak audience of 23 million, the highest audience for a single channel that year and surpassed only by the 28 million viewers who watched the funeral of Queen Elizabeth II (broadcast by numerous channels) (Jones, 2022). In a similar vein, PSM can also provide the focal point for a shared cultural experience that spans the entire duration of major national/international sports competitions or events. For example, in the UK, over the four weeks of the tournament, the BBC's television coverage of the 2022 FIFA World Cup reached an audience of 38.8 million (BBC, 2022a). Even more starkly, in France, France Télévisions' coverage of the 2023 edition of cycling's Tour de France reached a total television audience of 42.5 million viewers, as well as gaining 22 million views for its online content (Sim, 2023a). With the escalation in the value of rights and the limited financial resources of PSM (see below), the continued ability of PSM to enhance cultural citizenship in this way is increasingly dependent on the existence of major/listed events legislation. In numerous European countries, as well as some beyond Europe (e.g. Australia, South Africa, and India), major events legislation effectively ensures that certain major national/international sporting events remain available on free-to-air television. The ongoing political debate over the need for such legislation and how it should (if at all) be updated so that it remains effective in the age of streaming and platformisation is discussed in detail in Chapter 8.

A second way that PSM enhances cultural citizenship is by providing access to sports coverage for viewers that are unwilling, or unable, to pay for subscription services. This is a significant proportion of citizens. A survey commissioned by the European Broadcasting Union (EBU), an alliance of PSM based mainly, but not exclusively in Europe, found that while 44 per cent of television viewers enjoyed watching sport, two-thirds of sports fans in Europe did not have access to premium sports channels (Oxford Economics, 2024, p.10). The popularity of sport on PSM also suggests that many viewers enjoy watching sport, even if they do not subscribe to pay-tv services. Perhaps most notably, in the UK, in 2022, PSM (BBC, ITV, Channel 4, and Channel 5) accounted for just 6 per cent of all sport broadcast on television, but delivered around 60 per cent of the total viewing of sport (McCaskill, 2023a). The enduring popularity of the BBC's flagship *Match of the Day* programme, which provides weekly highlights from the English Premier League, is also testament to the value attached to sports coverage on PSM by large numbers of viewers. Despite the growth of pay-tv in the UK over the last 25 years, in the early 2020s, *Match of the Day* (and other football highlights programmes on the BBC) still accounted for two-thirds of all (domestic) Premier League football viewing (BBC, 2021). Since 2021, the availability of 'near-live' highlights of Premier League matches (without a subscription), via the pay-tv broadcaster Sky's YouTube channel, has seen a significant decline in *Match of the Day*'s average audience, from around 2 million to just over 1.5 million weekly viewers, but the programme continues (annually) to reach over 50 per cent of the UK television audience (Ampere Analysis, 2022, p.38).

In light of the rising living costs experienced in Europe during the early 2020s, European PSM view universally available sports coverage as an increasingly important way to serve all segments of society (Oxford Economics, 2024, p.10). Beyond Europe, in countries where disparities of wealth and income are even more acute, PSM provision of sport can be just as important a source of cultural citizenship, if not more. For example, in South Africa, the 'provision of national sports, developmental and minority sports' is a specific part of the SABC's legal mandate (SABC, 2019, p.5). To this end, SABC provides free-to-air coverage of a host of international and national sports events, including: the 2022 FIFA World Cup and Africa Cup of Nations (AFCON) 2024 football tournaments; local Heritage Cup and (French) Top 14 rugby; and NBA basketball (SABC, 2023, pp.41–2). Most significantly, in 2024, SABC's live coverage of the South African men's national football team – the Bafana Bafana – at the AFCON in Ivory Coast reached 21.8 million viewers, more than double the 10 million viewers who watched via South Africa's leading pay-tv broadcaster, SuperSport, which also offered live coverage of AFCON matches (Seleme, 2024). For supporters of PSM, these viewing figures highlight the importance of providing sport on free-to-air television. As put by SABC sports presenter, Xoliswa Zondo, 'had the national broadcaster not acquired the rights to air AFCON games, over 20 million people would've been denied the privilege of seeing Bafana games' (Seleme, 2024).

A third way that PSM utilise sport to build cultural citizenship is by providing representation for regional identities and/or minority groups. In the UK, for example, different sporting events are of major importance to particular national audiences. Consequently, BBC television coverage of rugby union test matches involving Wales is often watched by more than two-thirds of the Welsh population (BBC, 2021). In a similar vein, in 2023, for the first time, BBC Northern Ireland provided live coverage of the All-Ireland Gaelic football championships, a sport followed predominately by the country's Catholic nationalist community (BBC, 2022b). The BBC's coverage was watched by almost one million viewers in Northern Ireland (Tunney, 2023). Even more clearly, in the UK, in accordance with its specific remit to provide public service for minorities, since 2012, the commercially funded PSM, Channel 4, has provided extensive coverage of the Paralympics. For example, in 2021, the PSM offered more than 1,300 hours of coverage of the Paralympics from Tokyo, including a 'staggering' 17.5 hours each day on its flagship channel, Channel 4 (Sweney, 2021). Furthermore, Channel 4's coverage of the Paralympics has been credited with helping to change public perceptions of disability sports, with audience research suggesting that viewers have developed 'a greater appreciation of Paralympic sport as an elite sporting event' and 'an awareness of emerging cultural citizenship concerning disability rights-based discourses through greater disability media representation' (Pullen et al., 2020, p.480).

Alongside the intrinsic goal of promoting cultural citizenship, it should also be noted that PSM have a more pragmatic reason for providing coverage of national and international sport. Faced with increased competition from (national and international) subscription video-on-demand (SVoD) services, such as Netflix, PSM in most, if not all, countries are experiencing declining audiences. For example, in Europe's largest markets (France Germany, Italy, Spain, and the UK), between 2017 and 2023, the proportion of viewers that 'engaged with at least one PSM service' (linear or on demand) fell by an average of 15 per cent (Ampere Analysis, 2023). Amidst ongoing policy debates over the future funding and remit of PSM, sport provides a valuable means for PSM to demonstrate their continued relevance and value to audiences. For example, in the UK, no doubt with PSM coverage of major sports events in mind, such as the 2022 FIFA World Cup, in 2023, 65 per cent of viewers agreed that PSM 'deliver on broadcast events that bring the nation together for a shared viewing experience' (Ofcom, 2023, p.25). In addition, with falling engagement with PSM 'particularly prominent among younger age groups', the ability of sport to reach younger audiences is increasingly valuable (Ampere Analysis, 2023). For example, ITV's coverage of England's defeat to France at the 2022 FIFA World Cup was the most viewed programme of the year on television on any channel by young adults (16–34 year-olds), with 2.5 million viewers (ITV, 2022). Similarly, the young British tennis player, Emma Raducanu's, victory in the 2021 US Open tennis final recorded a 48 per cent share of young adult (16–34 year olds) viewers (Sherwin, 2021).

Challenges and Opportunities for PSM Sport

Over the last decade, PSM looking to utilise sport in order to enhance cultural citizenship, as well as their own status with viewers and policy makers, have faced two major challenges. First, increased competition, from both established pay-tv broadcasters and, more recently, SVoD services, has fuelled a rapid escalation in the value of sports rights – particularly premium rights (see Chapters 2 and 3). For example, in the UK, between 2015 and 2019, total spending on sports programming increased by 25 per cent (in real terms) (Ofcom, 2021). PSM have felt the impact of sports rights inflation particularly acutely because it has coincided with the second major challenge, namely significant reductions in their own funding. Albeit with some national variations, over the last decade, PSM in Europe have faced reduced or, at best, static levels of funding. In Europe, between 2012 and 2022, funding for PSM experienced a 'decade of stagnation' (EBU, 2024a, p.6). In 2013, financing for PSM for the entire EBU region (i.e. EU and non-EU) was €34.7 billion and, by 2019, it remained close to that level, at €35.8 billion, an increase so small (3.3 per cent) that for all intents and purposes it could be regarded as a 'freeze' (EBU, 2024a, p.6). Between 2020 and 2022, in the aftermath of the COVID pandemic, there was a 'rebound' in PSM funding, with increases of 6.6 and 2.8 per cent respectively in 2021 and 2022 (EBU, 2024a, p.6). However, these were only nominal increases in funding. Between 2012 and 2022, when adjusted for inflation, the value of PSM funding in the EBU region fell by 5.8 per cent (EBU, 2024a, p.9).

More specifically, some of Europe's leading PSM, particularly those with governments less supportive of PSM, have experienced severe cuts to their funding and this has had a significant impact on their capacity to spend on sports rights. Perhaps most notably, in the UK, in 2010, as part of the newly elected Conservative-led coalition government's plans to cut public spending, the BBC was required to make annual savings of around £700m for the next five years (Kanter, 2013). As a result, the BBC cut its sports rights budget by 15 per cent and committed itself to limit spending on sports rights to an average of 9p in every licence fee pound received (BBC, 2010, p.32). In 2015, the (now fully) Conservative government also announced that the BBC would take on from the government the £600 million-plus annual cost of providing free TV licences for people aged over 75. This prompted further reductions in the BBC's spending on sports rights, with an additional annual saving of £35 million targeted by the Corporation (Slater, 2015a). Finally, in 2022, the Conservative government announced that the annual cost of a television licence (the BBC's main source of funding) would be frozen for the next two years (at £159), which against a backdrop of rising inflation equated to a significant real-terms funding cut, requiring the BBC to find annual savings of around £285 million (Waterson, 2022). Against this backdrop, the BBC is, as put by its Director of Sport, Barbara Slater, 'on a mission to do the very best with the budget we've got', even though that means 'difficult choices' over how to spend limited resources (McCaskill, 2023a). In smaller countries like Belgium, PSM with much less resource than the BBC face very similar difficult choices (see Box 4.1).

BOX 4.1 THE CASE OF VRT IN BELGIUM

VRT is the PSM for the Flemish, Dutch-speaking, region of Belgium. Like other PSM in Europe, over the last decade it has experienced budget cuts and hostile political lobbying from commercial broadcasters. As a result, VRT (north) has had to significantly reduce its sports coverage. Most notably, the Corporation has gradually lost the rights for various major football competitions and cycling events, by far the most popular sports in the region, to pay-tv broadcasters (Telenet and Proximus) and free-to-air commercial broadcasters (VTM and Play Media). Specifically, over the last decade or so, VRT has lost the highlight rights for Belgium's domestic football league (since 2011) and the live rights for UEFA's major European club competitions: the Champions League (since 2006), the Europa League (since 2024), and the Conference League (since 2024) (De Moor, 2023). However, as a long-standing member of the EBU, VRT continues to broadcast (and stream) matches involving the men's and women's national football teams at the UEFA European Football Championships and the FIFA World Cup, although its commercial rival, VTM, has, since 2016, secured the rights for international friendly matches, qualifiers, and the UEFA Nations League. Traditionally, VRT has excelled in its television coverage of major national and international cycling events, but new commercial competitors, most notably Discovery/Eurosport, have recently acquired the pan-European rights for a number of key events, including the Italian-based races, Milan–Sanremo and the Giro d'Italia (Sporza, 2017). VRT continues to cover most major UCI World Tour cycling races, including the Tour of Flanders, Paris–Roubaix, and the Tour de France, as free-to-air coverage of these events is protected by Belgium's listed events legislation (see Chapter 8). However, VRT has lost its exclusive rights to cover cyclo-cross, a hugely popular form of off-road cycling that involves courses with barriers and obstacles. This sport (and VRT's coverage) has produced a host of major sports stars in Belgium, such as Mathieu van der Poel and Wout van Aert. However, due to budget constraints, VRT has been forced to share the rights for various major cyclo-cross races with pay-tv operator, Telenet, while the rights to other races have completely migrated to pay-tv. Faced with a limited budget and increased competition for premium sports rights, VRT has increasingly focused on providing more coverage of minority and/or traditionally underrepresented sports, including gymnastics, volleyball, basketball, and women's cycling. This approach has enabled VRT to fulfil the legal requirements of its public service remit and, particularly in the case of women's cycling, has enabled it to attract large numbers of viewers. Most notably, fuelled by the success of the Belgian rider, Lotte Kopecky, VRT's coverage of the UCI Cycling World Championships achieved a 66 per cent audience share (UCI, 2023).

Beyond Europe, the financial pressures faced by PSM over the last decade or so have been just as, if not more, severe. For example, in Australia, from around 2014, the ABC faced cuts of AUS$254 million (2014–19) and $84 million (2019–22), largely due to the Australian government's unwillingness to sanction inflation-linked increases to the level of its government grant (ABC, 2018). In 2022, the ABC lamented that 'budgetary constraints and the increased cost of production and rights' meant the Corporation was only able to provide 'limited coverage of sporting events on television [...] and broadcast major events only sporadically' (ABC, 2022, pp.1–3). Even more starkly, in South Africa, for more than a decade, the largely commercially (advertising) funded SABC has faced a series of political and financial crises. Despite a R3.2 billion government 'bail out' in 2019, by 2023, the Corporation was again 'technically insolvent' (Jacobs, 2023). Throughout this period the SABC has frequently complained that 'the exorbitant cost of sports rights' combined with 'limited potential for revenue generation' makes investment in 'premium sports content [...] prohibitive' (SABC, 2023, p.23).

Almost inevitably, the combination of rights inflation and reduced budgets has led many, if not all, PSM to lose the rights to cover numerous popular sports events. For example, in 2015, the BBC lost the live rights to the Open Golf Championship to the pay-tv broadcaster, Sky, bringing to an end 61 years of live coverage of the event on free-to-air television (Slater, 2015b). In the same year, the Corporation also announced that it had decided to end ahead of schedule its contract with Formula One (originally due to end in 2018) (Slater, 2015a). In a similar vein, in Italy, with a reduced programming budget, Rai has been forced to cede live coverage of a host of major and minor sporting events, including the 2014 Sochi Winter Olympics and the 2018 FIFA World Cup, to the pay-tv broadcaster, Sky Italia, and commercial free-to-air broadcaster, Mediaset, respectively (Callea, 2023, p.101).

PSM and Women's Sport

In response to the twin challenges of escalating rights fees and reduced budgets, PSM have adopted several interrelated sports media rights strategies. First, and arguably most significantly, over the last decade, PSM in Europe and beyond have made a deliberate and concerted effort to begin to redress the media's historic underrepresentation of women's sport. The relative lack of media coverage given to women's sport is long established and well documented (see, e.g. Cooky et al., 2021; Godoy-Pressland, 2014). By markedly increasing their coverage of a range of different women's sports, PSM have been able to promote the cultural citizenship of (female and male) viewers while also demonstrating to policy makers and regulators the distinctiveness of their output in comparison to that of their commercial counterparts. For PSM, the cost of the rights to cover women's sports has also been relatively affordable, while for many women's sports organisations the exposure offered on free-to-air television (and online) by PSM has been viewed as a valuable means to increase their sport's public exposure to commercial sponsors and/or new audiences. In this sense, PSM and women's sport have enjoyed a mutually beneficial relationship.

The BBC's coverage of women's sport provides a clear illustration of the symbiotic nature of the relationship between PSM and women's sport (see Box 4.2), but this relationship is just as evident in smaller countries with less well-resourced PSM. For example, in 2015, in Sweden, the country's PSM, SVT, began working actively on providing gender-equal sports coverage, in terms of both live events and sports news. To this end, between 2015 and 2021, SVT added coverage of around ten women's sports championships/leagues, including Damallsvenskan, the highest football league for women in Sweden, which was not broadcast at all before SVT acquired the rights (in 2017) (PMA, 2022). By 2021, SVT's coverage of men's and women's live sport was virtually equal. Similarly, in 2015, approximately 25 per cent of SVT's news coverage was about women's sports and this figure had doubled by 2022 (PMA, 2022). Similarly, in Ireland, from around the mid-2010s, Ireland's PSM, RTÉ, has played a significant role in the promotion of women's sport. For example, in 2019, for the first time, RTÉ provided live coverage of the women's FIFA World Cup (Liston et al., 2024, p.862). Subsequently, RTÉ's audience research found evidence of more viewers for women's sport and 75 per cent of male respondents said they had 'changed their mindset positively towards women's sport' (Liston et al., 2024, p.868). When, for the first time, the Irish women's team qualified for the FIFA World Cup, in 2023, RTÉ's coverage of their matches achieved record viewing figures. Most notably, the team's second match (versus Canada) became the most-watched women's sports event in Irish TV history, with an average of 551,000 viewers, which equated to a 68.9 per cent audience share, plus 234,883 livestreams on RTÉ's streaming service, RTÉ Player (Cunningham, 2023).

BOX 4.2 THE BBC AND THE PROMOTION OF WOMEN'S SPORT

Over the last decade, the BBC and women's sport have enjoyed a mutually beneficial relationship. This has been particularly evident in relation to the Corporation's growing coverage of women's football, most notably successive women's FIFA World Cups and UEFA European Championships. With this coverage, the BBC has helped build the profile of women's football and, in turn, has itself enjoyed steadily increasing audiences. For example, 28.1 million people watched the BBC's coverage of the 2019 FIFA World Cup, compared with 12.4 million for the 2015 FIFA World Cup (House of Lords (Communications Committee), 2019, p.28). Even more impressively, England's win over Germany in the final of the 2022 Women's European Championships achieved a peak television audience of 17.4 million, making it the most-watched women's football game on UK television of all-time and the most-watched UK television programme of 2022 (BBC, 2022c). Furthermore, for the BBC, the rights to international women's football have also proved particularly good value for money. For instance, in a joint deal with FIFA, the BBC and ITV secured the rights for the 2023 FIFA World Cup for £9 million, 'a fraction' of the price they paid for the rights to the men's World Cup (McCaskill, 2023b).

The popularity of international football on the BBC (and other UK PSM) has prompted increased interest in acquiring the rights to women's sport from UK pay-tv broadcasters, chiefly Sky. As a result, in 2021, the BBC and Sky agreed a joint three-year deal for the live rights to top-level English domestic women's football, the Women's Super League (WSL). At around £8 million per season, this 'landmark' deal was the biggest broadcast rights deal for any professional women's football league in the world (Wrack, 2021). With increased coverage of a host of women's sports, including football, cricket, and netball, Sky now provides many more hours of women's sport than the BBC. In 2023, Sky Sports broadcast 6,217 hours of women's sport, compared to the BBC's 838 and ITV's 133 (WST, 2024, p.12). However, the public exposure provided by PSM remains invaluable for women's sport. In 2023, the BBC and ITV accounted for only 11 per cent of the total number of hours of women's sport broadcast on UK television, but they represented 77 per cent of the total viewing (WST, 2024, p.11). Furthermore, increased public exposure has also been vital to the wider social and cultural impact of the BBC's coverage of women's sport, most notably increased attendances at women's sports events and increasing levels of public participation. Between 2016 and 2023, attendance at women's sports events in the UK increased from 0.4 million to 2.6 million, including record-breaking attendances for WSL matches (WST, 2024, p.47). Just as significantly, in 2022, the English Football Association's participation tracker – a monthly online survey run across adults aged 16 and over – showed that 43 per cent of surveyed grassroots women's football participants felt 'inspired to start playing football' by watching the England Women's team at the UEFA Women's Euro 2022 championships (UEFA, 2023, p.27). In these ways, the BBC's coverage of women's sport has made a significant contribution to cultural citizenship in the UK.

In numerous other European countries, the underlying popularity of football has seen PSM coverage of women's major football tournaments prove just as popular as in Ireland. In Spain, RTVE's coverage of the country's 2023 FIFA World Cup victory was watched by an average audience of 5.6 million viewers, a 56.2 per cent audience share and the highest ever television audience in Spain for a women's football match (Reuters, 2023). Even more impressively, in Germany, ARD recorded a record peak audience of 21.8 million and an average audience share of 64.8 per cent for its live coverage of Germany's defeat to England in the 2022 UEFA Women's European Championships final, making it the most watched women's football match in Germany of all time (EBU, 2022). Alongside football, the particular sporting preferences and traditions of different countries/regions have also been reflected in the output and popularity of women's sport on PSM. For example, in France, the 2023 Tour de France Femmes attracted a total viewership of nearly 20 million viewers via France Télévisions (Sim, 2023b). In Belgium, PSM coverage of women's cycling has also been particularly popular (see Box 4.1). Similarly, PSM outside Europe have also been keen to promote women's sport. For example, in 2023, SABC launched a public campaign, #GAMECHANGEHER, to celebrate women's sports events 'from international to local' and provided coverage of numerous women's sporting events/competitions, including the ICC Women's T20 World Cup cricket final between South Africa and Australia (SABC, 2023, p.51).

PSM, Minority Sports, and Rights Partnerships

While mainly focused on major national and international sporting events (see Chapter 2), PSM in Europe and beyond have also long been committed to providing coverage of a range of minority/niche sports. In the UK, for example, Saturday afternoon sports magazine programmes from both the BBC (Grandstand, 1958–2007) and ITV (World of Sport, 1965–85) offered coverage of a host of minority sports, including horse racing, rugby league, golf, gymnastics, swimming, and athletics (Boyle and Haynes, 2009, pp.38–40). With increased competition for the rights to cover many minority sports, as well as reduced programming budgets, PSM have adopted two main strategies. First, PSM continue to emphasise how they are able to offer sports organisations far greater public exposure for their sports than subscription services, which enables them to attract commercial sponsors and grow their sports. Most notably, the EBU emphasises how, as of 2021, free-to-air television has the potential to reach a total European population of 800 million, compared with a potential audience of 170 million for premium sports channels (Oxford Economics, 2024, p.29). Furthermore, to maximise this potential competitive advantage in the sports rights market, the EBU's Sport Division, Eurovision, agrees collective rights deals with sports organisations on behalf of its members and can also coordinate production and/or distribution with EBU members in Europe and beyond. In 2023–24, Eurovision's 'rights catalogue' included the rights to a host of different sports, including athletics, swimming, cycling, and skiing (Eurovision Sport, 2023). At least some commercial rivals of PSM view the collective buying of rights by the EBU as anti-competitive (see Chapter 7), but for many minority sports the combination of public exposure and efficiency offered by Eurovision is an attractive proposition. For example, European Athletics has had rights agreements with the EBU since 1981 and over that time has seen significant growth in television audiences and sponsorship revenue, as well as grassroots participation (Oxford Economics, 2024, p.27). Similarly, the International Biathlon Union (IBU) is the governing body for biathlon, a winter sport that combines cross-country skiing and rifle shooting. It is an especially popular sport in the Nordic region and the IBU has had an exclusive media rights deal with Eurovision since 2000. In 2020, when its deal with Eurovision was last renewed, television exposure to the IBU Biathlon World Championships was three times the level it had been in 2000, in terms of total hours viewed, and several EBU members had achieved 'stellar live market shares for their coverage', including NRK in Norway (82 per cent), SVT in Sweden (79 per cent), and Yle in Finland (73 per cent) (EBU, 2020).

Albeit often more due to budgetary concerns than a preferred strategy, a second related way that PSM have attempted to retain (at least some of) their coverage of minority sports is via rights partnerships with other PSM, or commercial media organisations. In the UK, this approach has been utilised by the BBC across a number of different sports. For example, in 2015, the BBC and ITV agreed a joint six-year deal to offer live coverage of Six Nations Rugby, with ITV offering all England, Ireland, France, and Italy home matches and the BBC covering Wales and Scotland home matches (Rees, 2015). Renewed in 2021 for a further four years, this deal has enabled the BBC and ITV to share the costs of the rights to the competition while preserving its availability on PSM (Dixon, 2021). In a number of other cases, including FA Cup football (McCaskill, 2024) and the WSL (see Box 4.2), the BBC has shared rights with UK pay-tv broadcasters, Sky or TNT Sports (formerly BT Sport). With these rights partnerships, the impetus behind the deals is not so much the need for the BBC to reduce costs, but rather the desire of sports organisations to complement the greater revenue provided by pay-tv with the audience reach offered by PSM. The value of including PSM, and specifically the BBC, in a rights partnership is illustrated particularly well by the case of English cricket. In 2017, the ECB, the governing body of cricket in England and Wales, agreed a landmark five-year deal with Sky and the BBC, worth £1.1 billion, which meant that, while Sky would continue to show the vast majority of England's (men's and women's) international cricket fixtures, the BBC would offer exclusive coverage of two men's and one women's T20 internationals, plus ten men's matches and eight women's matches from the ECB's new city-based competition, subsequently named The Hundred (Dudley, 2017). What made this deal particularly significant was that it signalled the return of international cricket to free-to-air television for the first time since 2005. By migrating from free-to-air PSM to pay-tv, the ECB had significantly increased the revenue it received from the sale of its rights (Evens et al., 2013, p.116). However, without free-to-air coverage, England cricket suffered much-reduced public exposure and a significant decline in levels of participation (Smith, 2017). In the ten years after English cricket went behind a paywall, the number of adults who played the sport at least once a week dropped by almost 20 per cent (Bull, 2019). As put by the BBC's cricket correspondent, Jonathan Agnew, the ECB's 2017 deal with the BBC (and Sky) amounted to a tacit admission that 'cricket needs to be on free-to-air TV' (quoted in BBC Sport, 2017). Delayed by the COVID pandemic, when, in 2021, The Hundred eventually launched, in its first year it reached a total of 16.1 million viewers and of these viewers 57 per cent had not watched any cricket on television previously that year (ECB, 2021).

PSM, Sport, and Online Platforms

Albeit to varying degrees, a third key strategy employed by PSM to enhance their sports coverage has been to utilise their respective online platforms to deliver both live and recorded sports content. To a large degree, this approach can be seen as part of the more general shift from public service broadcasting to PSM (Donders, 2019). In this regard, with both the extensive distribution of existing programmes online and the provision of digital-only content, the BBC is widely regarded to have the most 'mature' online strategy of the established public service broadcasters (Donders, 2019, p.1018). This is certainly evident in the Corporation's approach to sport. First, the BBC has long used its online platform, the iPlayer, and/or its BBC website/app, to stream live coverage of major events also being covered via its broadcast channels, most notably the 2012 London Summer Olympics (see Chapter 8), as well as numerous FIFA World Cup and UEFA European Championship international football tournaments. While still significantly less popular than traditional broadcast coverage, over the last decade, online streaming has become an increasingly popular means for viewers to access the BBC's coverage of such major events. For example, during the 2022 FIFA World Cup, matches were streamed a 'record breaking' 104.7 million times on the BBC iPlayer and BBC Sport Online (BBC, 2022a). Furthermore, the final (between France and Argentina), watched by a peak audience of 14.9 million on BBC television, was also streamed 7.1 million times via the BBC (BBC, 2022a). Similarly, in Italy, alongside its broadcast coverage, Rai provided live coverage of every match at the 2022 FIFA World Cup via its online platform, RaiPlay, including specific online viewing options, such as a 'tactical camera', which followed the game from above (Callea, 2023, p.106). As well as providing viewers with an additional way to view major sporting events, for PSM, the provision of such coverage also serves a wider strategic objective, namely attracting large numbers of viewers to their online platforms. For example, in the run-up to the 2024 Paris Olympics, France Télévisions detailed how it plans to use its online coverage of the games to increase the 'visibility' of its streaming platform, france.tv (Paoli-Lebailly, 2024). By taking advantage of the Games, France Télévisions intends to showcase its recent overhaul of the platform. As put by France Télévisions' President, Delphine Ernotte, 'with the Olympic Games, everybody is going to connect [to france.tv]. We want to strongly accelerate and launch a new generation platform' (Paoli-Lebailly, 2024).

The BBC and other PSM have also increasingly used their online platforms to provide additional live coverage and increased exposure for minority sports. Most notably, in 2017, the BBC announced 'the biggest increase of live sport in a generation', whereby, in partnership with a host of relatively small sports organisations, including British Swimming, British Basketball, and the WSL, it would make available over a thousand additional hours of live sport via its BBC Sport app and the BBC iPlayer (BBC, 2017). Subsequently, the BBC has adopted the same approach to offer coverage of a host of other minority sports and/or niche sports events, including: weekly matches from the Netball Super League (BBC, 2024); (men's) Olympic qualifier hockey matches (Gilmour, 2024); and all Great Britain's matches in the Billie Jean King Cup (women's tennis) (LTA, 2022). At a European level, the EBU has also recently adopted the same type of approach. In 2024, the EBU announced the launch of a new digital streaming platform, Eurovision Sport, to provide 'free public access to sports content across Europe' (EBU, 2024b). Supplementing the coverage provided by national PSM (broadcast and online), the new platform will provide additional coverage of a range of minority sports, such as athletics, gymnastics, skiing, and swimming (Saleh, 2024).

A third way that PSM have made use of their respective online platforms to enhance their sports coverage is through the provision of on-demand video clips and/or highlights. For example, in the UK, on-demand short clips of key moments (e.g. wickets, boundaries, etc.) have become an increasingly important feature of the BBC's coverage of international cricket. With pay-tv broadcaster, Sky, providing exclusive live television coverage, the BBC offers a combination of text updates and video clips via BBC Sport Online, as well as live audio coverage via *Test Match Special*. In 2023, the BBC Sport website received nearly 500 million page views for the men's and women's Ashes across both series, nearly 60 million video views, and 194 million views on social media platforms in the UK (BBC, 2023). For the BBC, and other PSM, the provision of on-demand clips has become an increasingly vital part of their sports coverage. For example, in the case of the 2023 Ashes, video views via BBC Sport Online were 60 per cent higher than the 34.8 million received in 2019 (BBC, 2023). At least in part, the popularity of digital on-demand clips reflects wider changes in audience behaviour, particularly younger audiences (see Chapter 1). For example, in the UK, between 2011 and 2021, the average reach of television sports channels amongst 16–34 year olds fell from 20 to 15 per cent, a trend 'broadly mirrored' in the BBC's own coverage of major sport events (BBC, 2023). However, younger audiences (16–34) are more likely to view BBC Sport coverage online, with younger viewers consuming 15 per cent of their 'BBC TV viewing in sport' via the iPlayer, compared to 6 per cent for all audiences (BBC, 2023, p.27).

Finally, it should be noted that PSM also use a range of different social media platforms to promote their sports coverage, often with the distribution of short-form audio-visual content. For example, the BBC delivers 'a continuous stream of sports information on Twitter [now known as X]' (Rojas-Torrijos and Ramon, 2022, p.933). Social media platforms provide PSM with a further opportunity to promote cultural citizenship through the promotion of minority and/or historically under-represented sports, most notably women's sport. To date, however, Europe's leading PSM, including the BBC, Rai, RTVE, France Télévisions, and RTÉ, have tended to 'perpetuate a fairly restricted and routinized agenda', with social media content dominated by (men's) football and limited coverage of sportswomen and disabled athletes (Rojas-Torrijos and Ramon, 2021, p.233). PSM can (and should) make better use of social media platforms to promote cultural citizenship via sport.

References

ABC (2018). 'ABC indexation freeze amounts to cuts', 8 May. Available at: https://www.abc.net.au/about/media-centre/press-releases/abc-indexation-freeze-amounts-to-cuts/103724688 (Accessed: 7 May 2024).

ABC (2022). 'ABC: Submission to the review of the anti-siphoning scheme', December. Available at: https://www.infrastructure.gov.au/sites/default/files/documents/assr–australian-broadcasting-corporation-abc.pdf (Accessed: 8 May 2024).

Ampere Analysis (2022). *Trends and Dynamics in the Sports Broadcasting Sector – Abridged Report for Ofcom.* Available at: https://www.ofcom.org.uk/__data/assets/pdf_file/0019/240553/Ampere-abridged-report.pdf (Accessed: 1 May 2024).

Ampere Analysis (2023). 'Europe's public service media in need of support to overcome market challenges', 21 August. Available at: https://www.ampereanalysis.com/press/release/dl/europes-public-service-media-in-need-of-support-to-overcome-market-challenges (Accessed: 3 May 2024).

BBC (2010). *BBC Strategy Review: Supporting Analysis.* Available at: http://downloads.bbc.co.uk/bbctrust/assets/files/pdf/review_report_research/strategic_review/supporting_analysis.pdf (Accessed: 2 May 2024).

BBC (2017). 'More sport for more people as the BBC announces biggest increase of live sport in a generation', 3 November. Available at: https://www.bbc.co.uk/mediacentre/latestnews/2017/live-sport (Accessed: 7 May 2024).

BBC (2021). 'DCMS committee - Major cultural and sporting events inquiry: BBC written evidence', May. Available at: https://committees.parliament.uk/writtenevidence/36269/html/ (Accessed: 1 May 2024).

BBC (2022a). 'BBC breaks streaming records for World Cup 2022 as peak of 14.9 million tune into thrilling final on BBC One', 19 December. Available at: https://www.bbc.co.uk/mediacentre/2022/bbc-breaks-streaming-records-world-cup (Accessed: 7 May 2024).

BBC (2022b). 'BBC agrees new landmark broadcast deal with the GAA', 25 October. Available at: https://www.bbc.com/mediacentre/2022/bbc-agrees-new-landmark-broadcast-deal-with-the-gaa (Accessed: 7 May 2024).

BBC (2022c). 'England's Women's Euro 2022 final victory breaks TV viewing record', 1 August. Available at: https://www.bbc.co.uk/mediacentre/2022/englands-womens-euro-2022-final-victory-breaks-tv-viewing-record (Accessed: 8 May 2024).

BBC (2023). 'Record numbers turned to the BBC for the Ashes', 8 August. Available at: https://www.bbc.com/mediacentre/2023/record-numbers-turned-to-the-bbc-for-the-ashes (Accessed: 9 May 2024).

BBC (2024). 'BBC Sport secures Netball Super League rights deal', 14 February. Available at: https://www.bbc.com/mediacentre/2024bbc-sport-secures-netball-super-league-rights-deal (Accessed: 9 May 2024).

BBC Sport (2017). 'BBC to broadcast live TV coverage of English international and domestic cricket', 30 June. Available at: https://www.bbc.co.uk/sport/cricket/40455556 (Accessed: 7 May 2024).

Boyle, R. and Haynes, R. (2009). *Power Play: Sport, the Media and Popular Culture.* Edinburgh: Edinburgh University Press.

Bull, A. (2019). 'Keeping the Six Nations on free-to-air TV should not be up for debate', *The Guardian*, 20 March. Available at: https://www.theguardian.com/sport/2019/mar/20/rugby-union-future-cricket-free-to-air-tv (Accessed: 4 May 2024).

Callea, D. (2023). Rai, Public Service Media, and Sport: Exploring the Historical Bonds and Current Challenges between Italian Rai and Global Sporting Events.

MedieKultur: Journal of Media and Communication Research, 39 (75), pp. 94–113.

Carp, S. (2021). 'EURO 2020 final delivers mammoth TV figures in UK and Italy', *SportsProMedia*, 13 July. Available at: https://www.sportspromedia.com/news/euro-2020-final-tv-figures-bbc-itv-rai-england-italy (Accessed: 6 May 2024).

Cooky, C., Council, L., Mears, M., and Messiner, M. (2021). One and Done: The Long Eclipse of Women's Televised Sports, 1998–2019. *Communication and Sport*, 9 (3), pp. 347–371.

Cunningham, E. (2023). 'Ireland's first WWC appearance leads to coverage records for RTE', *Sportcal*, 22 August. Available at: https://www.sportcal.com/news/irelands-first-wwc-appearance-leads-to-coverage-records-for-rte (Accessed: 5 May 2024).

De Moor, M. (2023). 'Voetbalaanbod op VRT nog meer uitgekleed: Europees clubvoetbal verhuist naar Play Media', *De Standaard*, 1 December. Available at: https://www.standaard.be/cnt/dmf20231201_93977916 (Accessed: 28 May 2024).

Dixon, E. (2021). 'Report: Six Nations to remain on BBC and ITV in TV rights renewal', *SportsProMedia*, 19 May. Available at: https://www.sportspromedia.com/news/six-nations-rugby-bbc-itv-tv-rights-renewal-fta-cvc (Accessed: 4 May 2021).

Donders, K. (2019). Public Service Media beyond the Digital Hype: Distribution Strategies in a Platform Era. *Media, Culture and Society*, 41 (7), pp. 1011–1028.

Dudley, G. (2017). 'Sky Sports and BBC get broadcast rights to English cricket', *SportsProMedia*, 30 June. Available at: https://www.sportspromedia.com/news/sky-sports-and-bbc-get-broadcast-rights-to-english-cricket (Accessed: 30 May 2024).

EBU (European Broadcasting Union) (2020). 'Eurovision Sport and IBU sign long-term exclusive media rights agreement', 19 February. Available at: https://www.ebu.ch/news/2020/02/eurovision-sport-and-ibu-sign-long-term-exclusive-media-rights-agreement (Accessed: 12 May 2024).

EBU (European Broadcasting Union) (2022). 'EBU Members on a high after record UEFA Women's EURO TV viewing figures', 3 August. Available at: https://www.ebu.ch/news/2022/08/ebu-members-on-a-high-after-record-uefa-womens-euro-tv-viewing-figures (Accessed: 4 May 2024).

EBU (European Broadcasting Union) (2024a). *Funding of Public Service Media.* Available at: https://www.ebu.ch/files/live/sites/ebu/files/Publications/MIS/login_only/funding/EBU-MIS-Funding_of_PSM_2023_Public.pdf (Accessed: 4 May 2024).

EBU (European Broadcasting Union) (2024b). 'EBU launches Eurovision Sport streaming platform boosting free public access to live sport across Europe', 5 February. Available at: https://www.ebu.ch/news/2024/02/ebu-launches-eurovision-sport-streaming-platform-boosting-free-public-access-to-live-sport-across-europe (Accessed: 14 May 2024).

ECB (2021). 'More than 16m tune in to The Hundred as competition welcomes new fans to cricket', 23 August. Available at: https://www.ecb.co.uk/news/2230059/more-than-16m-tune-in-to-the-hundred-as-competition-welcomes-new-fans-to-cricket (Accessed: 4 May 2024).

Eurovision Sport (2023). *Sports Rights Catalogue: 2023–2024.* Geneva: EBU. Available at: https://www.ebu.ch/files/live/sites/ebu/files/Services/Sport/EBU_Sports_Rights_Catalog.pdf (Accessed: 4 May 2024).

Evens, T., Iosifidis, P., and Smith, P. (2013). *The Political Economy of Television Sports Rights.* Basingstoke: Palgrave Macmillan.

Gilmour, R. (2024). 'GB Hockey aims for TV boost with BBC deal', *The Hockey Paper*, 12 January. Available at: https://www.thehockeypaper.co.uk/articles/2024/01/12/gb-hockey-aims-for-tv-audience-boost-with-bbc-deal (Accessed: 10 May 2024).

Godoy-Pressland, A. (2014). 'Nothing to Report': A Semi-Longitudinal Investigation of the Print Media Coverage of Sportswomen in British Sunday Newspapers. *Media, Culture and Society*, 36 (5), pp. 595–609.

House of Lords (Communications Committee) (2019). *Public Service Broadcasting: As Vital as Ever. 1st Report of Session 2019*. Available at: https://publications.parliament.uk/pa/ld201919/ldselect/ldcomuni/16/16.pdf (Accessed: 1 August 2024).

ITV (2022). 'England v France watched by 23 million on ITV', 11 December. Available at: https://www.itv.com/presscentre/press-releases/england-v-france-watched-23-million-itv (Accessed: 4 May 2024).

Jacobs, S. (2023). 'SABC got a R3.2 billion bailout — and now it's worse off', *MyBroadband*, 17 November. Available at: https://mybroadband.co.za/news/broadcasting/515623-sabc-got-a-r3-2-billion-bailout-and-now-its-worse-off.html (Accessed: 4 May 2024).

Jones, R. (2022). 'Qatar 2022: England's World Cup quarter-final defeat to France scores 19.4m viewers on ITV', *SportsProMedia*, 12 December. Available at: https://www.sportspromedia.com/news/england-v-france-tv-ratings-viewers-itv-qatar-2022-world-cup (Accessed: 4 May 2024).

Kanter, J. (2013). 'Hall Calls for the Consultants', *Broadcast*, 19 July, p. 1.

Liston, K., Hellstrand, L., and O'Leary, C. (2024). Public Service Broadcasting and Gender Equal Coverage: Reflections on Research and Practice in Ireland and Sweden. *Sport in Society*, 27 (6), pp. 860–876.

LTA (Lawn Tennis Association) (2022). 'BBC and BT Sport as domestic broadcasters for Billie Jean King Cup Finals', 31 October. Available at: https://www.lta.org.uk/fan-zone/billie-jean-king-cup/news/bbc-and-bt-sport-as-domestic-broadcasters-for-billie-jean-king-cup-finals/ (Accessed: 4 May 2024).

McCaskill, S. (2023a). 'BBC Sport's Barbara Slater on the power of free-to-air, making difficult choices, and how PSBs can help sports grow in the digital era', *SportsProMedia*, 16 June. Available at: https://www.sportspromedia.com/insights/analysis/bbc-sport-barbara-slater-interview-womens-sports-fta-broadcasting-iplayer/ (Accessed: 5 May 2024).

McCaskill, S. (2023b). 'BBC admits nerves over last-minute Women's World Cup deal but proud of coverage', *SportsProMedia*, 19 October. Available at: https://www.sportspromedia.com/news/fifa-womens-world-cup-tv-deal (Accessed: 4 May 2024).

McCaskill, S. (2024). 'BBC "agrees deal" with TNT Sports for live FA Cup coverage from 2025', *SportsProMedia*, 7 March. Available at: https://www.sportspromedia.com/news/bbc-tnt-sports-fa-cup-tv-uk/ (Accessed: 5 May 2024).

Miller, T. (2014). Before, During, and After the Neoliberal Moment: Media, Sports, Policy, Citizenship. In: J. Scherer and D. Rowe (eds.), *Sport, Public Broadcasting, and Cultural Citizenship: Signal Lost?* (pp. 30–47). London: Routledge.

Ofcom (2021). *Small Screen: Big Debate. Recommendations to Government on the Future of Public Service Media*. Available at: https://www.smallscreenbigdebate.co.uk/__data/assets/pdf_file/0023/221954/statement-future-of-public-service-media.pdf (Accessed: 4 May 2024).

Ofcom (2023). *Media Nations: UK 2023*. Available at: https://www.ofcom.org.uk/__data/assets/pdf_file/0029/265376/media-nations-report-2023.pdf (Accessed: 4 May 2024).

Oxford Economics (2024). *The Economic Impact of the Sports Activities of Public Service Media*. Available at: https://www.oxfordeconomics.com/resource/the-economic-impact-of-the-sports-activities-of-public-service-media (Accessed: 10 April 2024).

Paoli-Lebailly, P. (2024). 'Olympic Channel for France Télévisions', *Advanced Television*, 15 January. Available at: https://advanced-television.com/2024/01/15/olympic-channel-for-france-televisions/ (Accessed: 4 May 2024).

PMA (Public Media Alliance) (2022). 'SVT Sport: A world leader in equal sports coverage', 18 July. Available at: https://www.publicmediaalliance.org/svt-sport-a-world-leader-in-equal-sports-coverage/ (Accessed: 4 May 2024).

Pullen, E., Jackson, D., and Silk, M. (2020). Watching Disability: UK Audience Perceptions of the Paralympics, Equality and Social Change. *European Journal of Communication*, 35 (5), pp. 469–483.

Rees, P. (2015). 'BBC and ITV join forces to stop Sky winning Six Nations broadcast rights', *The Guardian*, 9 July. Available at: https://www.theguardian.com/sport/2015/jul/09/bbc-itv-join-forces-sky-six-nations (Accessed: 4 May 2024).

Reuters (2023). 'Women's World Cup final draws record TV figures in Spain, England', 22 August. Available at: https://www.reuters.com/sports/soccer/womens-world-cup-final-draws-record-tv-figures-spain-england-2023-08-21 (Accessed: 4 May 2024).

Rojas-Torrijos, J. and Ramon, X. (2021). Exploring Agenda Diversity in European Public Service Media Sports Desks: A Comparative Study of Underrepresented Disciplines, Sportswomen and Disabled Athletes' Coverage on Twitter. *Journalism Studies*, 22 (2), pp. 225–242.

Rojas-Torrijos, J. and Ramon, X. (2022). Public Service Media, Sports and Cultural Citizenship in the Age of Social Media: An Analysis of BBC Sport Agenda Diversity on Twitter. *International Review of the Sociology of Sport*, 57 (6), pp. 918–939.

SABC (South African Broadcasting Corporation) (2019). SABC Submission on the Draft Sports Broadcasting Services Amendment Regulations, 15 March. Available at: https://www.icasa.org.za/legislation-and-regulations/sabc-submission-on-the-draft-sports-broadcasting-services-amendment-regulations (Accessed: 1 August 2024).

SABC (South African Broadcasting Corporation) (2023). *Annual Report 2023*. Available at: http://web.sabc.co.za/digital/stage/Corporate/SABC_Annual_Report_2023_Final.pdf (Accessed: 4 May 2024).

Saleh, T. (2024). 'EBU launches new streaming service to enhance coverage of Olympic sports', *Sportcal*, 5 February. Available at: https://www.sportcal.com/media/ebu-launches-new-streaming-service-to-enhance-coverage-of-olympic-sports (Accessed: 4 May 2024).

Scherer, J. and Rowe, D. (eds.) (2014). *Sport, Public Broadcasting, and Cultural Citizenship: Signal Lost?*London: Routledge.

Seleme, R. (2024). '21 million: SABC doubled Supersport's Afcon viewership', *The South African*, 24 February. Available at: https://www.thesouthafrican.com/lifestyle/21-million-sabc-doubled-10-million-supersports-afcon-viewership-bafana-bafana/ (Accessed: 8 May 2024).

Sherwin, A. (2021). 'Emma Raducanu: 9.2 million watch US Open triumph on Channel 4 after deal with Amazon', *The i*, 12 September. Available at: https://inews.co.uk/news/emma-raducanu-9-2-million-watch-us-open-triumph-channel-4-deal-amazon-1195043 (Accessed: 4 May 2024).

Sim, J. (2023a). 'Tour de France total viewership on FTV shoots up to 42.5m', *SportsProMedia*, 27 July. Available at: https://www.sportspromedia.com/news/tour-de-france-viewership-france-televisions-eurosport-tv-ratings/ (Accessed: 4 May 2024).

Sim, J. (2023b). 'Tour de France Femmes total viewership close to 20m viewers on France Télévisions', *SportsProMedia*, 27 July. Available at: https://www.sportspromedia.com/news/tour-de-france-femmes-2023-tv-viewership-france-televisions-eurosport-social-digital-engagement (Accessed: 5 May 2024).

Slater, B. (2015a). 'BBC Blog: Formula 1', 21 December. Available at: https://www.bbc.co.uk/blogs/aboutthebbc/entries/d65fc069-ca52-41dd-a7be-674ca1614e14 (Accessed: 4 May 2024).

Slater, B. (2015b). 'BBC Blog: BBC Coverage of the Open Championship', 30 September. Available at: https://www.bbc.co.uk/blogs/aboutthebbc/entries/d07a6acf-403f-4ddc-a7cd-d034cbffc274 (Accessed: 5 May 2024).

Smith, P. (2017). Playing under Pressure: Sport, Public Service Broadcasting and the BBC. *International Communication Gazette*, 79 (2), pp. 203–216.

Sporza (2017). 'Italiaanse topkoersen niet meer op Sporza, alle andere wél: "We blijven relevant"', 2 March. Available at: https://sporza.be/nl/2017/03/02/italiaanse-topkoersen-niet-meer-op-sporza-alle-andere-wel-we-bli-1-2906207 (Accessed: 28 May 2024).

Sweney, M. (2021). 'Wider, stronger, longer: Channel 4's coverage will break Paralympic record', *The Guardian*, 22 August. Available at: https://www.theguardian.com/sport/2021/aug/22/wider-stronger-longer-channel-4s-coverage-will-break-paralympic-record (Accessed: 4 May 2024).

Tunney, L. (2023). 'BBC's celebrity filled All-Ireland football final coverage reaches 800,000 viewers', *Belfast Telegraph*, 2 August. Available at: https://www.belfasttelegraph.co.uk/sport/gaa/bbcs-celebrity-filled-all-ireland-football-final-coverage-reaches-800000-viewers/a1398212477.html (Accessed: 4 May 2024).

UCI (Union Cycliste Internationale) (2023). 'Spectacular TV and digital audiences for 2023 UCI Cycling World Championships in Glasgow and across Scotland', 17 October. Available at: https://www.uci.org/pressrelease/spectacular-tv-and-digital-audiences-for-2023-uci-cycling-world/3KSV2mdsYiRRoPBupy1tDT (Accessed: 4 May 2024).

UEFA (2023). *Turbo-charging Women's Football: UEFA European Women's Championship 2022: Post-Tournament Report.* Available at: https://editorial.uefa.com/resources/0283-186cff205f72-b18d4799cb75-1000/uefa_women_s_euro_2022_post-tournament_report.pdf (Accessed: 4 May 2024).

Waterson, J. (2022). 'BBC announces raft of closures with CBBC and BBC Four to be online only', *The Guardian*, 26 May. Available at: https://www.theguardian.com/media/2022/may/26/bbc-announces-raft-of-closures-cbbc-four-online-only (Accessed: 4 May 2024).

Wrack, S. (2021). 'A huge step forward': WSL announces record-breaking deal with BBC and Sky', *The Guardian*, 22 March. Available at: https://www.theguardian.com/football/2021/mar/22/a-huge-step-forward-wsl-announces-record-breaking-deal-with-bbc-and-sky (Accessed: 4 May 2024).

WST (Women's Sport Trust) (2024). *Visibility Uncovered: 2023 - The Year in Review.* Available at: https://www.womenssporttrust.com/latest-research-from-womens-sport-trust-delves-into-visibility-and-fandom-of-womens-sport-in-2023 (Accessed: 4 May 2024).

5

SPORTS ORGANISATIONS

Previous transformations of the media industries have had implications for covering live sports and have boosted the economic value of sports media rights, as well as the omnipresence of sports content in general (see Chapter 2). Sports rights owners have previously benefited from new developments in distribution technology, such as the introduction of satellite television and the success of digital television. Similarly, platformisation and the rise of internet-distributed television create plenty of opportunities for sport organisations to enhance the economic value of their media rights by taking advantage of the expansion of the sports broadcasting value chain. As more and more sports fans opt for streaming platforms as their preferred destination for entertainment and sports programming, and reside in social media to interact with fan communities, media rights strategies are increasingly led by digital plenitude. The launch of a sports-branded, direct-to-fan (D2F) platform is perhaps one of the most spectacular developments in this ongoing platformisation of sports broadcasting. This chapter critically assesses the opportunities for both premium and lower-tier sports and claims that there is no one-size-fits-all approach for all sports organisations. D2F platforms confront sports organisations with the key challenge of maximising income from digital distribution without undermining existing, and way more lucrative, revenue streams created by more traditional broadcasting partners. After discussing the main challenges for D2F platforms, the chapter examines two crucial strategic dilemmas of a D2F strategy, which very much resemble the dilemmas rights owners have long faced when dealing with traditional broadcasting partners. A first dilemma relates to the issue of whether D2F platforms are really a realistic substitute for pay-tv deals and, if so, whether a D2F service should provide exclusive live coverage or not. The section discusses different models of how to position D2F platforms vis-à-vis pay-tv

DOI: 10.4324/9781003401988-8

services. A second dilemma concerns the classical trade-off between maximising audience reach by offering coverage to free-to-air platforms and maximising media income by selling rights to a subscription-based service. Despite new technology being involved, it becomes clear that these strategic choices for sports organisations reflect the same 'old' issues that have been faced since the early 1990s when pay-tv was introduced. This reinforces the key argument at the heart of the book, namely that the rise of sports streaming is best seen as an evolution, rather than a revolution, in the sports media rights market.

Sports in the Digital Plenitude

The relationship between sports and broadcast media has often been described as symbiotic and said to create a win-win situation for both sports rights owners and media organisations (Nicholson et al., 2015). Professional sports provide the kind of exciting entertainment that draws large and diverse audiences for media platforms, but also became dependent on the lucrative income from broadcast rights. In 2023, the 20 richest football clubs in the world generated about 40 per cent of their revenue from broadcasting, their largest income source (Deloitte, 2024). The omnipresence of media has transformed the traditional spectator-based model of sports into a business model that relies primarily on commercial income from media rights, sponsorship, and merchandising (Andreff and Staudohar, 2002). In addition to its ability to draw large audiences, the economic value of a sport depends on its flexibility and adaptability to the demands of the media. Almost addicted to the high levels of broadcast income, sports leagues and competitions have difficulty resisting demands from media partners, and have subscribed to the logic of mass media to maximise their suitability and attractiveness for television coverage (Frandsen, 2014). For example, major US sports leagues, with their multiple in-game breaks and timeouts, are tailor-made to suit advertising-funded broadcasters. The media's impact on timing and scheduling has eventually transformed viewing habits with evening and midweek matches. New-media technologies such as real-time statistics, slow-motion replays, dashboard cameras, or reverse angle shots add extra value to the sports broadcast. Furthermore, sporting events were restructured or reformatted to increase sporting rivalry and uncertainty of outcome by introducing knockout phases, championship play-offs, or shorter games. Tickell et al. (2021) coined the term 'redbullization' of sports to refer to this media-driven spectacularisation of sports. Television also opened up the possibility for television-created sports, mostly spectacular sporting events that primarily satisfy the needs of media platforms. For example, Rallycross (RX) was created by and for television, and started as a TV show for ITV's *World of Sport* programme. The motorsports series aimed to overcome existing constraints and issues for televising motorsports, such as scheduling, lighting, and bad-weather cancellations, and was said to provide exciting and spectacular motorsports (Haynes and Robeers, 2019).

The financialisation of sports is thus driven mainly by a sport's ability to transform itself into a media-friendly product and create commercial opportunities for sponsors and advertisers. The more mediated a sport, the larger its fan base and television viewership, and the higher its ability to extract income from sponsorship and broadcasting deals. This 'unruly trinity' (see Rowe, 1999) is particularly effective at explaining why some franchises, such as the Summer Olympics, Super Bowl, or Tour de France, have turned into media-led events that attract significant attention, viewership, and participation around the world. Wenner and Billings (2017) acknowledged that the creation of these commodified, global, and supersized spectacles would not have been possible without the media. Middle-tier and niche sports, on the contrary, could not achieve significant financialisation because they struggle to fit into the tight programming schedules of television broadcasters, do not (yet) have a wide audience and fan base, have limited access to geographical markets, or simply lack the level of drama, dynamics, narrative, or spectacle that television audiences expect. Rosner and Shropshire (2011, pp.99–100) identified four nonexclusive categories of such lower-tier championships. First, minor leagues, in which the league does not represent the top level of competition in its sport (like secondary divisions or youth competitions). Second, leagues that do represent the top level of competition in the sport but that fail to gain much financial stability and success (like martial arts, volleyball, or cycling). Third, leagues that are indoor variations of established outdoor leagues (like indoor soccer or table tennis). Fourth, gender-specific leagues that take benefit from the increased interest in women's sports (like the WNBA or Tour de France Femmes). For all these categories of niche sports to achieve long-term financial success, television presence is of utmost importance to grow interest from audiences and sponsors.

The last couple of decades have witnessed an almost constant process of technological change within the media industries, which has seen the development of new broadcast delivery technologies, such as satellite and digital television, as well as the growth of new-media technologies, chiefly internet-distributed television and social media. Hence, the digital transformation of the media industries further affects the mediatisation of sports, both major and niche. Hutchins and Rowe (2009) pointed at the evolving dynamics of the media industries and the implications for media sport. The long-established broadcast model, in which only a limited number of broadcasters possessed the production and distribution capacity and financial means to deliver sports content, is gradually being challenged. Broadcasting may remain the prime outlet for live sports, but internet-distributed television creates 'digital plenitude':

> Significantly lower barriers of access and cost have multiplied the number of media companies, sports organisations, clubs, and even individual

> athletes who can produce and distribute content for online consumption and allowed large numbers of users to appropriate, modify, and share digital sports footage through web sites.
>
> *(Hutchins and Rowe, 2009, p.356).*

Through social media, sports fans consume game highlights, but also actively engage in producing their own forms of sports-related content. As a result, the media sports industry is said to evolve from a live game-based to a platform ecosystem model, which requires a new approach to create, distribute, and monetise sports content, both live and non-live, in multiple formats (Zheng and Mason, 2018). For Bolter (2019, p.5), disruption of the traditional broadcasting model means that the media industry could get rid of gatekeepers, which allows literally every sports organisation to approach fans directly, for example through D2F services. This could tilt the power balance more in favour of sports rights owners, who could benefit from ubiquitous digital distribution and turn into a successful digital brand (Duncan, 2020).

Whether all sports franchises will benefit equally from the, at least theoretical, opportunities made possible by this 'digital land of plenty' remains a matter of debate. For some, the streaming era could bring about a bright future for niche sports. Using digital distribution, niche sports could find more exposure and address new fans, most notably younger audiences that rely primarily on social media and video streaming (Draper, 2018). Streaming technology provides an opportunity for sports that are ill-suited to fit inflexible programming structures – for example because they have an inconsistent duration or last for multiple days rather than hours – to circumvent strict broadcasting schedules. Niche sports, especially those that are difficult to televise, generally do not get widespread media coverage and may find an outside option to show games and provide engaging sports content via the internet (Tickell, 2022). Changing distribution technology and lower associated technical costs could also play in favour of niche sports. Unlike traditional live broadcast feeds, which bring about substantial delivery costs including satellite trucks, uplink and downlink fees, fibre circuit charges, and so on, cloud delivery demands rather minimal infrastructural and operational set-up requirements, so that niche sports organisations with limited financial means can stream sports events. Sports organisations often rely on third-party service providers to produce and distribute the content, without the need for broadcast partners to pick up the feed (Secular, 2018; SVG Europe, 2021). Partnerships with or ownership by media corporations bring in the required expertise in the production and marketing of sports content, which partly explains the involvement of Red Bull Media House in the World Rally Championship (WRC) as well as Liberty Media's purchase of Formula One (F1) and MotoGP (Evens et al., 2023; Tickell et al., 2021). Streaming technology thus helps to overcome the complexity of the traditional content delivery process and opens an unprecedented window of opportunity for long-tail, even non-professional, sports to produce high-quality content and control its distribution. No matter how popular a sports championship is, cloud production and distribution infrastructure as well as artificial intelligence and automation enable sports organisations to further monetise live and on-demand game content.

Others are, however, more sceptical about the opportunities of digital plenitude for middle-tier and niche sports. According to Meier, Hagenach, and Jetzke (2020), major sports will be the prime beneficiaries of these technical developments and can benefit from the competition between different distribution platforms to maximise media exposure and drive up the value of media rights. They claim that niche sports broadcasting is in a crisis. While digital plenitude certainly increases the distribution options of niche sports, it also decreases the chances of finding an audience. Unlike major sports, niche sports hardly benefit from social network externalities (Boardman and Hargreaves-Heap, 1999), which lowers their visibility in the land of plenty. Branding power and sports popularity matter in a hypercompetitive media landscape populated by numerous streaming platforms. Niche sports organisations are able to launch a platform on their own, but may face difficulties in standing out from the competition and drawing audiences to their platform. Hence, de-bundling sports content would prove detrimental for niche sports (Tickell et al., 2024). Although niche sports traditionally rely on loyal and dedicated fan bases, limited willingness to pay for niche sports may also limit the viability of such a platform (see Box 5.1). Due to the growing audience fragmentation and declining viewing figures for linear television, general-interest broadcasters have become more risk-averse and have turned down niche sports with limited audience appeal. Public service broadcasters in Europe have been severely impacted by austerity policies and have reduced their expenditure on sports rights (see Chapter 4). Other broadcasters continue to focus on major sports and especially soccer – hence the 'soccerization' of European broadcasting (Meier, Hagenach, and Jetzke, 2020). For these reasons, we argue that digital plenitude will affect distinct sports in a differential manner, and reinforce the dominance of a few leading sports rather than enhancing the visibility of a series of middle-tier and niche sports. In contrast to the optimistic rhetoric of flourishing long-tail sports, it seems most likely that only a handful of sports will dominate the emerging digital media landscape. This, however, does not rule out the vast opportunities that new-media technology creates for niche and lower-tier sports to position themselves in the digital sports ecosystem.

BOX 5.1 THE RISE AND FALL OF THE WWE NETWORK

Since the mid-1980s, World Wrestling Entertainment Inc. (WWE), the American professional wrestling promoter, had been broadcasting pay-per-view events including its flagship franchise WrestleMania in partnership with satellite pay-tv provider Dish. WWE Network was launched in February 2014 as a subscription-based, stand-alone video streaming platform owned by WWE. In addition, partnerships sealed with multiple pay-tv operators made the network available in the US and elsewhere as a premium service. WWE Network announced it had reached 1 million subscribers by January 2015 and about 1.5 million by April 2018. Since then, however, the number of subscribers more or less plateaued, and remained well short of the public goal of 3 million.

In 2019, digital intermediary Endeavor Streaming replaced BAMTech as its operating partner. The decision followed the acquisition of BAMTech by Disney (see Box 1.1), which caused concerns over how WWE's relationship with BAMTech would be affected by the sale, especially since WWE was seeking greater control over its operations. Endeavor would provide the infrastructure and billing services, whereas Massive Interact would develop a new front-end and mobile apps (Weich, 2019). The new WWE Network platform launched in July 2019 and provided a range of new functionalities that would enhance the fan experience. Alongside its premium tier with additional features, a free tier with 15,000 hours of content was launched. This advertising-supported free tier was intended primarily to promote WWE's weekly programmes and pay-per-view events.

After NBCUniversal/Comcast had acquired the exclusive US distribution rights to WWE Network (as part of a five-year deal worth US$1 billion), the service folded into the conglomerate's streaming platform, Peacock, in early 2021. WWE Network would be hosted by a branded channel as part of Peacock's premium tier; the free tier was abandoned altogether. This event also marked the end of WWE Network as a stand-alone service in the US. WWE's decision to merge under Peacock eventually paid off: it was reported that more than 3 million Peacock subscribers had tuned in to WWE Network programming, much more than the sports franchise was able to draw as a stand-alone service (Hayes, 2022). A ten-year partnership with Netflix, agreed in 2024, marked the global phase-out of WWE Network. The WWE case shows that the success of direct-to-consumer models, at least as a primary distribution strategy, is not guaranteed, even for popular sports franchises, and that rights owners need to find a balance between reach and revenue.

D2F Platforms

The launch of sport-branded, D2F platforms is perhaps one of the most spectacular developments of the ongoing platformisation of the sports media industry. Digital infrastructure provides sports organisations with an opportunity to lower their dependency on television broadcasters and develop a commercial approach that enables them to take, at least partial, control over the distribution and monetisation of their content. Over the last couple of years, many sporting competitions – from premium-tier sports franchises like

FIFA, NBA, and Formula One; to middle-tier sports like golf, tennis, and rugby; to niche sports like triathlon, motor racing, and volleyball – have been providing D2F offerings. With mixed results, however, as the example of WWE Network shows (see Box 5.1). Sports-branded D2F platforms may not be guaranteed success, but are likely to remain an essential part of the marketing strategy of sports teams, leagues, and competitions in the future. The D2F landscape consists of a wide variety of value propositions and revenue strategies built on a direct relationship with the fan base. Some franchises provide exclusive live coverage of sporting events whereas others offer complementary, non-live programming. Some franchises provide their content for free and rely on advertising, merchandising, and even betting as revenue sources whereas others put their content behind a paywall and try to turn fans into paying subscribers. To date, middle-tier and niche sports have been leading the D2F landscape, whereas premium-tier sports competitions have been reluctant to dip their toes fully into the D2F water.

This reluctance of premium-tier sports has for the most part to do with the lucrative broadcasting contracts they are attached to and, more specifically, the substantial amount of revenues that media rights generate for these organisations. Although limited in number, premium-tier sports competitions command the lion's share of media rights income and would probably have much more to lose than to win if they were to launch a pure D2F platform with exclusive live coverage of their events. As long as sports broadcasters and online platforms remain willing to pay significant sums to secure exclusive coverage, premium sports properties will continue to be in a relatively comfortable position. Essentially, it is a matter of economics: a huge financial gap remains between what sports properties *do* get from media rights deals and what they *could* get from selling subscriptions to their global fan base. Although this may change over time, selling media rights to broadcasters is still way more profitable than operating a pure D2F offering. In other words, the sports rights licensing business is still a much better business than selling subscriptions direct to sports fans. As discussed in Box 5.2, top-flight soccer leagues such as the English Premier League and the Bundesliga have repeatedly been considering, or at least threatening, to launch their own league-branded subscription service, especially in international markets with limited competition between pay-tv operators or low pay-tv penetration. The Spanish La Liga was the first European major soccer league to launch its own streaming platform: the free service boosts the visibility of second-division games, but does not feature live top-tier games (Carp, 2019). Premium sports properties may experiment with the D2F model in non-premium markets, but it is unlikely this will be a game-changer in premium markets anytime soon. It is fair to say that they prefer their guaranteed media income to pay the heavy player contracts and other long-term commitments over the risky and volatile business of media service subscriptions.

BOX 5.2 PREMFLIX: A STREAMING PLATFORM FOR THE ENGLISH PREMIER LEAGUE?

With every new tender process for the English Premier League, rumours about a possible launch of Premflix – a Netflix-style streaming platform featuring live Premier League games – are growing. The launch of a stand-alone subscription-funded service would move the league away from the traditional broadcasting model and end long-standing partnerships with pay-tv broadcasters, such as Sky Sports and TNT Sports. It would allow the Premier League to bypass these broadcasters and go D2F with its own global streaming service. Holding back the exclusive media rights to launch its own Premflix streaming service would mean nothing less than a radical break in the way European premium sports are monetised. The Premier League is the world's leading soccer league, being aired in 188 countries and commanding about £6.7 billion in broadcasting revenue (2025–29 deal). However, such a move would come with a series of financial risks and strategic challenges that would seriously affect the feasibility of such a platform.

The commercial logic behind a possible Premflix is obvious. By exploiting the global popularity of its championship, the Premier League could increase revenues from media rights. Since 2016, the value of the Premier League's domestic rights has more or less plateaued and the chances that any newcomer will shake up the UK broadcast market are rather low, especially since Viaplay has withdrawn from the UK and neither Apple nor Netflix have shown any interest in acquiring Premier League rights. This stagnation in the value of domestic rights has been offset by a spectacular surge in international media rights sales. However, international pay-tv markets are seeing declining subscriber rates due to cord-cutting, subscription fatigue, and price hikes. By marketing live games in-house, Premflix would be able to control its own product and provide a convenient, lower-cost alternative to the expensive pay-tv bundles provided by Sky and its international equivalents. There might be opportunities to gain more revenue from merchandise and sponsorships, and remain relevant for a growing group of digital-only media consumers. By circumventing the long-standing 3pm blackout rule – a rule in place since the 1960s to preserve the stadium attendance of lower-tier league clubs (see Box 2.2) – the service could also address a substantial group of fans currently unable to watch their team.

While there is certainly huge market potential for a Premflix service, the league has shown little appetite for going all-in on streaming. A D2F model could create instability within the league and remove the financial predictability given by media rights income. The most popular clubs, such as Manchester City or Liverpool, might be keen to simply market their games individually via their club-owned platforms, ultimately breaking solidarity with smaller clubs, like Crystal Palace, which could end the idea of a united Premier League altogether. But more importantly, it is a misconception that, for the

Premier League, the D2F streaming model would be more profitable than the current business of rights licensing. If successful, gross margins and revenue per subscriber may be higher for D2F, but overall revenue may be lower compared to traditional licensing – especially in the UK market. The economics of Premflix, and any other subscription-funded streaming service, command substantial costs of production, marketing, infrastructure, and customer acquisition and retention. Hence, it is questionable whether Premflix would prove more profitable than the current broadcasting contracts. Nevertheless, the league may use the potential of a D2F service as a bargaining chip to extract more revenue from its broadcast partners, and explore the model in non-premium markets to create more brand visibility.

For middle-tier and niche sports, on the contrary, D2F platforms provide the largest opportunity to generate more reach and create commercial value. Some of these sports competitions, such as the PGA Tour (golf), ATP/WTA/Grand Slams (tennis), or MotoGP, have several broadcasting deals in place that secure them the much-needed free-to-air coverage (in addition to income generated by pay-tv contracts). However, for competitions such as WRC and World Snooker, these contracts may not necessarily bring in significant media revenue, but mainly serve to create reach that can be turned into sponsorships. Other competitions may be even worse off and fail to generate interest from mainstream media partners for some of the reasons discussed above. In those cases, streaming provides the only avenue to deliver a mix of content – full-length and short-form, live and non-live – to find more exposure, create awareness, and build a fan base. Because broadcasters are not interested in scheduling these competitions, D2F platforms are the only way fans can watch these competitions. As a result, super-fans may be willing to pay for such services. In 2018, World Triathlon, the international governing body for the multi-sports disciplines of triathlon, duathlon, and aquathlon, entered into a long-term partnership with rights agency Infront to develop sponsorship opportunities and digital strategies (Holmes, 2018). It launched TriathlonLIVE, a subscription-based streaming platform that provides exclusive coverage of every elite World Triathlon Series race. The platform is instrumental in engaging a wider fan base and showing demand to broadcasters, and forms a starting point for turning triathlon into a televised sport.

There may be several incentives both for premium-tier and for lower-tier sports organisations to launch a league-branded D2F platform. First, by self-exploiting media rights, sports franchises gain entire control of the distribution and marketisation of their media content. In the traditional broadcasting model, sports franchises sell their rights to media platforms, which then assemble a sports product bundling several sports competitions and events. Additionally, sports broadcasters may provide too wide an array of competitions and are, therefore, too expensive for a significant portion of fans that want to pick their favourite competition, team, or even individual athlete. Previously, sports organisations had almost no say in how their brand was presented to the audience. A D2F model allows sports organisations to keep control of how the streaming product is built, branded, segmented, and delivered to their fans. Through D2F, sports franchises can deliver personalised, interactive content to engage specific target groups that are hardly catered for by traditional broadcasting. Digital distribution allows sports organisations to offer individualised, tailor-made, à la carte packages for fans that want greater freedom, choice, and flexibility in terms of the content they want to see. Newcastle United fans might not be interested in how Arsenal and Liverpool perform so some may be willing to subscribe to watch 'The Magpies' only instead of having to subscribe to watch all Premier League games. Although most major leagues and competitions seem rather reluctant to move quickly, the NBA is at the forefront of digital innovation. Along with many other subscription schemes, the NBA Team Pass, for example, gives paying fans access to their favourite team games for the entire season and offseason. This is just one example of how leagues can rethink distribution and monetisation models. Future marketing strategies of sports rights owners will, therefore, need to be much more sophisticated and address emerging media consumption habits and evolving expectations of digital-savvy generations of fans.

Second, D2F platforms allow sports organisations to leverage their brand in the wider media sports industry and create a unique identity that resonates with the audience. This may reinforce fans' willingness to pay for the service. Digital distribution enables sports organisations to address audiences all over the world, create global reach, and develop their sport as a global brand. Premium-tier leagues with global appeal will certainly benefit from this strategy, but this also provides a huge opportunity for smaller sports franchises to explore and unlock their popularity. Indeed, D2F platforms can serve territories where rights were left unsold, grow the popularity of the sports, and create market interest from potentially interested broadcasters. Digital touchpoints such as Golf's R&A TV or FIS TV (International Ski and Snowboard Federation) have an increased focus on direct-to-consumer relationships, which are instrumental in increasing engagement and fan loyalty worldwide. Loyal fans become advocates for the brand, promoting the sports through word-of-mouth, social media, and other digital platforms. Powerful brand ambassadors ensure the longevity of the sport: their support helps to maintain the sport's popularity and media relevance over the long term. Through digital storytelling and transmedia marketing successful brands are able to build engaged online communities, which establish emotional connections with and between fans (McClearen, 2017). Such a shared identity, in turn, enhances the overall experience of being a sports fan and increases customer satisfaction and retention. Satisfied customers are more likely to continue to follow and subscribe to the league's platforms. Moreover, digital fan engagement attracts sponsors and potential partners to invest in the sport. In 2022, the NBA launched its global NBA App, the all-in-one destination for NBA fans of every team. The app provides a highly personalised experience and features social-style vertical video content, exclusive behind-the-scenes content, and much more. Additionally, it contains NBA ID, a global membership programme offering fan benefits and rewards including ticket promotions and members-only experiences from NBA partners. Ultimately, digital technology helps sports organisations to collect digital data and understand customers more accurately.

Third, this advanced datafication of customer behaviour is key to the digital strategy of any sports league or team. Through D2F platforms sports franchises can interact directly with fans and collect valuable customer data. Fans subscribe to, or at least sign up for, a franchise's digital platform and leave personal information. In addition, they leave digital traces while using digital platforms. This allows sports organisations to better understand customer needs, preferences, and behaviour, enabling them to personalise commercial offers and provide a more relevant fan experience. Having control of the customer relationship allows sports organisations to own and analyse customer data, enabling data-driven decisions, optimised marketing strategies, development of new products and services, and much more. Instead of relying on third-party data delivered by social media channels, streaming platforms, or advertising tools, league-owned platforms can extract first-party data to achieve their commercial objectives. The collection of first-party data is crucial because third-party data are put under pressure by data and privacy regulations such as the General Data Protection Regulation (GDPR) and the Californian Consumer Privacy Act (CCPA) that restrict tracking consumer behaviour in Europe and the US, respectively. Armed with rich data, sports organisations can boost stadium attendance and ticket sales, enhance recruitment of sponsors and advertisers, and target fans with personalised sports content and commercial offers. Although the commercial value of first-party data is obvious, especially middle-tier and lower-tier sports leagues find difficulties in extracting and understanding data on fan behaviour. Unlike premium-tier sports, niche sports face a huge challenge making sense of data. This has, of course, to do with the relatively limited scale and number of users of these D2F platforms, but also with the lack of financial muscle to invest in data analytics expertise (Tickell et al., 2024). In 2019, however, the Swedish Football Association (SvFF) successfully launched the Min Fotball subscription service, a second-screen platform with match feeds, commentary, data, and livestreaming of lower-tier football games. The platform increases engagement around amateur and youth football and activates sponsor packages (Bassam, 2021).

Ultimately, leagues may create extra revenue streams through their D2F platforms, and integrate merchandising, sponsorship, betting, and ticket sales into a single data-driven platform. By eliminating traditional sports broadcasters as middlemen, rights owners avoid paying margins to distributors, keep greater control of operating profits, and solve the issue of double marginalisation (Abito and Wright, 2008). Moreover, D2F allows sports organisations to monetise ancillary and international rights that were left unsold. It enables leagues to expand internationally and target markets with limited pay-tv penetration or with relatively limited interest in the sport. Instead of selling their rights below price to broadcasters in particular international markets, sports organisations can choose to self-exploit these rights and keep control of how the sport is promoted in these markets. Through their D2F services, sports leagues generally provide out-of-market games, games which are available outside of the designated broadcast regions. NFL, for example, provides out-of-market games via subscription services such as NFL Sunday Ticket, NFL Game Pass International, or NFL+. Finally, other sports leagues have been using the (possible) launch of a D2F service as an outside option to influence the outcome of rights auctions and negotiate more favourable deals with television broadcasters. Having an own league-branded premium service is said to create more leverage in negotiations and would allow franchises to take unsatisfactory rights deals off the table because live coverage of games in these respective markets would be guaranteed via the service. In the end, this could induce broadcasters to come up with a better financial offer to win the exclusive coverage of the league in their market. In this context, it was rumoured that, in 2023, Italy's Serie A was interested in purchasing Sky Italia to build its own Serie A TV channel. The rumour came as Serie A's clubs discussed the sale of domestic rights, which were ultimately sold to TIM and sub-licensed to DAZN (Sim, 2023).

However, a D2F subscription platform brings about a few challenges for sports organisations. While some are common to all kinds of streaming services – related to monetisation, scalability, distribution, branding power, or infrastructure – probably the most important challenge for league-branded D2F services is to find a difficult balance between disrupting the media sports value chain and keeping traditional allies happy. For many years, sports rights owners have relied on sports broadcasters as traditional rights buyers and built partnerships to grow the sport. By launching a D2F platform, sports rights owners risk jeopardising long-standing relationships with sports broadcasters who previously invested heavily in rights deals and, in doing so, financed the development of their sport. Adopting a direct-to-consumer approach may upset broadcasters and pay-tv operators, as it eats directly into their revenues and profit margins, and could create conflicts of interest in the value chain. An overly opportunistic strategy by the rights owners to launch may pay off in the short term, but may prove problematic in the longer term, for example when the subscription service would need to partner with pay-tv platforms for distribution to generate additional reach (via the set-top box or non-exclusive licensing). Or the D2F strategy may fail and sports competitions would have to negotiate with broadcasters again, figuratively with their tails between their legs. For some leagues, a D2F approach may work, especially for those lower-tier sports that have almost no contractual broadcasting strings attached. However, D2F also creates significant commercial uncertainty for leagues, so they are most likely to live with a less generous broadcast deal than to put their entire media rights model at risk with a new model whose commercial sustainability has yet to prove itself.

D2F Strategies

As discussed above, a large number of sports organisations have been experimenting with D2F platforms as part of their digital marketing mix. However, a D2F strategy comes with many strategic options and business model choices, and there simply does not exist a one-size-fits-all approach that may work for all sports franchises. Notable differences between premium and lower-tier sports exist because of differing dependence on broadcast income, brand appeal, or willingness to pay, but there are also significant variations within the segments of premium and lower-tier sports. In the remaining part of this chapter, emphasis is, therefore, placed on the strategic dilemmas league-branded D2F platforms may face in terms of value proposition (exclusivity of rights) and go-to-market strategy (pricing).

A first dilemma relates to the issue of whether D2F platforms should carry exclusive live rights and how these offerings then would relate to traditional sports channels held by broadcasters or other media platforms. It is important to stress the complementarity of D2F compared to the existing broadcasting model: D2F is not going to replace broadcasting as the main distribution outlet anytime soon, but just adds another layer of distribution to reach a digital-only audience. To date, D2F as a primary distribution strategy does not seem a really viable strategy. As it stands, D2F platforms are generally complementary to the fully-fledged live sports subscription services operated by broadcasters, pay-tv operators, and streaming platforms. Sports organisations have no interest in creating head-to-head competition with established pay-tv broadcasters and emerging streaming platforms – a battle they can never win – and seek to serve fans with a differentiated offering. It is fair to say most of these offerings have been rather modest and usually target superfans that primarily want supplementary content, such as behind-the-scenes documentaries, off-season games, player interviews, podcasts, or archival content. When these D2F services do offer live coverage, this is generally because sports leagues or individual clubs were entitled the rights to transmit the event. First, this happens when live rights for particular territories have remained unsold or were left unused (like FIFA+). In those cases, leagues can use a bespoke D2F platform or other digital platforms such as YouTube or TikTok to stream live games in these markets. This strategy is inexpensive, has a relatively low distribution cost, and allows the extraction of customer data in these markets. Second, individual clubs are generally awarded some live rights for self-exploitation. In the Spanish La Liga, for example, clubs can broadcast games played at home on a delayed basis upon completion of each match round via their official club channels. Similarly, MUTV, a premium channel operated by Manchester United, broadcasts a selection of live and exclusive preseason friendly matches, in addition to live coverage of United's U21 Premier League 2 matches, United U18 Premier League matches, and Man United Women's FA WSL matches.

Premium-tier sports rights owners continue to see the most value in the model of rights exclusivity, although practice shows an erosion of this model in certain markets (see Chapter 4). Under this model, broadcasters obtain control over rights packages and this increases revenue for the rights owners. Rights may be split into several rights packages and sold to different broadcasters, but there is actually no duplication of availability for viewers. As long as multiple broadcasters are interested to join the bidding process, this model of exclusivity will remain in place. This may lead to an extensive fragmentation of the rights spread across multiple platforms, and possibly causes inconvenience and incurs extra costs for consumers (see Chapter 6). However, every distribution platform also creates an additional touchpoint to cater to different groups of fans. Hence, most premium-tier leagues may continue to implement exclusive selling and welcome streaming platforms as possible buyers to keep up, or further increase, the value of their rights. Under this 'contemporary classic' model (Tickell et al., 2024), exclusivity is maintained and streaming is just added as a supplementary distribution avenue to the rights marketing mix. Most US major sports leagues and the European top-flight soccer competitions continue to adhere to this lucrative rights-selling model.

Formula One (F1) is probably one remarkable premier-tier exception to this traditional media rights model. The Liberty Media–owned franchise combines lucrative non-exclusive television contracts with live coverage via its premium-tier F1 TV Pro streaming platform in over 80 markets including Brazil, France, the Netherlands, and the US. Basically, F1 follows a 'fusion' approach: it tends to negotiate free-to-air and pay-tv broadcasting deals, for example with Band Sports (Brazil), Canal+ (France), and ESPN (the US), while retaining digital rights for its own F1 TV Pro platform in the same market. In other markets where broadcasters hold exclusive rights to F1, the premium platform is geo-blocked, preventing fans from watching live content – Sky Sports has extended its exclusive pay-tv deals with F1 in its key markets (Germany, Ireland, Italy, and the UK); beIN Sports secured a multi-year contract for its Asian markets; Tencent obtained the rights to stream F1 in China; Foxtel is the exclusive home of F1 in Australia, and so on.

The emergence of internet-distributed television and the opportunities produced by digital plenitude led certain lower-tier sports franchises such as the Fédération Internationale de Volleyball (FIVB), European Professional

Club Rugby (EPCR), and the World Rally Championship (WRC) (see Box 5.3) to adopt a more hybrid strategy. They abandoned the business model of rights exclusivity because of limited reach and revenue, and switched to what Tickell and Evens (2021, p.268) label the 'betting on two horses' strategy. Under this model, sports organisations become, more or less, a global broadcaster by exploiting a bespoke streaming service while also negotiating broadcasting deals in national or regional markets, possibly with multiple partners in a single market. It allows sports franchises to combine traditional broadcasting with an innovative internet-distributed service and puts sports organisations in a more advantageous negotiating position regarding interested media and commercial partners. The model helps to overcome tight programming schedules and leads to more coverage than is possible under the traditional broadcasting model. Such an approach provides subscribers with flexible viewing options that catch up with emerging consumer habits, and provides a model to commercialise media coverage of the sport. In most cases, the streaming service is available worldwide, and varies only slightly due to local television broadcast restrictions, cultural specificities, or language preferences. However, it remains uncertain whether many smaller sports organisations are too risk-averse to experiment with such entrepreneurial models and leave the traditional broadcasting model behind.

BOX 5.3 WRC'S 'BETTING ON TWO HORSES' STRATEGY

WRC+ All Live was the official subscription-based livestream and video platform of the World Rally Championship (WRC), a global motorsports competition consisting of a series of rally events driven on public roads. Rallye Monte-Carlo and Rally Finland are considered among the most prestigious events in the Championship. WRC+ All Live was the sport's flagship media product, providing 25 hours or more of live coverage through a rally weekend. Since the 1990s, the championship had failed to seal lucrative broadcast deals, mainly because the complicated structure of a rallying event did not fit smoothly into strict broadcasting schedules. Consequently, WRC was flirting with bankruptcy until 2012 when Red Bull Media House and KW25 took over and provided financial stability for the sport (Tickell et al., 2021). The new promoter was not bound by existing broadcast contracts and established, in 2014, the WRC+ streaming service, which provided only limited coverage of the races. Four years later, WRC+ All Live was introduced, providing live coverage of all stages run at each event of the WRC series, along with other non-live content including season reviews, historical specials, documentaries, and best-of programmes. To deliver the high-definition streaming content, broadcast technology partners NEP Group and Tata Communications were employed for production and distribution assistance (McLean, 2019). In 2023, WRC+ was replaced by Rally.TV, which became the new home of WRC, as well as live coverage of the European Rally Championship (ERC) and World Rallycross (World RX).

By taking control of its own production and launching a worldwide streaming service, Red Bull Media House was able to overcome the constraints of traditional television schedules while maintaining the ability to negotiate rights deals in individual markets. WRC+ All Live enabled the motorsport to revamp its media strategy and to complement a streaming platform by offering live and highlight packages to interested broadcasting and streaming services. As Tickell and Evens (2021) discuss, operating a bespoke platform fits perfectly within a wider strategy of the WRC to make its product more attractive to media and commercial partners without undermining the value of third-party rights contracts. On the contrary, WRC+ All Live enabled the championship to create a fallback position, which changed the negotiation power balance between the WRC promoter and interested broadcasters. Following the extended WRC coverage and growing fan base, the championship was able to negotiate deals both with pay-tv and with free-to-air broadcasters worldwide and also extend long-term partnerships with leading pay-tv operators Canal+, BT Sport (now TNT Sports), and Sky Italia. Moreover, the motorsports streaming service is also available on third-party platforms such as Stan sport, ITVX, and C More. Hence, its availability as a worldwide streaming service did not seem to cannibalise the WRC's potential to tap into different revenue pools. WRC even resisted pressure to geo-block in territories where the sport is highly popular (like Estonia and Finland).

In addition to generating income from subscription revenue, WRC's digital media strategy allows the championship to commercialise its brand and respond to new media consumption patterns. The streaming service functions as part of a transmedia storytelling strategy that not only targets existing rally fans, but also draws new viewers, especially younger generations that are hard to reach, into the motorsport. Tickell (2022) discussed how funnelling through social channels drives engagement and increases interaction. Short clips like onboard coverage from stages or crashes, but also gaming such as eSports WRC, generate interest in the sport and build a relationship with motorsport fans. Transmedia guide people through the fanship journey, starting from seeing and commenting on social videos and leading eventually to the linear sports experience, with a future prospect of raising subscription revenues. Audience data have proved vital to understanding how fans think and act online. Data generated by the streaming platform and meshed with those collected from social channels help to raise revenues from sponsorship, but also allow the WRC to introduce customised features and create pathways to 'dip [fans] in and out of the live broadcast' (p.148).

A second dilemma relates to the trade-off between maximising audience reach and maximising media income, which basically boils down to the long-standing question of whether sports organisations should provide live coverage to advertising-funded (free-to-air) or subscription-funded (pay-tv) broadcasting or streaming platforms (Solberg, 2002). Whereas free-to-air broadcasting remains the prime outlet for US major sports, most domestic soccer leagues in Europe have migrated to pay-tv channels that are willing to pay significant amounts for, preferably exclusive, broadcasting rights – even with declining subscriptions due to cord-cutting. By playing off multiple providers of pay-tv platforms against each other in a bidding process, rights owners can select the option that provides the best financial offer and secure higher revenue, at least when the competition is not legally required to be available via free-to-air television (see Chapter 8). Assuming these sports have already built sufficient popularity and command significant willingness to pay among their fans, rights owners may prioritise financial considerations and opt for coverage on pay-tv. Despite increased income from media rights, a pay-tv distribution strategy may come at a serious cost, too. This is illustrated by Formula One's switch to pay-tv. After decades of exclusive free-to-air coverage on the BBC, it was announced that, from 2012, Sky Sports (the entire season) and the BBC (ten races) would share the rights to broadcast Formula One races in the UK. The move boosted Formula One's rights fee by 110 per cent to an estimated £105 million. Despite full coverage of the championship, the number of viewers almost halved from 4.15 million per race to 2.2 million per race, eventually resulting in a loss of about 25 million viewers (Sylt, 2015). Since 2019, live Formula One coverage has moved entirely behind the Sky paywall – a development that is also visible in other broadcast markets, also with a detrimental effect on viewership, however. In Germany, for example, after Formula One coverage shifted from free-to-air broadcaster RTL to Sky, viewing rates fell from 4.55 million per race to 816,000 per race. On the one hand, this reduction in the number of viewers could reduce the interest from potential sponsors and the sponsorship rates teams can command. On the other hand, this potential loss in sponsorship revenue was generously compensated for by a steep increase in broadcast income. Moreover, despite a reduction in Formula One viewership, Sky subscribers are likely to have a higher disposable income and higher affection for the sport, which in turn may make them more valuable to Formula One sponsors. In a similar vein, Formula One opts to license live content to subscription-funded streaming services, either third-party platforms such as DAZN, ESPN+, Tencent, and Viaplay or its bespoke F1 TV Pro. Advertising-funded platforms such as YouTube and Twitter's X are used primarily to show highlights and clips, and to reach out to a younger audience that is less willing and able to pay.

Unlike top-tier sports, maximising the value of broadcast rights may not always be a priority for middle-tier and niche sports that are seeking to grow the fan base and boost the value of sponsorship deals. For these organisations, sponsorship rather than media rights represents by far the largest source of revenue. Instead of sacrificing long-term sports success for short-term financial gain, smaller sports generally prefer free-to-air broadcast deals to generate exposure and increase audience reach in earlier stages of development. Free-to-air broadcasting – be it live coverage or highlights – helps to raise awareness, attract new audiences, and generate interest from sponsors. Even the English Premier League initially opted for free-to-air coverage to let the popularity of the championship in the US grow (Robinson and Clegg, 2019). Public service broadcasters sometimes have a remit to devote considerable attention to smaller sports, which may help to build a wider fan base. In other cases, however, sporting organisations pay broadcasters for coverage – this also happened with Formula One in large markets such as India in which broadcasters were initially not keen to bring the sport on screen. Also MLS, with its inaugural season being played in 1996, had to pay US broadcasters for much-needed television exposure until it managed to sell its rights in a pivotal broadcast deal in 2007 (Evens et al., 2013). Niche sports have also been approached by pay-tv platforms, for whom smaller sports are often inexpensive 'platform fillers' that possibly address unserved target groups. However, such a move is not without any risks. Meier, Schreyer, and Jetzke (2020) present a case study of DKB Handball-Bundesliga (HBL), the top German professional handball league, and found that the move to pay-tv distribution led to a significant decrease in audience reach. Moreover, exclusive pay-tv coverage tends to limit the audience to hardcore fans and makes it much harder for casual fans to dip into the game. Hence, niche sports, much more than premium sports, need a hybrid rights strategy that allows rights owners to grow future audiences and generate commercial interest. Free-to-air broadcast platforms, but also YouTube or TikTok, therefore, are deemed necessary to create fan engagement and reach, and can be supplemented with a paid-for offering provided by subscription-funded platforms to generate additional revenue. It goes without saying that a franchise-branded D2F platform forms a crucial part in this marketing mix, no matter its value proposition and go-to-market strategy.

References

Abito, J. M. and Wright, J. (2008). Exclusive Dealing with Imperfect Downstream Competition. *International Journal of Industrial Organization*, 26 (1), pp. 227–246.

Andreff, W. and Staudohar, P. D. (2002). European and US Sports Business Models. In: C. P. Barros, M. Ibrahimo, and S. Szymanski (eds.), *Transatlantic Sport: The Comparative Economics of North American and European Sports* (pp. 23–49). Cheltenham: Edward Elgar.

Bassam, T. (2021). '"We're in the game now": How Sportswik helped the SvFF connect Swedish soccer from top to bottom', *SportsProMedia*, 15 July. Available at: https://www.sportspromedia.com/analysis/swedish-football-association-svff-sportswik-min-fotboll-app-social-media/ (Accessed: 23 July 2023).

Boardman, A. E. and Hargreaves-Heap, S. P. (1999). Network Externalities and Government Restrictions on Satellite Broadcasting of Key Sporting Events. *Journal of Cultural Economics*, 23 (3), pp. 167–181.

Bolter, J. D. (2019). *The Digital Plenitude: The Decline of Elite Culture and the Rise of New Media*. Cambridge, MA: MIT Press.

Carp, S. (2019). 'La Liga launches OTT service to boost visibility of Spanish sport', *SportsProMedia*, 25 March. Available at: https://www.sportspromedia.com/news/la-liga-ott-streaming-platform-launch/ (Accessed: 7 August 2023).

Deloitte (2024). 'Football Money League'. Available at: https://www2.deloitte.com/uk/en/pages/sports-business-group/articles/deloitte-football-money-league.html (Accessed: 4 July 2023).

Draper, K. (2018). 'The era of streaming niche sports dawns', *The New York Times*, 17 July. Available at: https://www.nytimes.com/2018/07/17/sports/streaming-sports.html (Accessed: 17 July 2018).

Duncan, S. (2020). *The Digital World of Sport: The Impact of Emerging Media on Sports News, Information and Journalism*. London: Anthem Press.

Evens, T., Iosifidis, P., and Smith, P. (2013). *The Political Economy of Television Sports Rights*. Basingstoke: Palgrave Macmillan.

Evens, T., Tickell, S., and Næss, H. E. (2023). Ecclestone out, Liberty Media in: A Look into the Shifting Ownership Structure of Formula One. In: D. Sturm, S. Wagg, and D. Andrews (eds.), *Lives in the Fast Lane: Essays on the History and Politics of Motor Racing* (pp. 592–603). Basingstoke: Palgrave Macmillan.

Frandsen, K. (2014). Mediatisation of Sports. In: K. Lundbye (ed.), *Mediatization of Communication* (pp. 199–226). Berlin: Mouton de Gruyter.

Hayes, D. (2022). 'WWE reports big streaming lift since Peacock move, with 3.5M paid subscribers viewing its content', *Deadline*, 3 February. Available at: https://deadline.com/2022/02/wwe-streaming-peacock-fourth-quarter-1234926352/ (Accessed: 13 July 2023).

Haynes, R. and Robeers, T. (2019). The Need for Speed? A Historical Analysis of The BBC's Post-War Broadcasting of Motorsport. *Historical Journal of Film, Radio and Television*, 40 (2), pp. 407–423.

Holmes, E. (2018). 'International Triathlon Union appoints Infront to drive commercial growth', *SportsProMedia*, 21 February. Available at: https://www.sportspromedia.com/news/international-triathlon-union-infront-drive-growth/ (Accessed: 18 July 2023).

Hutchins, B. and Rowe, D. (2009). From Broadcast Scarcity to Digital Plenitude: The Changing Dynamics of the Media Sport Content Economy. *Television & New Media*, 10 (4), pp. 354–370.

McClearen, J. (2017). "We Are All Fighters": The Transmedia Marketing of Difference in the Ultimate Fighting Championship (UFC). *International Journal of Communication*, 11, pp. 3224–3241.

McLean, H. (2019). 'FIA World Rally Championship talks live OTT and remote production at 200km per hour', *SVGE News*, 14 March. Available at: https://www.svgeurope.org/blog/headlines/fia-world-rally-championship-talks-live-ott-and-remote-production-at-200km-per-hour/ (Accessed: 10 February 2023).

Meier, H. E., Hagenach, J., and Jetzke, M. (2020). Aggregation as the Remedy for the Decline of Niche Sports Broadcasting: A Case Study of the European Championships. *International Journal of Sport Communication*, 13 (4), pp. 719–743.

Meier, H. E., Schreyer, D., and Jetzke, M. (2020). German Handball TV Demand: Did it Pay for the Handball-Bundesliga to Move from Free to Pay TV? *European Sports Management Quarterly*, 20 (5), pp. 618–635.

Nicholson, M., Kerr, A., and Sherwood, M. (2015). *Sport and the Media*. London: Routledge.

Robinson, J. and Clegg, J. (2019). *The Club*. London: John Murray.
Rosner, S. R. and Shropshire, K. L. (2011). *The Business of Sports* (2nd ed.). Burlington, MA: Jones & Bartlett.
Rowe, D. (1999). *Sport, Culture and the Media. The Untruly Trinity*. Buckingham: Open University Free Press.
Secular, S. (2018). Games without Frontiers: Streaming Sports and the Evolution of Digital Intermediaries. *Media Industries Journal*, 5 (2). Available at: https://doi.org/10.3998/mij.15031809.0005.209 (Accessed: 13 July 2023).
Sim, J. (2023). 'Reports: Serie A considers Sky Italia takeover bid', *SportsProMedia*, 15 March. Available at: https://www.sportspromedia.com/news/serie-a-sky-italia-takeover-bid-acquisition-media-rights/ (Accessed: 12 July 2023).
Solberg, H. A. (2002). The Economics of Television Sports Rights. Europe and the US – A Comparative Analysis. *norsk medietidsskrift*, 9 (2), pp. 57–80.
SVG Europe (2021). 'Variety is the spice of life: Maximising the reach of niche sports', *SVGE News*, 21 April. Available at: https://www.svgeurope.org/blog/headlines/variety-is-the-spice-of-life-maximising-the-reach-of-niche-sports/ (Accessed: 13 July 2023).
Sylt, C. (2015). 'F1 loses 25 million viewers driven by switch to pay TV', *Forbes*, 13 December. Available at: https://www.forbes.com/sites/csylt/2015/02/01/f1-loses-25-million-viewers-driven-by-switch-to-pay-tv/ (Accessed: 1 August 2023).
Tickell, S. (2022). *'It was Never Made for TV': Niche Sports in the Age of Digital Plenitude: A Case Study of the World Rallying Championship (WRC)*. PhD thesis, Universiteit Gent.
Tickell, S. and Evens, T. (2021). Owned Streaming Platforms and Television Broadcast Deals: The Case of the World Rally Championship. *European Journal of International Management*, 15 (2–3), pp. 266–282.
Tickell, S., Næss, H. E., and Evens, T. (2021). Powerful Owners and Powerful Legacies. What Drives Change in the World Rally Championship? *Journal of Global Sport Management*, 8 (4), pp. 943–964.
Tickell, S., Sobral, V., and Meier, H. E. (2024). Finding a Niche in Digital Plenitude: Sport Media Strategies of Smaller European Football Leagues. *European Sports Management Quarterly*, 24 (4), pp. 876–897.
Weich, C. (2019). 'WWE Network 2.0: How WWE rebuilt its streaming service after a split with Disney', *The Verge*, 10 September. Available at: https://www.theverge.com/2019/9/10/20857446/wwe-network-streaming-redesign-george-barrios-interview-disney-price-subscription-downloads (Accessed: 13 July 2023).
Wenner, L. A. and Billings, A. (2017). The Curious Case of the Megasporting Event. In: L. A. Wenner and A. Billings (eds.), *Sport, Media and Mega-Events* (pp. 3–18). London: Routledge.
Zheng, J. and Mason, D. S. (2018). *Brand Platform in the Professional Sport Industry. Sustaining Growth through Innovation*. Cham: Springer.

PART 3

The Regulation of Sports Rights

6

COPYRIGHT LAW AND SPORTS PIRACY

Copyright law enables authors to protect their 'literary and artistic works' (e.g. films, books, photographs, music, etc.) from being appropriated without permission. Albeit with significant national variations, particularly in relation to enforcement, over 180 countries operate a form of copyright law based on a series of international agreements coordinated by the World Intellectual Property Organisation (WIPO), an agency of the United Nations (WIPO, 2024a). However, while sports fans may beg to differ, in legal terms sports events are not generally regarded as 'artistic' or 'creative works' (EAO, 2021, p.11). Unlike a novel or a film, for example, with a plot and/or a script, sports events are defined by (at least some degree of) unpredictability and randomness. On this basis, in Europe, the US, India, Australia, as well as numerous other countries, sports events are not deemed to be 'works of authorship' that qualify for protection under copyright law (Asser Institute, 2014, p.29; Boyle, 2015; Kariyawasam and Tsai, 2017; Robertson, 2015; Sharma, 2018). Yet, copyright law remains vital for sports and media organisations in two related areas: recording and broadcast rights. First, the audio-visual recording of a sports event (whether by a sports organisation itself or a nominated producer) almost always involves a host of creative choices (e.g. choice of camera angles, players to be filmed, etc.) and as such is protected by copyright law (EAO, 2021, p.14). Second, often referred to as (copyright) 'related rights', broadcasters have the exclusive rights to authorise the rebroadcasting, 'fixation' (i.e. recording), reproduction, and/or communication to the public of their broadcasts (WIPO, 2024b; EAO, 2021, p.16). Taken together, these legal protections have underpinned the growth of the sports rights market, but their application and enforcement in the age of streaming are more challenging than ever.

Some forms of media content, such as films, music, and video games, have long histories of being subject to extensive copying and/or distribution

DOI: 10.4324/9781003401988-10

without the copyright holder's permission, commonly referred to as piracy (Cvetkovski, 2013). By contrast, piracy of sports content (at least to any significant degree) is a relatively recent phenomenon. This stems largely from the fact that the value of sports content resides almost wholly in live coverage (see Chapter 2). Thus, for example, whereas, during the 1980s and 1990s, piracy of Hollywood films, via video cassettes and then DVDs, grew from 'niche to mass market' (McDonald, 2015, p.84), there was no equivalent boom in sports piracy. From around the early 1990s (and slightly earlier in the US), the illegal supply of unauthorised decoder cards to access (encrypted) pay-tv services without payment (to the official provider) enabled some growth in sports piracy, but, in most, if not quite all, countries, this was relatively limited. Not least because, as put by Paul Segre, chief executive officer of video security technology specialist company, Synamedia, the 'traditional conditional access systems' used by satellite and cable television operators to restrict access to paying subscribers were 'rock solid. Super secure' (Leaders, 2021, p.12). However, over the last couple of decades, with the development of the internet into an increasingly reliable medium for the distribution of live audio-visual content, piracy has become a significant feature of the global sports right market. According to one industry study, sports and media organisations could 'unlock' as much as $28.3 billion in new annual revenue by tackling online piracy (Synamedia, 2021a, p.4). This chapter examines in more detail the significance of piracy for the contemporary sports rights market. This first part highlights the global scale, but different national patterns of online sports piracy, as well as the various ways sports fans access pirated content. The second part then details the range of technical and/or legal solutions pursued by media and sports organisations, together with policy makers and regulators, in their attempts to tackle sports piracy. The chapter concludes by arguing that providing easily accessible and affordable legal routes to view sports content is likely to be the most effective way to reduce online sports piracy.

The Scale and Patterns of Sports Piracy

By its very nature the exact scale of any form of piracy is difficult to ascertain, but international and national survey evidence suggests that online sports piracy is ubiquitous. One of the most comprehensive surveys, carried out by Ampere Analysis on behalf of Synamedia (2020a), questioned over 6,000 sports fans (aged between 18 and 64) across ten different national markets (Brazil, Egypt, Germany, India, Italy, Jordan, Malaysia, Saudi Arabia, the UK, and the US). It found that over half (51 per cent) of sports fans consumed sports content from pirate services at least once a month (Synamedia, 2020a, p.6). At the national level, sports piracy largely conforms with 'conventional wisdom' on international rates of media piracy, with piracy rates inversely (and loosely) tracking wider measures of socioeconomic development, such as GDP (gross domestic product) (Karaganis, 2011, p.10). In this way, national levels of sports piracy reflect the established 'geography of media piracy', whereby, while piracy is evident almost everywhere, certain countries, mostly 'emerging economies', such as Brazil and India, are regarded, particularly by major copyright owners based in the West, as 'piracy hotspots' (McDonald, 2021, p.73). Thus, for example, in Australia, a government-commissioned survey found that 26 per cent of 'live sport consumers' accessed 'at least some content unlawfully' (AGD, 2023, p.89). Similarly, in the UK, the government's Intellectual Property Office (IPO) survey of 'online copyright infringement' recorded that 36 per cent of individuals watched pirated live sports (IPO, 2023). Whereas, by contrast, Brazil has been described as a 'hotspot for illegal live sport viewing', with 88 per cent of all sports fans watching pirate streams weekly (Synamedia, 2020b, p.20). And, in India, the prevalence of sports piracy is perhaps best illustrated by the fact that around 50 per cent of sports fans are estimated to 'pay for piracy services', a figure much higher than, for example, the UK and the US, at 17 and 22 per cent, respectively (Synamedia, 2020a, p.21). At the same time, however, even though piracy is less prevalent in some of the most valuable national sports rights markets, such as the US, UK, and Australia, the underlying wealth of these markets means they account for a relatively high proportion of the total global revenue estimated to be lost to illegal sports viewing – well over one-third (Synamedia, 2021a, p.6).

In much the same way as the legal global sports rights market (see Chapter 2), patterns of online sports piracy are also largely shaped by national/regional sporting preferences. Reflecting its global popularity, football is 'the planet's most pirated sport', with domestic leagues the focus of piracy in a number of major national markets in Europe and South America, including Italy, Germany, the UK, and Brazil (Synamedia, 2021b, pp.7–9). In Europe, levels of sport piracy can even be traced directly onto the calendar of the main football leagues, with 'maximum levels' in April and between September and October, but 'minimum values' in June and July (EUIPO, 2023, p.56). The UK also provides a particularly good illustration of how sports piracy can be dominated by a single popular sport, namely football. A UK survey reported that 73 per cent of those who had watched 'illegal sports broadcasts' had done so to watch football, around three times more than the next most pirated sport (YouGov, 2023). Albeit with different sports, much the same pattern is evident in other nations and regions. For example, cricket is by far the most pirated sport in India, the NFL (American football) in the US, and badminton 'features disproportionately' in Malaysia (Synamedia, 2021b, pp.9–10). At the same time, however, national patterns of sports piracy may also reflect other key market conditions, most notably cost and/or (lack of) availability (both of which are discussed in more detail below). For example, in the UK, even though other sports, such as cricket and rugby, may be more popular, boxing is the UK's second most pirated sport, with around 24 per cent of those that 'watch sport via illegal broadcasts' watching boxing (YouGov, 2023). This stems largely from the relatively high cost of watching major boxing events, which are often sold on a 'pay-per view' basis. For example, in March 2024, to view (legal) live coverage of the heavyweight contest between Anthony Joshua and Francis Ngannou (which, in the event, lasted only six minutes), UK viewers were required to pay (DAZN or Sky) £20. According to 'internet analysts', Yield Sec, around 100,000 UK viewers opted to watch via illegal streams (Hughes, 2024). Furthermore, its high viewing cost has also led boxing to be labelled 'a gateway sport' to piracy in the UK, because it is the sport that most often leads viewers to seek out an illegal streaming service and take their 'initial step into the world of illicit consumption' (Synamedia, 2021b, p.9). In national markets, patterns of piracy may also be driven by the relative lack of availability of a particular sport/competition via legal television services. For example, in the US, while the most popular sports are still the most pirated overall, fans of the major sports leagues (i.e. NFL American football, NBA basketball, MLB baseball, and NHL hockey) are markedly less likely to watch pirate streams than fans of less popular sports, at least in part due to the variety of (free and pay) legal viewing options available. Whereas, US sports fans who favour other sports that are not so widely (or freely) available, particularly international football leagues and tournaments, have been found to be far more likely to be watching them from pirate sources (Synamedia, 2021b, p.18).

Viewers use a variety of methods to illegally access sports content online. One of the most common is the sharing of passwords with family, friends, and/or others in order to access subscription video-on-demand (SVoD) services without (full) payment. From its inception, this type of improper password sharing has been a prominent feature of the SVoD market. With their initial focus on achieving rapid subscriber growth, the practice was 'largely ignored' by leading SVoDs, most notably Netflix (Grimes, 2022). For example, in the UK, in 2023, it was estimated that around one-quarter of Netflix's 15 million subscribers shared their password with others (Brignall, 2023). However, amidst a slowdown in subscriber growth, in 2022, Netflix announced a 'global crackdown' on password sharing (Rushe, 2023). Initially, it was feared that this move would further undermine subscriber growth, but in fact, by 2024, Netflix's stricter approach to password sharing was widely viewed as a chief driver behind record subscriber growth (Grimes, 2024a). Subsequently, other SVoDs have also looked to adopt a stricter approach to password sharing, including key players within the sports rights markets, such as Discovery+ (Warner Bros. Discovery), ESPN+ (Disney), Viaplay, and DAZN (Grimes, 2024b; Thomas, 2024). Password sharing is certainly widespread amongst sports fans. More than one in five of all sports fans say they share passwords with people outside their household (Synamedia, 2020b, p.11). Perhaps most notably, the dedicated sports streaming service, DAZN, has faced particularly severe problems with password sharing.

In one of its most significant national markets, Italy, DAZN launched its service, in 2018, with a 'dual user' option for subscribers that allowed simultaneous viewing of content on two different devices with the same account. However, DAZN's internal monitoring found that the feature was widely 'misused by users', who would commonly sell on one of their 'subscriptions' (Pekic, 2021). In 2022, as part of a wider 'crackdown on content sharing', DAZN limited simultaneous access via two devices to the same home IP address and introduced a higher-cost premium subscription, DAZN Plus, for those wanting to stream simultaneously on more than one device from any location (Pekic, 2022).

Sports fans also often access illegal content online by simply searching for streams of live events on mainstream social media sites, such as Facebook Live, Twitch, and X (formerly Twitter), or internet search engines, such as Google. For example, in November 2020, Stefan Brost, the Team lead for Public Affairs of the German Football Association (DFB), estimated that around 350,000 different illegal Bundesliga streams are made available each match day on platforms, such as YouTube, Facebook, or Twitter (EPRS, 2020, p.3). The vast majority of fans that use social media to access coverage of a particular event do so without the need for any additional payment, or subscription. According to Synamedia (2020a), around 70 per cent of fans that access illegal sports content online view 'free-to-view' coverage only (p.6). Categorised as 'casual viewers', such fans use social media platforms to view illegal content from individual pirates, who make streams available using a variety of 'P2P exchange platforms' and/or by sharing credentials for live streams using communication apps, such as WhatsApp and Telegram (EUIPO, 2019, pp.35–6). Alternatively, 'casual viewers' may also use dedicated pirate aggregator sites to find streams of live sports events. These 'link aggregators' typically maintain a vast catalogue of links to live television channel streams online and, in much the same way as individual 'free-to-view' pirates, generate revenue through indirect sources, including 'pay-per-click' payments from advertisers and/or by spreading malware (EUIPO, 2019, p.29).

In contrast, more committed consumers of online illegal sports content regularly pay to access pirate services and can be categorised as 'long term viewers' (EUIPO, 2019, p.36). The most common 'business model' is where a 'package' of unauthorised online television (IPTV) services is offered through a dedicated website, or IPTV app, usually for a monthly subscription fee (EUIPO, 2019, pp.26–9). Some 'long-term viewers' also opt to purchase specific hardware to keep permanently connected to their television set, such as a set-top box, or streaming stick, which has been, or can be, adapted to facilitate the reception of illegal online content (EUIPO, 2019, p.34). Perhaps unsurprisingly, far fewer sports fans go to the trouble of installing, configuring, and using IPTV apps and/or purchasing hardware devices in order to subscribe to pirate services than 'casually' access free-to-view streams. Not least because becoming a 'long-term viewer' often requires at least some level of technical expertise. According to Synamedia (2020a, p.6) just over one-quarter (29 per cent) of sports fans who access content online pay for such services. Nonetheless, this still represents a significant number of 'long-term viewers'. For example, in the EU, in 2019, an estimated 7.6 million subscriptions were made to 'illegal broadcast platforms' (EPRS, 2020, p.11). And, in national/regional 'piracy hotspots', where the proportion of 'long-term viewers' is above average, such as India (50 per cent), Malaysia (35 per cent), and MENA (Middle East and North Africa) (30 per cent), the number of subscribers to illegal online television services is likely to be even higher (Synamedia, 2020a, p.21).

Tackling Sports Piracy

Major media organisations, perhaps most notably beIN Media and DAZN, regularly describe online sports piracy as a form of 'organised crime' that 'costs the industry tens of billions of dollars every year' (Thomas, 2023). Given the sophisticated nature of many sports piracy distribution networks, this description is difficult to dispute. Subscription-based piracy services, in particular, often act as 'super-aggregators' of illegal content and involve a whole host of different actors, including: 'industrial scale professional hackers, criminal technology experts [working] with content aggregators, content wholesalers and content resellers' (Leaders, 2021, p.5). Or, as put by Cameron Andrews, legal director at beIN Media Group, 'it's like a drugs network... You've got suppliers or manufacturers, those who are copying the channels... then you have aggregators above that, and then resellers and restreamers, so it's a kind of spider's web' (SportsProMedia, 2021). Media organisations can be seen to lose out from sports piracy in two related ways. First, the media organisation's content is stolen and viewed for free. Each time a viewer opts to watch pirated live sports content, rather than the legitimate offering, the broadcaster loses revenue (advertising and/or access fee). Second, media organisations also lose out through the opportunity cost of that same viewer not buying a subscription to a full service because of the illegal alternatives available to them. In this sense, sports broadcasters have 'their pockets picked twice' by piracy (Leaders, 2021, p.10). The exact value of the losses suffered by media organisations is inherently difficult to measure. One approach is to attempt to calculate the total amount of revenue earned by illicit broadcasting platforms. Using the method, EPRS (2020, p.11) estimated that, in 2019, EU broadcasters lost out on around €522 million. Alternatively, industry consultant Synamedia's (2021a, p.10) figure of $28.3 billion for the 'cost of global sports piracy' is arrived at by measuring the value of those consumers who claim they would be willing to switch to legitimate pay-tv services and ignoring the about one-quarter of illegal viewers who say they will never pay for content. Whatever method is used, such estimates should certainly be treated with a degree of caution, not least because (as discussed more below) media/sports organisations have a clear incentive to maximise such estimates when lobbying for tougher copyright laws and/or enforcement measures. Nevertheless, it is beyond doubt that sports piracy significantly reduces the revenue of legitimate media organisations.

With revenue from the sale of media rights almost always received in advance, the nature of the threat posed by piracy to sports organisations relates not to an immediate loss of income, but rather to the long-term value of their rights. As discussed in Chapter 2, top-level sports organisations generate a significant proportion of their total revenue from the sale of media rights, often over 50 per cent. For sports organisations, the sale of media rights is therefore a vital part of the 'virtuous circle of sports revenues', whereby, particularly in Europe, revenues from elite sport fund grassroots facilities and financial solidarity arrangements, as well as stadiums and athlete salaries at the elite level (EPRS, 2020, p.2). The potential danger for sports organisations is that piracy threatens the profitability of investing in sports rights for media organisations to such a degree that they reduce the amounts they are prepared to pay for rights, or even opt to not invest in sports rights at all. As pointed out by Mark Lichtenhein, Chair of the Sports Rights Owners Coalition (SROC), a forum representing over 50 international and national sports bodies, including UEFA, the English Premier League, the European (golf) Tour, the International Cricket Council (ICC), and the Indian Premier League, if piracy threatens income from the sale of rights, then it is 'potentially disastrous' for the entire sports industry (Leaders, 2021, p.8). While exceptional in that it involved unprecedented levels of piracy sponsored by a nation state, the case of beoutQ in Saudi Arabia provided a real-world demonstration of how, if left unchecked, piracy can lead to the collapse of a national/regional sports rights market (see Box 6.1).

BOX 6.1 BEIN SPORTS, BEOUTQ, AND STATE-SPONSORED SPORTS PIRACY

Part of the Qatari state-owned Al Jazeera Media Network, beIN Sports was officially launched in 2012 and, in the same year, came to prominence with the acquisition of the domestic rights for France's leading football competition, Ligue 1 (Slater, 2022). Focused mainly on the MENA region, but also with a significant presence in a host of other national/regional markets, including France, Australasia, and North America, by the mid-2010s, beIN Sports had established itself as one of the world's leading sports broadcasters, with a rights portfolio valued at around $15 billion (Leaders, 2019, p.4). Perhaps most notably, beIN Sports had secured exclusive live rights across the MENA region for each of the widely followed 'big five' national European football leagues, as well as the FIFA 2018 and 2022 World Cups. With the latter tournament also to be hosted by Qatar, beIN Sports was a key part of Qatar's strategy to use sport to build 'global prestige and soft power' (Ahmed and Al Omran, 2018). However, between 2017 and 2021, the status of beIN (and Qatar) was challenged by an unprecedented wave of sports piracy backed by the state of Saudi Arabia.

As part of a long-running geopolitical rivalry, in summer 2017, Saudi Arabia and its allies, namely, Bahrain, Egypt, and the UAE, severed all diplomatic and trade ties with Qatar and also began a land, sea, and air blockade of their rival. In what was a 'war by any other means', sports piracy was deployed as a weapon against Qatar by Saudi Arabia (Slater, 2022). To begin with, beIN Sports was prevented from operating in Saudi Arabia. Credit card payments to the broadcaster were blocked, criminal sanctions were threatened against any distributors, and its set-top boxes were confiscated across Saudi Arabia (Leaders, 2019, p.4). Soon afterwards, accompanied by an extensive social media campaign and championed by prominent Saudi figures, including Saud al-Qahtani, a senior adviser at the Saudi royal court, a new geo-blocked website, limited to Saudi Arabia, was launched, called beoutQ (Ahmed and Al Omran, 2018). The beoutQ website redistributed beIN's Arabic channels as its own, simply replacing beIN's on-screen branding with beoutQ (Carp, 2018a). A few months later, beoutQ was also available in Saudi Arabia via satellite, with a full High Definition service, offering ten live beoutQ channels and selling set-top boxes, advertising space, and subscriptions (Leaders, 2019, p.11). Throughout 2018 and into 2019, beoutQ offered live coverage of a whole host of premium sports events and competitions, including Premier League football, Formula One, Grand Slam tennis tournaments, and the 2018 FIFA World Cup. All without owning any of the rights (Carp, 2018a).

Taking legal action against beoutQ in Saudi Arabia proved practically impossible for both beIN Sports and various sports organisations. Nine different Saudi-based law firms 'chose not to act on behalf of the [English] Premier League and other soccer bodies' (Carp, 2020a). beIN Sports therefore sought legal redress via the World Trade Organisation (WTO), the global body that oversees the rules of trade between nations. First, beIN accused Saudi Arabia of failing to comply with its obligations under the WTO's 'TRIPS agreement', an international agreement that sets minimum standards for the protection and enforcement of intellectual property rights, including copyright. On this basis, beIN Sports made a claim for US$1 billion in damages to be paid by Saudi Arabia to compensate for 'the most widespread piracy of sports broadcasting the world has ever seen' (Carp, 2018b). Second, much the same case was also levelled against Saudi Arabia at the WTO directly by the state of Qatar itself.

The Saudi Arabian government consistently denied any involvement with beoutQ or in any way facilitating beoutQ's transmissions in Saudi Arabia (Ahmed and Al Omran, 2018). However, three widely respected technology groups – US-based Cisco, Swiss company Nagra, and Spain-based Overon – all produced findings that suggested beoutQ's satellite signal emanated from the

Saudi-based satellite provider, Arabsat (Leaders, 2019, p.15). At least partly as a result, Saudi Arabia also faced growing international criticism, including from the UK, the EU, and the US, who were all unconvinced by the Saudis' denials (Carp, 2020b). Most significantly, in 2019, the Office of the United States Trade Representative (USTR) upgraded Saudi Arabia's status in its renowned 'Special 301 Report' to 'Priority Watch List' and designated beoutQ a 'notorious market' (Impey, 2019a). A few months later, in August 2019, beoutQ's satellite transmissions suddenly ceased, although its set-top boxes remained widely available throughout Saudi Arabia and continued to be used to receive online pirated sports content from across the globe (Leaders, 2019, p.19).

In June 2020, the WTO ruled in Qatar's favour, concluding that there was 'prima facie' evidence that beoutQ was 'operated by individuals or entities under the jurisdiction of Saudi Arabia' (Farge and Blenkinsop, 2020). However, for beIN Sports, significant damage had already been done. At the height of the dispute, beIN lost more than 35 per cent of its total revenue and made hundreds of staff redundant (Slater, 2022). For several major sports organisations, the rise of beoutQ also proved costly. Scarred by the impact of beoutQ, in 2019, beIN Sports warned that, if left unchecked, the 'plague of piracy' could mean that in 'certain cases' the value of rights would 'fall off a cliff' due to a lack of exclusivity (Harwood, 2019). While beIN praised some sports organisations, such as the English Premier League, for their actions to counter piracy, it was less impressed by others and this was reflected in its revised rights strategy. Between 2019 and 2021, beIN opted not to bid to renew existing MENA region rights deals with Formula One, Serie A (Italy), and the Bundesliga (Germany), when previous deals had been worth US$30–40 million, US$500 million, and US$237 million, respectively (Bassam, 2020; Impey, 2019b; Nicholson, 2021).

From around late 2020, Saudi Arabia adopted a new geopolitical political strategy. Together with its allies, this began with the lifting of the blockade against Qatar. The Saudi government then invested 'tens of billions' developing its 'sports and entertainment infrastructure' in order to host top events, including Formula One, world championship boxing bouts, golf, and tennis, as part of a plan to 'project a new image of the country' (Ahmed and England, 2021). The purchase of the English Premier League club, Newcastle United, was also part of this plan. In April 2020, an initial bid to buy the club led by the Saudi Arabian Public Investment Fund (PIF) stalled, largely due to concerns within the Premier League about Saudi Arabia's involvement in beoutQ and a desire to preserve the League's existing commercial relationship with beIN Sports. However, in October 2021, against a backdrop of high-level political negotiations between football and government officials in the UK and the Middle East, it was widely reported that Saudi Arabia had promised that it would 'soon' lift the ban on beIN Sports operating in Saudi Arabia (Ahmed, 2021). A few days later, the Premier League allowed PIF to complete its purchase of Newcastle United in a deal worth £305 million (Ahmed and England,

2021). In December 2021, Saudi Arabia withdrew its appeal against the WTO's ruling and, in early 2022, Qatar and Saudi Arabia jointly agreed the formal 'withdrawal/termination' of their WTO dispute (WTO, 2022). Finally, although online sport piracy remains a significant feature of the MENA rights market, beIN Sports has subsequently agreed new rights deals for the MENA region with a number of leading sports organisations, including Formula One and the Bundesliga (Brittle, 2024; Nicholson, 2022).

Prosecuting the Sports Pirates

With the value of rights stable, or even rising, in most, if not quite all, national/regional markets, there is little evidence to suggest that online sports piracy will lead to a beoutQ-type collapse of the global sports rights market. At least in part, this is due to the combination of legal measures taken by media and sports organisations to protect the value of their rights. One way that media and sports organisations tackle piracy is by taking (criminal and/or civil) legal action against those involved in the distribution of illegal content. For example, in the UK, in 2023, following a rare private prosecution by the Premier League (i.e. not initiated by the state), five men were handed combined jail sentences of over 30 years for operating an illegal television service, known as Flawless, which, for just £10 per month (compared to around £80 per month to access legal pay-tv services in the UK), offered around 50,000 subscribers access to all Premier League football matches, as well as other pirated content, via dedicated online apps (Symonds and Grundy, 2023). Similarly, in France, in 2021, five defendants were convicted for operating an illegal sports streaming website and ordered to pay €7 million in damages to the country's leading sports broadcasters: beIN Sports, Canal+, and RMC Sport (Mann, 2021). However, despite the oft-mentioned links to organised crime and the scale of online piracy, cases like these are relatively rare. In Europe, in only three countries (Italy, Spain, and the UK) have the operators of infringing platforms/websites been imprisoned for 'massive copyright infringements' (EAO, 2021, p.23). Beyond Europe, in most countries, convictions of those involved in piracy are just as, if not even more, unusual. For example, in South Africa, in 2024, the Copyright Coalition, a group representing the country's creative industries, complained that 'only two' convictions had been made in well over a year (Forrester, 2024). Even more starkly, in India, the government's Committee on Piracy (CoP) has conceded that 'enforcement challenges' with copyright law mean that piracy is widely viewed as a 'low-risk high-reward' crime (Banerjee and Gane, 2022).

There are various interrelated reasons for the limited number of prosecutions made against those involved in online sports piracy. First, media and sports organisations have been keen to avoid the 'public relations disaster' experienced by the music industry during the early 2000s, when it attempted to tackle piracy by prosecuting ordinary music fans, including a 12-year-old girl from New York and a 71-year-old Texan grandfather (Hesmondhalgh, 2009, p.61). Largely as a result, media and sports organisations (as well as national governments) have made little, if any, attempt to prosecute individual sports fans for viewing illegal sports content online. Instead, as with both the UK and French cases cited above, their focus has been almost entirely on those involved in the systematic, commercially driven distribution of illegal sports content. However, this approach is itself far from straightforward. A second major challenge faced by media/sports organisations in their attempts to pursue legal action is identifying and locating the individuals responsible for providing illegal content. For example, in its response to a US government anti-piracy review, the Premier League detailed how those involved with supplying illegal content online almost always 'conceal their identities by using fake details, reverse proxy networks (such as Cloudflare) and privacy protection services (such as WhoisGuard)' (Premier League, 2023, p.9). A third related obstacle to successful prosecutions is the borderless nature of online piracy. This means that those involved in the distribution of illegal content may be located anywhere in the world and often spread across multiple different countries, which makes it even more difficult to establish who is supplying the content and adds layers of complexity to any attempted prosecution. Finally, the competing demands on the resources of local/national law enforcement agencies mean that the extensive support and expertise required to gather evidence for any subsequent prosecution(s) are often not available, particularly in so-called piracy hotspots. For example, in India, the CoP has noted that enforcement of copyright law is 'very low in terms of priority in the radar of law enforcement agencies' (Banerjee and Gane, 2022). Nevertheless, despite all these difficulties, prosecutions remain an important tool for media and sports organisations in their attempts to tackle piracy. As described by Cameron Andrews, the legal director of anti-piracy at beIN Media Group, 'old-fashioned investigation and legal prosecution... won't in itself stop piracy but it is important to send a message, deter people from doing it, obtain compensation and break the backs of these pirate networks' (SportsProMedia, 2021).

Take Down Notices, Blocking Orders, and a Never-Ending Game of 'Whack-a-Mole'

Given the inherent difficulty of prosecuting those involved in distributing illegal sports content online, media/sports organisations have instead focused most of their attention on attempting to remove and/or prevent access to pirated content. In legal terms, the first step to be taken by a rights holder when it discovers its content is being used without authorisation is usually to issue a 'cease and desist' notice to the relevant individual/organisation (Robertson, 2015, p.475).

However, as with criminal prosecutions, difficulties identifying and locating offenders mean that this option is often not practically possible. Or, the overt nature of the illegal activity may mean that any such legal notice is simply ignored. As a result, media and sports organisations have largely targeted their efforts to remove illegal online content at intermediaries, such as internet service providers (ISPs), social media platforms, and internet search engines, rather than those directly involved in sports piracy. In most countries, rights holders can have illegal online content removed by making a 'notice and take-down' (NTD) request to an online intermediary (Marsoof, 2015). For example, in the US, under the terms of the Digital Millennium Copyright Act 1998, in order to avoid being made liable for illegal online content accessed via their service (i.e. to retain 'safe harbour' status), online intermediaries are required to 'expeditiously' take down, or remove links to, any illegal content, as soon as they become aware of it. However, at least from the perspective of a number of major US sports organisations, a significant problem with this approach is that it relies too heavily on the goodwill and efficiency of online intermediaries. In 2023, in a joint submission to a US Patent and Trademark Office consultation on tackling piracy, the Ultimate Fighting Championship (UFC), NBA, and NFL complained that, while online service providers claim to be acting 'expeditiously', they had 'exploited ambiguity in the statutory language to delay removing content in response to takedown requests' and 'frequently take hours or even days to remove content' (UFC et al., 2023, p.3). Whether or not, as implied here, the approach of US-based online intermediaries has been driven by their own commercial incentives, it is certainly the case that an inherent problem with NTDs is the lack of an 'independent, unbiased and balanced mechanism' to oversee key decisions and their implementation (Marsoof, 2015, p.633).

Driven by their desire to guarantee online intermediaries act effectively to remove illegal content, over the last decade or so, media and sports organisations have increasingly sought to tackle piracy by securing formal legal blocking injunctions, rather than relying on NTDs. A blocking injunction, commonly known as a 'blocking order', generally refers to an order issued by a regional/national court (or specific regulatory agency), which requires 'intermediaries to block or disable access to infringing content made available through a website or a platform by putting appropriate technical measures in place' (EAO, 2021, p.42). In the US, during the early 2010s, attempts by Congress to legislate to allow such measures were abandoned over fears of 'censorship' and the impact on 'internet freedom' (Cory, 2022, p.2). However, in a host of other countries/regions, including most major sports markets, such as the UK, the EU, Australia, and India, blocking orders have become the main means by which media/sports organisations attempt to tackle sports piracy. For example, the first blocking order targeting illegal sports streaming was obtained, in 2013, in the UK, by the English Premier League and required 'the six main retail ISPs in the UK' to prevent users from accessing a website called FirstRow, an 'aggregation portal' offering illegal streams of Premier League matches (Robertson, 2015, pp.481–2). Similarly, in Australia, in 2015, amendments to copyright law facilitated the establishment of a 'website blocking scheme', which has been regularly used by the country's sports broadcasters. For example, Foxtel has had numerous applications for blocking orders agreed by the Federal Court, resulting in the blocking of over 350 piracy domains (Foxtel, 2023, p.1).

In practice, however, blocking injunctions have had only a very limited impact on the availability of illegal sports content online. This is because, to circumvent the blocking of a website, illegal content providers often simply create 'mirror' websites that share the same illegal content, but use a new website address (EAO, 2021, p.74). In response, media/sports organisations have adopted the use of 'dynamic' blocking injunctions, which extend the scope of a particular injunction to cover 'similar websites, including other domain names, Internet Protocol (IP) addresses or URLs, without the need to initiate new legal proceedings to obtain a new injunction' (EAO, 2021, p.74). With support from national governments and/or courts, dynamic injunctions have been widely adopted in Europe (Austria, Denmark, France, Germany, Greece, Ireland, Italy, the Netherlands, Portugal, Romania, Spain, Sweden, and the UK) (EAO, 2021, p.74). For example, in Spain, in 2020, the leading sports broadcaster Telefónica (Movistar+) secured a court-issued blocking order requiring the country's leading ISPs to prevent access to 44 pirate sites offering illegal access to live La Liga football matches. The 'dynamic' part of the injunction allowed Telefónica to notify the ISPs of new sites, URLs, domains, and IP addresses for blocking every week without having to refer to the court for permission (Maxwell, 2020). Similarly, beyond Europe, in Australia, in 2018, an amendment to the (2015) Copyright Law clarified the Federal Court's ability to make 'responsive orders applying to new or related online locations' (AGD, 2022, p.14). And, in Canada, in 2022, the Federal Court issued its first 'dynamic' blocking order to support the efforts of the country's leading sports broadcasters, Rogers and The Sports Network, to prevent illegal online streams of NHL ice hockey matches (Maxwell, 2022a).

Most recently, in some European countries, including Germany, the UK, Ireland, and Italy, the scope of blocking orders has been extended still further. On the grounds that blocking websites is no longer sufficient to combat sports piracy, 'live blocking orders' have been issued by courts, which require 'access to servers hosting, delivering and/or facilitating access to illegal streams of live sports events' to be blocked 'while the event is being broadcast' (EAO, 2021, p.82). This approach was first adopted in 2017, in the UK, when the Premier League secured a 'live blocking order' for the remainder of the 2016/17 season, and it has been regularly renewed since (Premier League, 2017). Live blocking orders are a key part of Italy's self-proclaimed piracy shield (see Box 6.2).

BOX 6.2 TACKLING SPORTS PIRACY IN ITALY: THE PIRACY SHIELD

Over the last decade, online sports piracy has become an increasingly significant feature of the Italian sports rights market. While piracy in other forms of media content, such as films and TV, has remained fairly stable, or even fallen, there has been significant growth in online sports piracy. In 2017, sports piracy accounted for just 7 per cent of piracy in Italy; by 2019, this figure had grown to 10 per cent and by 2022 it had grown again to 15 per cent (EPRS, 2020, p.11; Maxwell, 2022b). In 2022, there were 41 million acts of sports piracy, an annual increase of 26 per cent (Pekic, 2023a). Against this backdrop, Italy's leading sports broadcasters, most notably DAZN, have repeatedly called on the Italian government to take 'tougher' action against sports piracy (Pollina, 2023).

To this end, following the European Commission's Recommendation on tackling piracy of sports and other live events (see below), in 2023, the Italian government introduced a new anti-piracy law heralding the introduction of what has subsequently become known as Italy's 'piracy shield' (Pekic, 2023b). The underlying objective of the new law was to streamline the process of issuing and acting on blocking orders targeting illegal online sports content. To this end, first it gave the Italian communications regulator, AGCOM, the authority to issue 'dynamic' and 'live' injunctions against online service providers, whereas previously (and in most other countries) only courts had the power to perform this role. Second, the new law (and related regulations) also gave AGCOM the role of overseeing a semi-automated system of blocking orders being implemented by online intermediaries with the objective of disabling access to illegal content within 30 minutes. Finally, the law also increased the possible punishments for those involved in the supply/distribution of illegal streams and also individual consumers, who could be fined up to €5,000 (Maxwell, 2023).

Despite some initial delays, in February 2024, Italy's 'piracy shield' 'became operational' (Pekic, 2024). After its first month of operation, AGCOM reported that it had successfully issued blocking orders to protect a host of live sports events, including football from Serie A and Serie B, UEFA's main European club football competitions (the Champions League, Europa League, and Conference League), plus Formula One, MotoGP, Eurocup Basketball, and ATP/WTA tennis. In total, the regulator had blocked 3,127 domain names and 2,176 IP addresses (Maxwell, 2024). According to AGCOM, this meant that around 100,000 households had been prevented from illegally watching premium content (Pekic, 2024). In the long term, however, as with all attempts to tackle online sports piracy, the success of Italy's piracy shield will be judged by whether illegal online sports content remains easily available, rather than how much pirated content is blocked.

Despite their evolution in terms of scope and sophistication, media and sports organisations remain frustrated by the implementation of blocking orders. As in the US in relation to NTDs, their main complaint is that online intermediaries take far too long to block access to illegal streams. The SROC has repeatedly emphasised how the value of sports events 'is almost entirely in their live broadcast' and, in 2018, reported that only 'between 27.2 and 45' per cent of blocking requests sent by its members to ISPs resulted in the removal of illegal content within 30 minutes (SROC, 2018). With this in mind, in response to an ongoing EU debate on tackling online piracy, in 2022, the SROC called on the European Commission to introduce 'adequate measures' to guarantee that 'illegal content is taken down immediately and blocked before the live event terminates' (SROC, 2022). However, when, in May 2023, the European Commission issued its Recommendation on how Member States should combat 'online piracy of sports and other live events', it fell some way short of the action envisaged by the SROC, by merely encouraging the 'prompt' removal of illegal streams of live sports events (European Commission, 2023). The result is that for media and sports organisations, both within the EU and beyond, the task of tackling online piracy continues to resemble what many in the industry have described as a game of 'whack-a-mole', whereby, as soon as a rights holder manages to block one illegal source, a new one becomes available (Synamedia, 2020b, p.23).

Nevertheless, to at least some degree, blocking orders have enabled media and sports organisations to limit the availability of illegal sports content online. Sports organisations often claim to have removed thousands of illegal streams using blocking orders. For example, during the 2022/23 football season, the Premier League claimed to have removed 600,000 illegal streams (Thomas, 2023). Furthermore, while not focused solely on sports piracy, there is some evidence to suggest that blocking pirate sites can lead to an increase in the consumption of legal video content (Danaher et al., 2024). Perhaps most notably, in 2022, the Australian government reported that its 2021 Online Copyright Infringement survey had found that of the 11 per cent of respondents who had encountered a blocked website, the majority (59 per cent) subsequently gave up trying to access the material, and 18 per cent sought lawful access to the content instead (AGD, 2022, p.14). Ultimately, however, the most obvious illustration of the limited impact of blocking orders (and NTDs) is that illegal sports content remains widely available online.

Tackling the Causes of Sports Piracy: Availability and Cost

To date, the efforts of media and sports organisations to tackle piracy have focused almost entirely on law enforcement and on devising more efficient ways to enforce copyright law online. However, as has been noted in relation to other sectors of the media industries, piracy cannot be properly understood in isolation from 'the structure of the licit media economy' (Karaganis, 2011, p.iii). This is certainly the case for online sports piracy. According to Synamedia's international survey of sports fans, 74 per cent of those currently using illegal streaming services may be willing to pay to switch to legitimate providers (2021a, p.6). However, sports fans face two potential barriers to legally accessing the sports content they want to view: availability and cost. In relation to the former, it has been estimated that nearly one-third of sports fans who watch illegal content regularly claim they do so because the event they watch is not shown locally (Synamedia, 2020a, p.6). A clear example of how a lack of legal viewing options can fuel piracy is the use of television 'blackout rules' by sports organisations in an effort to protect levels of stadium attendance. Most notably, in the UK, to avoid the risk of undermining attendances at the vast majority of professional football matches with a traditional 3pm kick-off, since the 1960s, football's governing bodies have prevented any (live or recorded) domestic television coverage of football between 2:45pm and 5:15pm. This has meant that large numbers of games, including Premier League games, are not able to be viewed (legally) in the UK, even though all matches have long been available to international viewers. For instance, under the terms of the current Premier League television deal (2019/20–2024/25), only 200 out of a total of 380 matches each season are available to watch live on UK domestic television (McCaskill, 2023). Unsurprisingly, a recent UK survey found that, of the estimated over 5.1 million adults that admitted to watching sport illegally online, 40 per cent claimed to do so because 'the event I wanted to watch wasn't available in the UK' (YouGov, 2023; Slater, 2023).

The high cost of legal viewing options is a second, just as, if not more, important reason for why sports fans opt to view illegally online. According to Synamedia (2020b, p.6), 47 per cent of the lowest-income fans first used illegal services because they did not want to pay anything to watch a sports event. Furthermore, the cost factor is also just as much a key driver of sports piracy in wealthy countries as it is in poorer ones and piracy 'hotspots'. In the US, in 2023, a survey found nearly two in three NFL fans admitted to using illegal streaming services to watch games, primarily due to the high cost of legal or official streaming services (Hoefling, 2023). Against this background, a major concern for media and sports organisations looking to tackle sports piracy should be how increased competition and the growing fragmentation of rights in many national/regional sports rights markets risk increasing the level of illegal viewing. Ampere Analysis (2023) details how, between 2014 and 2022, the number of broadcasters holding rights to the 'top ten most popular sports competitions' increased in the US (from 8 to 12), the UK (from 4 to 6), Germany (from 3 to 7), France (from 3 to 8), and Italy (from 3 to 6); it only remained stable in Spain. Not only does such fragmentation make it more of a challenge for sports fans to locate the event/s they want to watch, but it has also increased the cost. For example, in Germany, during the early 2010s, Sky Deutschland was the sole broadcaster of the two leading football competitions in Germany, the Bundesliga and the UEFA Champions League. Following the arrival of new market entrants, such as DAZN, the value of the rights to these competitions has grown substantially, but the cost to watch all televised fixtures has increased by 54 per cent (Ampere Analysis, 2023, p.30). With the growing fragmentation of the sports rights market, it is difficult to avoid the conclusion that media and sports organisations are pursuing every legal and technical measure available to tackle online sports piracy, but, at the same time, also pursuing rights buying, selling, and distribution strategies that are likely to exacerbate the problem.

References

AGD (Attorney-General's Department) (2022). *Copyright Enforcement Review: Issues Paper*. Available at: https://consultations.ag.gov.au/rights-and-protections/copyright-enforcement-review/user_uploads/copyright-enforcement-review-issues-paper.pdf (Accessed: 2 March 2024).

AGD (Attorney-General's Department) (2023). *Consumer Survey on Online Copyright Infringement 2022*. Available at: https://www.ag.gov.au/sites/default/files/2024-05/consumer-survey-on-online-copyright-infringement-2022-report.pdf (Accessed: 5 August 2024).

Ahmed, M. (2021). 'How a Saudi-led consortium won control of Newcastle United', *Financial Times*, 8 October. Available at: https://www.ft.com/content/ed0d401a-ff9b-4199-9f5f-7a2a3e5727ca (Accessed: 3 March 2024).

Ahmed, M. and Al Omran, A. (2018). 'Pirated TV sport emerges as new Gulf battleground', *Financial Times*, 1 October. Available at: https://www.ft.com/content/970fc542-c173-11e8-95b1-d36dfef1b89a (Accessed: 3 March 2024).

Ahmed, M. and England, A. (2021). 'Saudi-led consortium completes £305m Newcastle United takeover', *Financial Times*, 7 October. Available at: https://www.ft.com/content/d93463e6-a6e0-400a-bec0-25d7c420b9f1 (Accessed: 3 March 2024).

Ampere Analysis (2023). *Fragmentation in the Sports Media Market*. Available at: https://www.ampereanalysis.com/report/fragmentation-in-the-sports-media-market (Accessed: 2 February 2024).

Asser Institute (2014). *Study on Sports Organisers' Rights in the European Union. Final Report for the European Union*. Available at: https://op.europa.eu/en/publication-detail/-/publication/138eb928-2981-11e7-ab65-01aa75ed71a1/language-en/format-PDF/source-233927641 (Accessed: 2 September 2023).

Banerjee, A. and Gane, N. (2022). 'Copyright piracy and cybercrime: Enforcement challenges in India', *WIPO Magazine*, December. Available at: https://www.wipo.int/wipo_magazine/en/2022/04/article_0008.html (Accessed: 5 March 2024).

Bassam, T. (2020). 'BeIN declines to renew Bundesliga rights over MENA piracy concerns', *SportsProMedia*, 22 September. Available at: https://www.sportspromedia.com/news/bundesliga-tv-rights-bein-mena-piracy-saudi-arabia-beoutq (Accessed: 5 March 2024).

Boyle, R. (2015). Battle for Control? Copyright, Football and European Media Rights. *Media, Culture and Society*, 37 (3), pp. 359–375.

Brignall, M. (2023). 'Netflix cracks down as it begins password-sharing purge in UK', *The Guardian*, 24 June. Available at: https://www.theguardian.com/media/2023/jun/24/netflix-cracks-down-as-it-begins-password-sharing-purge-in-uk (Accessed: 5 March 2024).

Brittle, C. (2024). 'F1 inks ten-year BeIN Sports broadcast rights deal in MENA and Turkey', *SportsProMedia*, 28 February. Available at: https://www.sportspromedia.com/news/f1-bein-sports-mena-turkey-saudia-arabia-broadcast-media-rights/ (Accessed: 2 March 2024).

Carp, S. (2018a). 'Walking the plank: Why the beIN-BeoutQ piracy saga has implications beyond Qatar', *SportsProMedia*, 14 December. Available at: https://www.sportspromedia.com/insights/features/from-the-magazine/bein-sports-beoutq-piracy-qatar-saudi-arabia-interview-feature/ (Accessed: 8 March 2024).

Carp, S. (2018b). 'beIN seeks US$1bn from Saudi Arabia over BeoutQ "piracy plague"', *SportsProMedia*, 2 October. Available at: https://www.sportspromedia.com/news/bein-sports-saudi-arabia-beoutq-piracy/ (Accessed: 8 March 2024).

Carp, S. (2020a). '"BeoutQ became a reliable piracy brand": The Premier League's ongoing battle with illegal streaming', *SportsProMedia*, 10 February. Available at: https://www.sportspromedia.com/insights/interviews/premier-league-piracy-bein-beoutq-illegal-streaming-singapore-interview/ (Accessed: 8 March 2024).

Carp, S. (2020b). 'Saudi Arabia criticised by European Commission over BeoutQ inaction', *SportsProMedia*, 28 January. Available at: https://www.sportspromedia.com/news/saudi-arabia-beoutq-european-commission-piracy-uefa-premier-league-la-liga/ (Accessed: 9 March 2024).

Cory, N. (2022). 'A decade after SOPA/PIPA, it's time to revisit website blocking', *Information Technology & Innovation Foundation*, 26 January. Available at: https://itif.org/publications/2022/01/26/decade-after-sopa-pipa-time-to-revisit-website-blocking/ (Accessed: 7 March 2024).

Cvetkovski, T. (2013). *Copyright and Popular Media: Liberal Villains and Technological Change*. New York: Palgrave Macmillan.

Danaher, B., Sivan, L., Smith, M., and Telang, R. (2024). The impact of online piracy website blocking on legal media consumption, Social Science Research Network. Available at: https://papers.ssrn.com/sol3/papers.cfm?abstract_id=4723522 (Accessed: 7 February 2024).

EAO (European Audiovisual Observatory) (2021). *Mapping Report on National Remedies against Online Piracy of Sports Content*. Available at: https://rm.coe.int/mapping-report-on-national-remedies-against-online-piracy-of-sports-co/1680a4e54c (Accessed: 10 March 2024).

EPRS (European Parliament Research Service) (2020). *Challenges Facing Sports Event Organisers in the Digital Environment: European Added Value Assessment*. Available at: https://www.europarl.europa.eu/RegData/etudes/STUD/2020/654205/EPRS_STU(2020)654205_EN.pdf (Accessed: 6 March 2024).

EUIPO (European Union Intellectual Property Office) (2019). *Illegal IPTV in the European Union: Research on Online Business Models Infringing Intellectual Property Rights - Phase 3*. Available at: https://op.europa.eu/en/publication-detail/-/publication/0617f865-1bc6-11ea-8c1f-01aa75ed71a1/language-en (Accessed: 5 March 2024).

EUIPO (European Union Intellectual Property Office) (2023). *Online Copyright Infringement in the European Union: Films, Music, Publications, Software and TV (2017–2022)*. Available at: https://op.europa.eu/en/publication-detail/-/publication/4e3fe9dd-672b-11ee-9220-01aa75ed71a1/ (Accessed: 10 March 2024).

European Commission (2023). Commission Recommendation of 4.5.2023 on combating online piracy of sports and other live events. Available at: https://ec.europa.eu/commission/presscorner/detail/en/ip_23_2508 (Accessed: 10 March 2024).

Farge, E. and Blenkinsop, P. (2020). 'WTO says Saudi broke global rules in Qatar broadcast dispute', *Reuters*, 16 June. Available at: https://www.reuters.com/article/us-trade-wto-saudi-qatar/wto-tells-saudi-to-obey-global-rules-in-qatar-broadcast-dispute-idUSKBN23N2A1/ (Accessed: 7 March 2024).

Forrester, C. (2024). 'South Africa: Piracy hurts DStv', *Advanced Television*, 1 February. Available at: https://advanced-television.com/2024/02/01/south-africa-piracy-hurts-dstv/ (Accessed: 3 March 2024).

Foxtel (2023). Copyright enforcement review. Available at: https://consultations.ag.gov.au/rights-and-protections/copyright-enforcement-review/consultation/view_respondent?uuId=199230222 (Accessed: 5 March 2024).

Grimes, C. (2022). 'Netflix shares jump after gaining 2.4mn subscribers', *Financial Times*, 19 October. Available at: https://www.ft.com/content/3b1e8a70-73e0-40a9-bd7d-7dcd6e015c42 (Accessed: 3 March 2024).

Grimes, C. (2024a). 'Netflix subscriber sign-ups blow past Wall Street expectations', *Financial Times*, 24 January. Available at: https://www.ft.com/content/0a3e8c61-8fd2-4f28-887a-7f86d9755629 (Accessed: 2 March 2024).

Grimes, C. (2024b). 'Walt Disney unveils $3bn buyback and lifts dividend ahead of activist battles', *Financial Times*, 8 February. Available at: https://www.ft.com/content/a66780ea-2cb5-4d1e-a45a-7b9af1d978c6 (Accessed: 3 March 2024).

Harwood, A. (2019). '"Piracy will see Premier League rights values drop off a cliff", warns BeIN Sports CEO', *SportsProMedia*, 9 October. Available at: https://www.sportspromedia.com/news/premier-league-tv-rights-value-pirate-steams-bein-sports-beoutq/ (Accessed: 2 March 2024).

Hesmondhalgh, D. (2009). The Digitalization of Music. In: P. Jeffcut and A. C. Pratt (eds.), *Creativity and Innovation in the Cultural Economy* (pp. 57–73). London: Routledge.

Hoefling, J. (2023). 'One in three fans admit to using illegal NFL streams, according to poll', *USA Today*, 21 September. Available at: https://eu.usatoday.com/story/sports/nfl/games/2023/09/21/illegal-nfl-streams-rising-in-popularity/70925341007/ (Accessed: 2 March 2024).

Hughes, M. (2024). 'Growing partnership between streaming and black-market bookmakers "threatens sport integrity"... after 500,000 viewers watched Anthony Joshua fight with Francis Ngannou illegally', *Mail Online*, 13 March. Available at: https://www.dailymail.co.uk/sport/boxing/article-13188575/Growing-partnership-streaming-black-market-bookmakers-threatens-sport-integrity-500-000-viewers-watched-Anthony-Joshua-fight-Francis-Ngannou-illegally.html (Accessed: 15 March 2024).

Impey, S. (2019a). 'US places Saudi Arabia on Watch List amid BeoutQ piracy case', *SportsProMedia*, 26 April. Available at: https://www.sportspromedia.com/news/us-government-saudi-arabia-watch-list-beoutq-piracy/ (Accessed: 2 March 2024).

Impey, S. (2019b). 'BeIN Sports opts out of F1 rights renewal amid BeoutQ standoff', *SportsProMedia*, 8 February. Available at: https://www.sportspromedia.com/news/bein-sports-f1-rights-renewal-beoutq-piracy/ (Accessed: 4 March 2024).

IPO (Intellectual Property Office) (2023). Online copyright infringement tracker survey (12th wave). Available at: https://www.gov.uk/government/publications/online-copyright-infringement-tracker-survey-12th-wave (Accessed: 3 March 2024).

Karaganis, J. (ed.) (2011). *Media Piracy in Emerging Economies.* Social Science Research Council. Available at: https://www.ssrc.org/publications/media-piracy-in-emerging-economies/ (Accessed 1 August 2024).

Kariyawasam, K. and Tsai, M. (2017). Copyright and Live Streaming of Sports Broadcasting. *International Review of Law, Computers & Technology*, 31 (3), pp. 265–288.

Leaders (2019). *BeoutQ: An Unprecedented Piracy Story*, 4 October. Available at: https://leadersinsport.com/sport-business/reports/leaders-special-report-beoutq-an-unprecedented-piracy-story/ (Accessed: 1 August 2024).

Leaders (2021). *The Super Aggregators: Sports IP Pirates Have Gone OTT*. Available at: https://leadersinsport.com/sport-business/reports/leaders-special-report-the-super-aggregators-sports-ip-pirates-have-gone-ott/ (Accessed: 2 February 2024).

Mann, C. (2021). 'French broadcasters win piracy damages', *Advanced Television*, 12 March. Available at: https://advanced-television.com/2021/03/12/piracy-damages-win-for-french-broadcasters/ (Accessed: 2 March 2024).

Marsoof, A. (2015). The Blocking Injunction: A Critical Review of its Implementation in the United Kingdom, within the Legal Framework of the European Union. *International Review of Intellectual Property and Competition Law*, 46 (6), pp. 632–664.

Maxwell, A. (2020). 'Court gives "dynamic" pirate site-blocking the green light in Spain', *TorrentFreak*, 20 February. Available at: https://torrentfreak.com/court-gives-dynamic-pirate-site-blocking-the-green-light-in-spain-200220 (Accessed: 2 March 2024).

Maxwell, A. (2022a). 'NHL broadcasters win Canada's first "dynamic" pirate IPTV blocking order', *TorrentFreak*, 8 June. Available at: https://torrentfreak.com/nhl-broadcasters-win-canadas-first-dynamic-pirate-iptv-blocking-order-220608/ (Accessed: 3 March 2024).

Maxwell, A. (2022b). 'Movie & TV pirates increase in Italy but they are pirating less than ever', *TorrentFreak*, 25 June. Available at: https://torrentfreak.com/movie-tv-pirates-increase-in-italy-but-they-are-pirating-less-than-ever-220625/ (Accessed: 5 March 2024).

Maxwell, A. (2023). 'Italian pirate IPTV customers risk a 5,000 Euro fine starting August 8, 2023', *TorrentFreak*, 28 July. Available at: https://torrentfreak.com/italian-pirate-iptv-customers-risk-a-5000-euro-fine-starting-august-8-2023-230728/ (Accessed: 7 March 2024).

Maxwell, A. (2024). 'AGCOM admits "piracy shield" blunder, Cloudflare urges users to complain', *TorrentFreak*, 21 March. Available at: https://torrentfreak.com/agcom-admits-piracy-shield-blunder-cloudflare-urges-users-to-complain-240321 (Accessed: 22 March 2024).

McCaskill, S. (2023). 'The Premier League's UK£6.7bn TV deal: The winners, what it means for Amazon and DAZN, and where English soccer goes from here', *SportsProMedia*, 7 December. Available at: https://www.sportspromedia.com/insights/analysis/premier-league-tv-rights-deal-explainer-sky-sports-tnt-amazon-dazn/ (Accessed: 23 March 2024).

McDonald, P. (2015). Piracy and the Shadow History of Hollywood. In: P. McDonald, C. Carman, E. Hoyt, and P. Drake (eds.), *Hollywood and the Law* (pp. 68–101). London: British Film Institute.

McDonald, P. (2021). Pirate-States: Imagining the Geography of Media Piracy. *International Journal of Cultural Studies*, 24 (1), pp. 72–89.

Nicholson, P. (2021). 'Serie A faces €150m drop in TV income after failure to back beIN over piracy row', *Inside World Football*, 7 April. Available at: https://www.insideworldfootball.com/2021/04/07/serie-faces-e150m-drop-tv-income-failure-back-bein-piracy-row/ (Accessed: 2 March 2024).

Nicholson, P. (2022). 'After 2-year gap, BeIN and Bundesliga patch up differences for new MENA rights deal', *Inside World Football*, 1 September. Available at: https://www.insideworldfootball.com/2022/09/01/2-year-gap-bein-bundesliga-patch-differences-new-mena-rights-deal/ (Accessed: 3 March 2024).

Pekic, B. (2021). 'DAZN to scrap dual user viewing', *Advanced Television*, 21 December. Available at: https://advanced-television.com/2021/12/21/dazn-to-scrap-dual-user-viewing/ (Accessed: 7 March 2024).

Pekic, B. (2022). 'Italy: DAZN changes policy to tackle account sharing', *Advanced Television*, 10 June. Available at: https://advanced-television.com/2022/06/10/italy-dazn-changes-policy-to-tackle-account-sharing/ (Accessed: 11 March 2024).

Pekic, B. (2023a). 'Data: Italian live sports piracy grows 26% YoY', *Advanced Television*, 29 June. Available at: https://advanced-television.com/2023/06/29/data-italian-live-sports-piracy-grows-26-yoy/ (Accessed: 2 March 2024).

Pekic, B. (2023b). 'Italy to deploy anti-piracy platform', *Advanced Television*, 11 December. Available at: https://advanced-television.com/2023/12/11/italy-to-roll-out-anti-piracy-platform/ (Accessed: 2 March 2024).

Pekic, B. (2024). 'Italy: Piracy Shield live but needs refining', *Advanced Television*, 19 February. Available at: https://advanced-television.com/2024/02/19/italy-piracy-shield-live-but-needs-retweaking (Accessed: 3 March 2024).

Pollina, E. (2023). 'DAZN urges Italy to introduce tougher rules to fight TV piracy', *Reuters*, 28 June. Available at: https://www.reuters.com/business/media-telecom/dazn-urges-italy-introduce-tougher-rules-fight-tv-piracy-2023-06-28/ (Accessed: 2 March 2024).

Premier League (2017). 'Premier League awarded High Court Blocking Order', 25 July. Available at: https://www.premierleague.com/news/442401 (Accessed: 4 March 2024).

Premier League (2023). US Department of Commerce - Patent and Trademark Office. Future strategies in anticounterfeiting and antipiracy: Premier League submission. Available at: https://www.regulations.gov/comment/PTO-C-2023-0006-0024 (Accessed: 4 March 2024).

Robertson, A. (2015). Internet Piracy of Sports Broadcasts: Finding the Solution in the United Kingdom and the United States. *Marquette Sports Law Review*, 25 (2), pp. 469–490.

Rushe, D. (2023). 'Netflix gains more new subscribers than expected following password-sharing crackdown', *The Guardian*, 19 July. Available at: https://www.theguardian.com/media/2023/jul/19/netflix-subscriber-growth-password-sharing (Accessed: 1 August 2024).

Sharma, S. (2018). Online Piracy of Live Sports Telecasts in India. *Marquette Sports Law Review*, 28 (2), pp. 433–462.

Slater, M. (2022). 'beIN Sports, its success and the uneasy truce with Saudi Arabia', *The Athletic*, 13 December. Available at: https://theathletic.com/3982136/2022/12/13/bein-sports-qatar-world-cup-saudi-arabia/ (Accessed: 5 March 2024).

Slater, M. (2023). '"Pirated live sport endemic in UK" as study suggests over eight million watching illegal streams', *The Athletic*, 21 August. Available at: https://theathletic.com/4792811/2023/08/21/premier-league-illegal-streaming-piracy/ (Accessed: 6 March 2024).

SportsProMedia (2021). '"There's an awful long way to go": BeIN's Cameron Andrews on tackling piracy in sport', *SportsProMedia*, 6 October. Available at: https://www.sportspromedia.com/insights/interviews/bein-sports-piracy-strategy-beoutq-cameron-andrews-interview/ (Accessed: 3 March 2024).

SROC (Sports Rights Owners Coalition) (2018). SROC Position on the possible measures to further improve the effectiveness of the fight against illegal content online. Available at: https://www.sroc.info/wp-content/uploads/2018/06/SROC-position-on-Measures-to-fight-illegal-content-online-.pdf (Accessed: 4 March 2024).

SROC (Sports Rights Owners Coalition) (2022). 'SROC supports call to end live piracy now', 5 October. Available at: https://www.sroc.info/sroc-supports-pledge-to-end-live-piracy-now/ (Accessed: 4 March 2024).

Symonds, T. and Grundy, T. (2023). 'TV fraud gang jailed for illegally streaming Premier League games', *BBC News*, 30 May. Available at: https://www.bbc.co.uk/news/uk-65697595 (Accessed: 2 March 2024).

Synamedia (2020a). *Charting Global Sports Piracy.* Available at: https://www.synamedia.com/wp-content/uploads/2022/08/Charting-Global-Sports-Piracy-Report.pdf (Accessed: 2 February 2024).

Synamedia (2020b). *Tackling Sports Piracy in an IP World.* Available at: https://www.synamedia.com/wp-content/uploads/2022/08/Tackling-Sports-Piracy-in-an-IP-world-Report.pdf (Accessed: 2 February 2024).

Synamedia (2021a). *Pricing Piracy: The Value of Action.* Available at: https://www.synamedia.com/whitepapers-reports/pricing-piracy-the-value-of-action/ (Accessed: 2 February 2024).

Synamedia (2021b). *Pirate Gateways: Assessing the Triggers for Sports Piracy.* Available at: https://www.synamedia.com/wp-content/uploads/2022/08/Pirate-gateways-assessing-the-triggers-for-sports-piracy-Synamedia-Ampere-Report.pdf (Accessed: 2 February 2024).

Thomas, D. (2023). 'Sky wins court order to block illegal streaming of hit shows and football', *Financial Times*, 30 July. Available at: https://www.ft.com/content/ed022ce0-521a-465f-86b8-b7ea2c403407 (Accessed: 7 March 2024).

Thomas, D. (2024). 'Warner Bros Discovery aims for global market with Europe launch of Max', *Financial Times*, 21 March. Available at: https://www.ft.com/content/1e3f71ba-9499-46c4-8af2-e20b0d6798f4 (Accessed: 22 March 2024).

UFC, NBA, and NFL (2023). UFC NBA NFL Joint Comment Letter- USPTO Antipiracy Anticounterfeiting Request. Available at: https://www.regulations.gov/comment/PTO-C-2023-0006-0041 (Accessed: 3 March 2024).

WIPO (World Intellectual Property Organisation) (2024a). Copyright. Available at: https://www.wipo.int/copyright/en/ (Accessed: 3 March 2024).

WIPO (World Intellectual Property Organisation) (2024b). Broadcasting & media rights in sport. Available at: https://www.wipo.int/en/web/sports/broadcasting (Accessed: 2 March 2024).

WTO (World Trade Organisation) (2022). DS567: Saudi Arabia — Measures concerning the Protection of Intellectual Property Rights. Available at: https://www.wto.org/english/tratop_e/dispu_e/cases_e/ds567_e.htm (Accessed: 5 March 2024).

YouGov (2023). 'One in ten Britons are watching illegal sports streams – but what are they watching?', 24 November. Available at: https://business.yougov.com/content/47949-one-in-ten-britons-are-watching-illegal-sports-streams-but-what-are-they-watching (Accessed: 9 March 2024).

7

COMPETITION ISSUES

The emergence of the streaming market for live sports programming adds a new dimension to the commercialisation of sports rights, which has the potential to impact the balance of power between sports and media organisations. In this context, the application of competition law to the sports media rights market remains as important as ever as a means to ensure free and fair competition. Although established competition remedies remain in place to tackle certain forms of market failure, such as dominant positions and exclusive selling, emerging issues typical to the streaming market may mean that existing regulatory approaches need to be amended. In other words, changing market conditions may put the effectiveness of existing remedies into question, and these may need to be abandoned in order to encourage competition in the evolving sports media rights marketplace. This chapter explores the application of competition law to each of the two main parts of sports media rights markets, namely the upstream sports rights market (i.e. the sale of rights) and the downstream sports programming market (i.e. the distribution of programming to consumers). To date, most regulatory attention has focused on the sports rights market, especially on the collective selling of rights. It is argued here that far more attention should be paid to the regulation of the sports programming market, with an emphasis on consumer interests in terms of choice and price. What is needed as part of a more future-proof competition regulatory approach is a better balance to preserve the interests of sports rights owners, sports broadcasters, and sports consumers.

A Primer on Competition Law

Competition law concerns government intervention in the marketplace when the competitive process is distorted, or when there is what economists refer

DOI: 10.4324/9781003401988-11

to as 'market failure' (Rodger and MacCulloch, 2009, p.1). To be more precise, underpinned by the principles of neoclassical economic theory, competition law is usually (but not always exclusively) designed to promote a competitive marketplace characterised by a high number of buyers and sellers, low entry barriers, and wide consumer choice. From this perspective, the antithesis of a competitive market is a monopoly, a market controlled by a single supplier. In a monopoly, a single company or business has the market power to provide goods or services on a 'take it or leave it' basis and can therefore reduce supply and force prices up so as to maximise its own profitability. Furthermore, a monopolist will also tend to be an inefficient provider, due to the lack of any competitive pressure to keep down costs and/or improve the product on offer.

On this basis, modern competition law was first introduced towards the end of the nineteenth century in the US (known in the US as antitrust law) with the passing of the Sherman Act of 1890, and was further substantiated with the Clayton Act of 1914. During the post-war period, the formation of the European Community (EC) led to the introduction of forms of competition law throughout much of Western Europe. By the early 2010s, more than 100 countries across the world had enacted a form of competition law (Papadopoulos, 2010, pp.15–17). Albeit subject to national variation, competition law has largely focused on three main areas:

- Monopoly: in practice, pure monopolies are rare so competition law tends to be focused on markets that, while not controlled by a single supplier, are dominated by companies or businesses with smaller, but still significant market shares. This may enable such companies or businesses to have power and influence over the market akin to that of a monopolist. Thus, Section 2 of the Sherman Act 1890 applies to 'every person who shall monopolize, or attempt to monopolize' trade or commerce. Similarly, under EC law Article 82 prohibits the 'abuse' of a 'dominant position' by an 'undertaking' (i.e. a business or company). The significance of this aspect of competition law is that a monopoly, or near-monopoly, position is not in itself illegal, but rather it is the attempt to act anti-competitively that is problematic. The Digital Markets Act addresses monopolistic conduct of very large online platforms such as Amazon, Alphabet, and Apple.
- Cartels: this term is used to describe forms of cooperation between firms who conspire, or agree to act together, so as to reduce competition. In effect, therefore, cartels carry the same threat to a competitive market as a monopoly. In the US, cartels are outlawed under Section 1 of the Sherman Act, which states, 'Every contract, combination in the form of a trust or otherwise, or conspiracy, in restraint of trade or commerce [...] is declared to be illegal.' In a similar vein, Article 81(1) of EC law prohibits 'decisions of associations and concerted practices that may affect

trade between member states and which have as their object the prevention, restriction or distortion of competition'. Major financial penalties are imposed on firms found to be involved in cartels, but such agreements are often difficult to prove, as almost by definition firms involved in these practices are unlikely to keep records of their illegal activities.

- Mergers: two or more companies may achieve a position of monopoly, or dominance, in a market by merging. The US Clayton Act of 1914 formally prohibits mergers 'where the effect of such acquisition may be substantially to lessen competition, or tend to create a monopoly'. Similarly, EU law is designed to prevent mergers that 'would significantly impede effective competition in the common market or in a substantial part of it' (European Commission, 2004). Typically, horizontal mergers, between two parties at the same level of the market, are the greatest concern for competition law. However, the competitive consequences of vertical mergers, between parties at different stages of the production process, may also raise concerns, particularly if the newly merged company could act to restrict competition at either level of the market.

The remainder of this chapter considers how competition law has been applied to the different sides of the sports broadcasting market – the sports rights market and the sports programming market (see Chapter 2) – and to what extent 'old' competition remedies are still effective to address the buying and exploitation of sports rights by 'new' streaming intermediaries.

Sports Rights Market

The sale of rights packages usually takes place in the sports rights market, or upstream market, where sports associations, sporting organisations, and rights intermediaries offer their rights and negotiate over the sale of rights with interested buyers. In both the US and Europe, the application of competition law to sports broadcasting has focused mainly on one controversial issue: the collective selling by sports leagues of the rights to broadcast exclusive live coverage of their sports.

Collective versus Individual Selling of Sports Rights

The main source of controversy in relation to the selling of broadcast sports rights concerns team sports. There has been much debate over whether broadcast rights should be exploited by the individual teams, or by a league (i.e. the competition organiser), usually acting as a joint venture between the teams, but occasionally as the rights owner itself (e.g. the UEFA Champions League in football). Fundamentally, in both the US and Europe, the key question was (and still is): to what extent should general competition law be applied to the selling of sports rights?

As discussed in Chapter 2, the case for the application of competition law to the selling of sports rights is based on the argument that by selling their rights collectively through a league teams act as a cartel. Indeed, sports rights markets are generally characterised by supply-side monopolies and demand-side rivalry, which creates considerable market power for sports associations marketing their rights to interested buyers. Collective selling agreements have repeatedly been criticised for being anti-competitive, and seen as a price-fixing mechanism that strengthens the market position of leading sports broadcasters because they are the only operators able to bid for all the rights in a package. This anti-collective viewpoint has received considerable support from a number of leading sports economists (Noll, 2007; Szymanski, 2002). Most sports economists agree that, to minimise market power, 'sports rights should be sold at the lowest "meaningful" level', which for team sports is the individual match (Cowie and Williams, 1997, p.631).

In defence of the collective selling of broadcasting rights, it is argued that sport, and in particular team sport, has a number of distinct economic characteristics which make the application of general competition law inappropriate. Most significantly, Gerrard (2006) highlights 'three economic peculiarities' that tend to characterise the sports industry. First, the production of sporting contests in professional team sports requires joint production by at least two individual teams. Consequently, unlike the underhand and/or secret behaviour that typifies cartels in other areas of business, team sports, by definition, need to cooperate and do so openly through leagues and tournaments. A second distinctive economic feature of team sports is the 'expressive allegiance of fans' to the teams that they support (Gerrard, 2006, p.29). For many sports fans, team allegiances are closer in intensity to family and religious allegiances, than they are to an economic trading allegiance (Sandvoss, 2003). For fans of a particular team, attendance at (or television viewing of) another team's matches is a very poor substitute for watching their own team. Competition within team sports for fans (if not trophies) is therefore inherently severely limited. Teams based in the largest cities and/or with long traditions of sporting success enjoy support and revenue that far exceed those of smaller teams operating within the same league. Finally, a league or competition is more exciting and attractive to fans (and broadcasters) if the outcome is uncertain. This underpins regulations designed to maintain fair and balanced competition within leagues, such as salary caps (more common in US than European leagues), transfer fees, sharing of gate receipts, and, most significantly here, the collective selling of broadcast rights. If individual teams are allowed to sell the broadcast rights to their matches, it could lead to significant income disparities between teams, which reduces the competitive balance and outcome uncertainty of the league, and, in turn, undermines the long-term popularity and economic value of the competition. Although some sports economists cast doubt that measures to equalise the distribution of rights income between teams will necessarily enhance competitive balance

(Szymanski and Kesenne, 2004), most leagues maintain that the collective sale of broadcast rights remains the most straightforward way to redistribute funds from richer to poorer teams. On this basis, it can be argued that the collective selling of broadcast rights is actually pro-competitive, rather than anti-competitive, and as such should be granted exemption from competition law.

Despite this pro-competitive case for collective selling, large teams, especially in European football, have been threatening to sell the broadcast rights to their home games individually as an outside option to negotiate, claim, and secure a larger share of the total media pool from collective selling. Recent controversies in European football have clearly illustrated the desire of the largest clubs to maximise their own individual rights revenue. Combined with the revenue losses experienced during the COVID-19 global pandemic, the lure of a potential revenue increase from individual rights selling, or at least sharing rights revenue with a smaller number of larger clubs, underpinned, first, in 2020, an initiative put forward by a handful of the English Premier League's biggest clubs – 'Project Big Picture' – to reorganise the league's governance and structures in order to give the bigger clubs greater control (Gardner, 2020). Second, in 2021, some of Europe's largest football clubs, including Real Madrid, Juventus FC, and FC Barcelona, announced they were going to launch a European Super League, in part because the other Big Five football leagues are financially falling behind the Premier League and its massive broadcast deals (Ahmed and Massoudi, 2021). The Super League, however, prompted a public backlash from fans, UEFA, and national governments, and was quickly abandoned. However, similar initiatives, or breakaway leagues, remain possible, if not likely. Third, European top leagues Italian Serie A, Spanish La Liga, French Ligue 1, and German Bundesliga (the Big Five except for the English Premier League) were all open to selling a stake in their media rights business to private equity funds and investment banks. Such outside investments would help to maximise the value of broadcast rights, but also supply the clubs with much-needed upfront capital to offset financial shortfalls suffered during the COVID-19 pandemic.

Moreover, as the streaming market for sports broadcasting is rapidly becoming mature, internet-distributed television creates another window of opportunity, especially for larger teams, to market their rights individually instead of adopting a rights-pooling and revenue-sharing strategy. With the growing value of digital rights, individual teams are experimenting with self-exploitation of ancillary rights (e.g. 'behind-the-scenes' footage, youth team matches, etc.) left unsold in deals with media organisations. Several European top-flight clubs have launched streaming services to serve and enlarge their global fanbase, deepen fan engagement, and generate revenue globally. Real Madrid (RM Play) and FC Barcelona (Barça One), among others, both launched a free, over-the-top video platform offering among others match clips, original content, and archive footage to fans around the world. Real Madrid were even one of the first football teams in the world to launch an in-house television station back in 1999 (McCaskill, 2023a). As livestreaming is soon to become a, if not the most, preferred way to serve and engage with sports fans, and accounts for a growing share of total media-related income for teams, these developments will put pressure on collective agreements as the dominant mechanism for selling rights and possibly give more leeway to bigger teams to market their rights individually somewhere in the not-too-distant future. To date, club-owned streaming platforms have predominantly focused on exploiting ancillary rights, but once they start to offer a viable business case more lucrative than the league-based selling model of exclusive live rights, it is plausible that large clubs, if legally possible, will withdraw from collective agreements, especially when these deals are not satisfactory, and turn to internet-distributed television to generate income by self-exploiting all rights. This would put smaller clubs at an even greater disadvantage as they will not be able to attract as much revenue for their matches and therefore be unable to compete with bigger clubs.

Regulation of Collective Selling in the US and Europe

Collective Selling in the US

While some sports economists may remain unconvinced by the case for the collective selling of sports rights, in both the US and Europe, the arguments put forward by sports leagues and their supporters have carried more weight with politicians and even some competition authorities. In the US, in 1961, the Supreme Court ruled that a lucrative 1960 NFL broadcast deal (with CBS for US$9.3 million) barring individual teams from selling their games to competing broadcasters was a violation of the Sherman Act. This prompted the NFL to lobby Congress for a change to the law and in 1961 Congress passed the Sports Broadcasting Act (SBA), which essentially reversed the court's decision and permitted national sports leagues to agree joint-selling agreements for the exclusive sale of broadcasting rights to free-to-air national and regional broadcasters. This exemption from antitrust law has enabled all the major US professional leagues for American football (NFL), basketball (NBA), baseball (MLB), and ice hockey (NHL) to agree lucrative collective deals with national broadcast networks. However, the exemption for the collective selling of broadcast rights provided by the SBA applies only to national 'sponsored' telecasters. Consequently, many of the teams from the major US leagues have agreed individual deals with local broadcasters or (paid) regional sports networks, alongside their collectively agreed national broadcast rights deal (Cave and Crandall, 2001, p.14).

However, the SBA was enacted in 1961, when free-to-air television was omnipresent and subscription-funded broadcasting provided by satellite, cable, and streaming technology was non-existent. Hence, the narrow exemption of sponsored telecasters under the SBA has been challenged by technological developments, first with the introduction of the NFL's exclusive Sunday Ticket offering on DirecTV (in 1994) and the NFL Network on premium cable (in 2003). For some time, the distinction between 'sponsored telecasters' and pay-tv channels for which subscribers have to pay a fee has been meaningless, since most of these premium channels also carry commercials and advertisements, or at least rely on a hybrid revenue model. The SBA, therefore, does not reflect the contemporary television markets. Nevertheless, in the *Shaw vs. Dallas Cowboys Football Club (1999)* case, the court argued that the SBA does not cover satellite and cable television, and that existing, as well as future, broadcasting contracts with cable and satellite could be found to be violating the Sherman Antitrust Act. Although modern legislative interpretation seems to suggest that pay-tv services, premium cable, and satellite are not included in the exemption of the Act, the Justice Department has not brought action against any of the leagues that agreed rights agreements with cable channels, ESPN, and TBS. However, the fading legal authority of the Act was also apparent when streaming platform YouTube became the exclusive home of the NFL Sunday Ticket (in 2022), Amazon got exclusive access to NFL's Thursday Night rights (in 2021), and Apple TV+ secured the exclusive rights to the MLS (in 2023), a league that is not even featured in the SBA. These contracts raised the issue of whether deals with subscription-funded streaming services are subject to the SBA and to what extent these deals may face antitrust scrutiny in the future. A 2019 ruling from the Ninth Circuit Court of Appeal did consider this issue and confirmed the strict interpretation of the SBA: media rights contracts with streaming partners could be at risk of violating the Sherman Antitrust Act. This ruling may give an indication of how courts will address streaming technology in future antitrust cases and may create incentives for fans, bars, and restaurants to file lawsuits against the NFL arguing the broadcasting contracts in place raise prices and lower the number of games being televised (James, 2021). While the US Congress, at least for now, seems reluctant to consider future broadcasting technology for inclusion in the SBA, it is up to the Supreme Court to rule whether deals with Amazon and others are included under the SBA antitrust exemption. The outcome of this ruling may have dire implications for how the NFL, as well as other leagues, will be able to organise its rights-selling model based on exclusivity in the future. Hence, the future of these exclusive deals with streaming platforms will depend crucially on whether the US Congress will recognise the need to update the SBA (and extend the notion of 'sponsored telecasting' to also include new forms of broadcasting technology) or whether the Supreme Court rules reverse the Ninth Circuit's ruling (Nathanson, 2023).

Collective Selling in Europe

Europe has also experienced widespread debate over the collective selling of, predominantly, football rights (see Box 7.1). At the national level, the collective selling of football rights has been favoured in the vast majority of countries, including the Big Five: England, Germany, France, Italy, and Spain. Following rulings from competition authorities, a number of football leagues did, during the late 1990s and early 2000s, move from a collective selling approach to the selling of broadcast rights by individual teams, but more recent regulatory interventions led these leagues to adopt a centralised system of rights selling. Portugal will be the latest country to move to a collective selling system after the Portuguese Competition Authority (AdC) intervened on several occasions to ensure competition in the Portuguese broadcasting rights market. In 2018, the AdC closed a series of investigations relating to football broadcasting rights and issued a recommendation to the government to adopt legislation concerning the football rights auction. Consequently, the government adopted Decree-Law No 22-B/2021, stating that the rights beyond the 2027/28 season must be marketed on a centralised basis (Carp, 2021). To date, Greece is the only remaining television market in Europe where individual selling is set to remain in place.

BOX 7.1 COMPETITION LAW AND THE SELLING OF FOOTBALL RIGHTS IN EUROPE'S BIG FIVE

England: In 1999, the collective selling of Premier League football broadcast rights was challenged by the UK competition authority, the Office of Fair Trading (OFT), at the Restrictive Practices Court (RPC). The RPC ruled against the OFT on the grounds that the existing deal operated in the 'public interest'.

France: Sports Law of July 16 (1984) amended by Law of 13 July 1992 states that 'the rights to a sporting event or competition shall belong to the organizer of that event' (article 18,1). Collective selling is therefore legally sanctioned, although exclusive contracts are limited to five years.

Germany: In 1994, the German competition authority, the Bundeskartellamt, prohibited the DFB, German football's governing body, from centrally marketing the broadcast rights for European matches involving German teams. However, in May 1998, the German Parliament passed a new law exempting the collective selling of broadcast rights to sporting events from the German Competition I Act.

Italy: In 1999, the Italian Competition Authority ruled against the collective selling of broadcast rights. Individual selling of rights was therefore made mandatory. However, in 2008, following continued controversy over the disparities in broadcast revenue between teams, the new Melandri Law was passed that removed the right of individual teams to sell broadcast rights to their matches and authorised the Italian football league to sell rights collectively.

Spain: In 1990, a new law (the Ley del Deporte) granted the Spanish football league (LNFP) authority to sell broadcast rights to league matches, which then negotiated an eight-year deal. However, in 1993, the Spanish competition court declared collective selling to be illegal, freeing teams to sell their rights individually from the 1993–94 season. Teams have turned to jointly selling since Article 7.1 of Royal Decree 5/2015 regulates the sale of media rights by Spanish football clubs and imposes a system of collective selling.

Source: Szymanski (2002); Szymanski and Zimbalist (2006); Tonazzi (2003).

At the EU level, the European Commission's approach to collective selling has also not been as hostile as might have been expected, particularly given its initial comments on the issue. Most significantly, during the early 2000s, the Commission negotiated a number of changes to the way that UEFA, the governing body of European football, sold the rights to its Champions League football competition, including (i) the introduction of a three-year limit to the length of any exclusive deal, (ii) the division of television rights into a number of separate packages, and (iii) the unbundling of new media rights. The Commission also accepted some of the advantages of UEFA's (modified) plan for the collective selling of Champions League rights, most notably the creation of a single point of sale (i.e. UEFA), particularly for an international tournament involving a large number of clubs from many different countries, and the potential for UEFA to create and develop the Champions League as a branded product (Toft, 2003). On this basis, the Commission granted UEFA an exemption under Article 81(3) of the EU Treaty. According to the Commission, UEFA's modified arrangements were sufficient to allow UEFA to continue to sell its rights collectively, 'to the benefit of all stakeholders in the game' (European Commission, 2003). The UEFA case proved particularly significant because it provided a template for the Commission's approach to other instances of the collective selling of football rights by national leagues, most notably the Bundesliga in Germany (European Commission, 2005a) and the Premier League in England (European Commission, 2005b).

With political support at both national and EU levels, collective selling remains the dominant model for the selling of broadcast rights to top-level football in Europe. Also in the streaming era, the antitrust exemption of collective selling is unlikely to be upended anytime soon. However, this does not mean to say that the way that sports rights are sold has remained unchanged. On the contrary, during the 2000s and 2010s, the (or even just the threat of the) application of competition law to collective agreements resulted in some important changes to the way that rights are typically sold. Most notably, the sale of all rights in single or large packages was replaced by a larger number of balanced packages sold as part of a transparent bidding procedure (European Commission, 2007, p.3.1.3.2). The unbundling of live rights in this way allowed newcomers to obtain the much-needed access to premium programming, although the lifecycle of some of these new entrants proved remarkably short. Also in the streaming era, carving up rights in multiple bundles allows new platforms to potentially join the audio-visual market and helps new entrants (try to) build a critical mass for their service. Overall, sports rights owners have been the prime beneficiary of this regulatory change. Extra demand for live rights, in combination with a supply-side monopoly, has led to an inflation of the fees paid for rights. The outcome for consumers is, as discussed in a later section, less convincing: unbundling has led to the fragmentation of rights supply so that live coverage of certain sports is scattered among a growing number of platforms, resulting in consumer frustration and, above all, extra costs.

Second, during the 2000s, several interventions from the European Commission led to a reduction in the duration of contracts for (exclusive) rights to three years. With this approach, the Commission aimed to prevent dominant pay-tv operators from extending their market control and to preserve recurrent competition in the rights market. Once again, this proved most beneficial for the rights owners, who experienced an increase in rights fees every time the rights were sold. While incumbent pay-tv operators were able to sustain their dominant position, competitors and often new entrants launched significant bids to position themselves in the market. Too long contracts, it was argued, would stifle competition and create little incentives for newcomers in the market. However, given the challenging market conditions for sports broadcasters and the rise of streaming, it seems sports leagues are now pushing regulatory authorities to abandon, or at least relax, these term limits more and more (see Box 7.2). While media rights values of most European top-flight football leagues have stagnated in recent years, longer deals are also welcomed by the leagues as they provide more financial guarantees. It is believed that a longer deal term will provide prospective media partners with more certainty, which will allow them to invest more in sports rights: a longer rights cycle would attract higher interest from incumbents and would provide new entrants with a longer timeframe to earn back their significant investments. Short-term contracts are also said to discourage investments in production and marketing, which would scare off newcomers from investing in the game (McCaskill, 2023b). Apart from these possible pro-competitive effects of longer broadcasting contracts, it is also fair to point to the likely anti-competitive effects such deals generate: long-term deals also have the ability to lock out rivals for a longer term and block access to the market. It is therefore recommended to combine such extended media contracts with unbundling remedies to offer as many rights packages to the market as possible. That is exactly what happened in the US, where the NFL and NBA have been creating several packages as part of their decade-long contracts with broadcasters and streaming services. It remains to be seen whether European competition authorities are open to such decade-long contracts, but premium sports leagues in Europe certainly envy the massive deals the NFL and NBA were able to agree during the early 2020s. As domestic rights deals start to flatten, pressure to introduce mechanisms to drive up the value of broadcasting contracts is likely to increase.

BOX 7.2 THE ENDING OF SHORT-TERM (THREE-YEAR) SPORTS RIGHTS CONTRACTS

Whereas long-terms rights deals are commonplace in the US, the duration of broadcast contracts in the EU was traditionally restricted to three years following a series of competition-related decisions. This would, it was argued, provide regular opportunities for rights owners to increase valuations, as well as prevent buyers from being locked into long-term deals. Recently, however, there has been a trend towards lengthier media contracts in Europe. Several football leagues were allowed to offer extended broadcast rights contracts and sell their rights for a much longer period than the regular three years. In Spain, for example, an amendment of the Royal Decree that governs the sale of centralised rights made it possible for La Liga, in 2020, to pursue long-term deals with broadcasters. However, while Telefónica (together with DAZN) was awarded the rights for five seasons (from 2022/23 to 2026/27), the National Commission on Markets and Competition (CNMC) questioned the duration of the contract against the backdrop of Telefónica's dominance in the market (under the terms of the telco's acquisition of pay-tv operator Digital+ in 2015). After scrapping these terms, Telefónica won the new tender process and was able to secure the rights (Sweeting, 2024). Similarly, Italian Serie A was permitted to sell its domestic rights for five seasons instead of three. AGCOM, the Italian communications regulator, approved the guidelines governing the marketing of the league's media rights for five seasons (2024/25–2028/29). These new guidelines followed an amendment to the Melandri Law, the 2008 legislation which imposed collective selling of media rights on professional sport in Italy (Sim, 2023). Under the new tender, DAZN and Sky were able to retain Serie A rights in a US$4.8 billion deal.

Collective Buying of Sports Rights

Whereas competition authorities have endorsed the practice of collective *selling*, collective *buying* agreements of sports rights have been viewed as more problematic. In Europe, the regulation of collective buying by broadcasters has predominantly been an issue raised in relation to the European Broadcasting Union (EBU). Established during the 1950s, the EBU was originally formed to further the interests of European public service broadcasters, although its membership has subsequently expanded to include some commercial broadcasters. By providing collective bidding power for its members, the EBU has traditionally enabled Europe's public service broadcasters to purchase and share the rights for international sports events, such as the Olympic Games and the European and World Cup football tournaments. However, rival commercial broadcasters have long viewed the EBU's activities as anti-competitive because they place non-members at an inherent commercial disadvantage (European Commission, 1991). In response, the European Commission has overseen some reforms to the EBU's rights-buying activities, including the opening up of the sub-licensing of rights to non-members on 'fair, reasonable and non-discriminatory' terms, but it has not moved to prevent the EBU's joint purchasing of sports rights altogether. On the contrary, in its 1993 Decision on the issue, the Commission praised the distinctive character of sports broadcasting provided by EBU members, 'who regardless of cost-revenue considerations, provide the widest possible range of sports programmes as part of their public service mission' (European Commission, 1993). Partly as a result, in this instance at least, the Commission has taken the view that the efficiency gains from not having to negotiate rights deals on an individual basis outweigh the potential losses that may arise from the collective buying of rights, hence the granting of an individual exemption under Article 81(3) of the EU Treaty (Hatton et al., 2007). However, the European Commission's view on the joint buying of rights by the EBU is not one shared by a number of leading international sports organisations, most notably the International Olympic Committee (IOC). Since the mid-2010s, the IOC has opted to negotiate the sale of their rights with individual broadcasters rather than with the EBU. Hence, the biggest threat to the EBU, and public service broadcasters in particular, may come from sports organisations keen to maximise the value of rights to their event (s) and the reduced purchasing power of public service broadcasters due to governments' austerity policies, rather than from competition law (see Chapters 4 and 8).

Competition authorities have always remained vigilant of the possible impact of collusion on the demand side (Evens and Smith, 2022). For this reason, horizontal mergers between pay-tv operators and vertical mergers between broadcasters and sports organisations, such as BSkyB's iconic attempt to control Manchester United (in 1999), have usually faced lengthy regulatory scrutiny. During the early 2000s, a number of major mergers between pay-tv broadcasters, including the formation of Sky Italia (Italy, 2003), Digital+/Canal+ (Spain, 2003), and Canal+ (France, 2006), prompted concerns from national and EU competition regulators over the creation of near-monopolies in pay-tv and monopsony (one buyer) in the sports rights market. Most of the issues raised by competition authorities related to the likely monopolisation within the sports programming market and the wider pay-tv market, but also the negative impacts of these mergers on the sports rights market, and especially the valuation of sports rights, were addressed in each case. In this context, a few recent cases are worth mentioning. While clearing the joint venture between BT Sport and Discovery, in 2022, Britain's Competition and Markets Authority (CMA) found, perhaps surprisingly, that the horizontal merger between sports broadcasters BT Sport and Eurosport (UK&I) would not lessen competition in the UK sports rights market. The CMA argued that both parties were not close competitors, indicating that BT Sport focused on premium rights (namely, rights for the English Premier League and Champions League football) and Eurosport on non-premium rights. Hence, the merger was unconditionally cleared because the merging parties were seen as complementary rather than substitutes in the sports rights market (CMA, 2022). However, the CMA did not address the implications of the merger for the sports programming market, despite the fact that the merger led to reduced consumer choice. A similar issue emerged in early 2024 when ESPN, FOX, and Warner Bros. Discovery announced the establishment of a joint venture to launch a sports streaming service, called Venu Sports. Its impact on the US sports rights markets seems to be negligible. The joint venture is unlikely to have a significant impact on rights sellers as the new service will not bid for rights itself, but the parties will continue to bid on sports rights independently. However, the undertaking may trigger several competition concerns in the sports programming market, by harming consumer welfare in terms of less choice and higher prices. The US Congress has raised concerns that the streaming joint venture will be anti-competitive and will result in unfair licensing terms for video distributors (Spangler, 2024). Similarly, Fubo, the all-sports streaming service, has sued the different parties for the possible anti-competitive effects of the joint venture on the market (McCaskill, 2024). Another notable competition case is the Reliance and Disney Hotstar joint venture, which would establish a streaming monopoly in the Indian sports streaming market. Together, JioCinema and Hotstar control the lion's share of streaming contracts, including the IPL and ICC, Premier League, and the Olympics. Given the vast popularity of cricket and soccer, the joint venture is poised to gain a significant advantage in negotiating contracts with sports rights owners, fixing advertising tariffs, and raising consumer prices. It is, therefore, expected that the Competition Commission of India (CCI) will intervene (Kaushik, 2024).

Sports Programming Market

As discussed in Chapters 2 and 3, in the era of streaming the ownership of exclusive live premium sports remains a source of market power within national, pay-tv, and/or wider communications and entertainment markets. Streaming platforms are turning to live sports to attract new customers and to lower churn among existing customers, and, consequently, are competing with both free-to-air and pay-tv broadcasters, who also remain keen to acquire sports rights. Access to sports rights continues to have a significant influence on commercial success, both for incumbent and for emerging media platforms, and create a competitive advantage in the sports programming market, or downstream market. In this primary market for sports programmes, sports broadcasters, pay-tv operators, and streaming platforms compete for viewers, subscribers, and/or advertisers. Therefore, competition issues raised by the behaviour of these parties seeking to use sports programming to ensure a competitive advantage over their rivals are just as significant as, if not more significant than, those already discussed in relation to the selling of sports rights. To some degree at least, market intervention in the form of competition law has improved free and fair competition within the sports rights market; however, without addressing competition issues within the sports programming market its impact is likely to be limited. It is fair to claim that regulators have so far put too much focus on the application of competition law in the sports rights market and not enough on the sports programming market. Considering the latest developments in the market for sports streaming, regulatory intervention should focus more on preserving consumer interests and balancing commercial interests of rights owners and broadcasters with the interests of consumers and society in general (Smith et al., 2015).

The risk of a breach of competition law within the sports programming market is plausible because most broadcasters, especially when live rights are concerned, rely on exclusivity to maximise the commercial value of the sports programming they offer. As part of merger control, in Europe and beyond, competition authorities have imposed a series of regulatory conditions, including a limited duration of exclusive sports rights contracts or the provision of wholesale access to third parties. The underlying idea of these remedies is to guarantee a sufficient level of competition in the sports programming market and to protect the benefits of the consumers in terms of choice, quality, and price. In each case, the underlying competition concern was that a dominant pay-tv operator could use its control of exclusive sports rights to undermine any prospect of the development of competition. In order to prevent this type of 'winner-takes-all' market and to facilitate new entry in the pay-tv market, competition authorities have often imposed an obligation to partially *unbundle* (i.e. dividing rights between different packages) and a *no-single-buyer* (NSB) rule, instead of awarding one broadcaster all rights (Evens and Lefever, 2011). However, the effect of each of these remedies on competition in the sports programming market has been, at least, questionable. Introducing earmarked packages with exclusive coverage of different matches had the intention to safeguard dynamic competition in pay-tv markets. Although this remedy actually led to the entrance of new players, increased competition provided by new entrants such as Setanta Sport, Kirch Media, or Sport7 proved relatively short-lived and did not really last over the longer term. At best, monopolies in pay-television markets were replaced by duopolies (e.g. Sky and BT in the UK; Sky Deutschland and Deutsche Telekom in Germany). At the time, rights packages were carved up for different delivery modes, ending up with free-to-air, pay-tv, mobile, digital, etc. (Evens et al., 2011). The growing importance of digital platforms means that most leagues, except in countries such as India where television and digital rights are still sold separately, now generally market their rights on a technologically neutral basis, with rights carved out on a temporal basis (live, near-live, highlights, clips, archive), rather than by means of delivery mode, that can be exploited across multiple platforms. This implies that streaming platforms previously had only access to smaller, often non-exclusive yet cheaper digital rights packages, but they are now able to secure more valuable live packages to provide exclusive coverage of sports events. Technology-neutral rights packages have generally helped streaming platforms to enter bidding processes for premium live rights and, consequently, also increased the value of these rights. A future challenge for competition authorities, however, will be to secure free and fair competition in digital markets, such as the streaming market, where network effects, global scale, and capital intensity push the market towards rapid consolidation and market dominance (Evens and Donders, 2018).

In addition to partial unbundling of sports rights into different packages, competition authorities have sometimes also obliged rights sellers to introduce mechanisms that prevent a single broadcaster from buying all the rights packages available, the so-called no-single-buyer (NSB) rule. The NSB rule thus posits that no individual broadcaster can obtain exclusive rights to all the matches. This can be implemented by awarding non-exclusive rights packages to broadcasters or by splitting up live rights in separate exclusive rights packages. Consequently, no single sports broadcaster can hold a monopoly on the coverage of a sport event as it has to share some of the rights with other competitors. In 2007, the NSB rule was introduced in the UK to end Sky's monopoly of live Premier League football coverage when a portion of the rights was awarded to Setanta Sport. After Setanta collapsed in 2009, the rights package was taken over by ESPN. Ever since, the rights to the Premier League have been divided between different pay-tv operators (or streaming platforms) claiming full exclusivity of matchdays or packages (Smith, 2010). In Germany, the Bundeskartellamt decided, in 2016, that the sale of Bundesliga media rights was subject to the NSB rule. From the 2017/18 season onwards, the German Football League (DFL) split the rights for the Bundesliga, Bundesliga 2., relegation, and Supercup games into 14 packages. Live coverage of Bundesliga games was marketed in separate exclusive, matchday-specific rights packages with an NSB clause. Sky Germany won all the pay-tv packages, except one smaller Friday evening package that was awarded to Eurosport. However, in 2024, the Bundeskartellamt ruled that the DFL was able to auction its rights without an NSB rule from the 2025/

26 season onwards. The competition authority reasoned that the NSB had facilitated competition in the pay-tv market and was now no longer needed. With competition between Sky and DAZN established, the competition authority decided to waive the rule that no single broadcaster is allowed to acquire the exclusive broadcasting rights to all Bundesliga games (Krieger, 2024).

However, the effects of the NSB rule, as well as other unbundling remedies, on consumer welfare have been repeatedly questioned. Budzinski et al. (2019) doubt whether these remedies have really served consumer welfare and claim these remedies have led to an increase, rather than a decrease, in retail prices and transaction costs; Heller et al. (2023) argue that the NSB rule harms consumers. First, the unbundling of media rights into separate packages has driven up competition for live rights and has, consequently, contributed to a rapid escalation in the cost of premium rights, which has primarily benefited sports organisations, most notably Europe's leading football clubs (and players). No doubt, this excessive expenditure on sports rights has been passed on to consumers. Paradoxically, for consumers, more competition has led to higher retail prices. Given the monumental rise in the value of UK sports rights, it is perhaps no surprise that subscribers to sports channels have faced some of the steepest price increases. Butler and Massey (2019) have examined the nature of competition in the broadcasting market for live English Premier League matches and found no evidence of a price-decreasing effect following more competition. Instead, the overall price as well as the price per game is higher with competing broadcasters than under a monopoly on the demand side. BT's entry in the UK sports broadcasting market, in 2013, has provided fresh impetus to the upwards trend in the cost for UK sports viewers: the cost of watching top-flight English football has increased dramatically ever since. However, consumers who do not subscribe to sports channels have also faced increased charges as a result of spiralling fees paid for sports rights. In 2014, just after BT had secured live Premier League rights for the first time, it imposed a significant increase in the cost of home phone and broadband packages on all its customers, a move described by some industry watchers as a 'football tax'. Similarly, Sky raised the cost of its 'family bundle', leading to suspicions that these family bundle subscribers were helping to pay for the expensive Premier League rights deal (Smith et al., 2016). However, it is fair to add that pay-tv retail prices (as part of a multi-product bundle) in the UK have been slightly decreasing since 2022, with the price of Sky Sports having the largest decrease. In turn, subscription video-on-demand (SVoD) platforms as well as fixed broadband have faced severe price increases above inflation rates in the same period (Ofcom, 2023).

Second, the obligations to unbundle live rights and to sell them to at least two different buyers have confronted consumers with the inconvenience (as well as extra costs) of subscriptions to multiple pay-tv services if they want to follow all of the matches of their favourite team within a particular competition. The broadcast rights to popular competitions are increasingly split across a growing number of video services (including pay-tv and streaming) in most markets: the fragmentation of sports rights has become a defining feature of today's premium sports rights markets. Under the 2025/26 Premier League deal, exclusive live rights are scattered between pay-tv channels Sky Sport (215 matches/season) and TNT Sports (52 matches/season) – previously Amazon also provided exclusive coverage of 20 matches per season. Similarly, under the ongoing deal (2022/23–2026/27) La Liga rights are split between Telefónica (205 matches/season) and DAZN (175 matches/season). Also the NFL rights are scattered across multiple cable channels (ESPN, NBC Sports) and streaming platforms (Amazon, YouTube, Peacock), alongside free-to-air coverage on ABC, CBS, NBC, and FOX. Because live rights become fragmented among several providers – both traditional pay-tv and streaming services – the aforementioned competition remedies eliminate a one-stop shopping option and, therefore, increase transaction and subscription costs for consumers, who become reliant on different services for supporting their favourite team (Budzinski et al., 2019). The emergence of new streaming platforms has reinforced, or even exacerbated, the fragmentation of sports programming markets and further highlighted the inadequacies of the existing regulatory approach. In Germany, for example, the number of broadcasters with the rights to the top ten sports competitions has been constantly growing. In 2014, all rights were owned by only three operators. By 2022, the same set of rights were split across seven broadcasters. Hence, this rights fragmentation and subsequent need for subscribing to different sports channels or platforms, in turn, increases household premium sports expenditure. According to a study by Ampere Analysis, this accessibility of sports coverage comes with a price and places sizeable financial barriers to access in front of core sports audiences. German sports fans currently take up an average of 3.3 paid streaming services per household, a figure that continues to rise (Dziadul, 2023). Against this background, it is perhaps no surprise that the viewing of live matches via illegal streams is an increasingly common practice in most markets across the globe (see Chapter 6).

One way to address the anti-competitive effects of exclusive dealing might be to simply impose a ban on exclusive deals for live sports rights. For example, Harbord and Szymanski (2004) recommend non-exclusive sale to multiple broadcasters as a means to tackle the persistent competition issues related to the buying and selling of English Premier League football. Such a move would be strongly opposed by sports organisations and (at least some) broadcasters, and could well fatally undermine the sports rights market. Non-exclusive allocation of sports rights may result in a situation in which multiple broadcasters offer competing sports coverage and in which consumers would benefit from an oligopolistic market with comparable offers and price competition between different providers. However, non-exclusive licensing may eventually lead to lower rights revenues for sporting organisations, which could likely have adverse effects on the organisations' ability to compete for the best sports talent. This decreased ability to compete internationally, in turn, could have negative consequences for sports consumers, who tend to care about the quality and competitiveness of the game (Heller et al., 2023).

The alternative approach adopted by competition law, particularly in Europe, at both the national and EU levels, has been to treat broadcast rights for exclusive sports programming, in particular football, in accordance with what is commonly known as the 'essential facilities doctrine' (Smith, 2007). The 'essential facilities doctrine' effectively denotes that certain upstream (i.e. sports rights) inputs are essential/indispensable for downstream broadcasters to compete in the relevant market (i.e. sports programming) and cannot easily be replicated without significantly raising costs. Following on from this, to facilitate competition, access is provided to the 'essential facility' for all market players on 'fair, reasonable and non-discriminatory' terms, which are overseen by broadcasting and/or competition regulators. Since the late 1990s, the 'essential facilities doctrine' has influenced the European approach to the regulation of a whole host of potential 'bottlenecks' or 'gateways' within the contemporary broadcasting industry to ensure access to dominant (satellite or cable) delivery platforms for channels not owned by the platform provider (Collins, 1998; Levy, 1999). Since the early 2000s, a whole host of mergers between European pay-tv operators have been accompanied by regulations to guarantee the wholesale provision of premium sports channels to other broadcasters and/or delivery platforms, including in Spain (between Via Digital and Sogecable to form Digital+, as well as more recently between Telefonica and Digital+) and France (between TPS and Canal Satellite to form Canal+ France) (see Smith et al., 2016).

The mandatory sub-licencing of exclusive sports rights forms a variation of this approach, and may be an alternative method to introduce competition in the sports programming market. However, Heller et al. (2023) do not find convincing evidence of the effect of such an approach. They argue that the potential benefit of winning the auction is reduced as the winner would be required to enter into a sub-licensing agreement. This may also discipline the height of the financial bid, and thus negatively affect total revenues for sports organisations. In 2023, Telefónica was fined by Spanish competition authority CNMC when it sub-licensed the exclusive broadcasting rights for Formula One competitions to DAZN. CNMC ruled that the operator had failed to comply with certain commitments made when acquiring Digital+ because it set out limitations on third parties acquiring these rights. Hence, the pay-tv operator was fined for not providing its wholesale supply under fair, reasonable, and non-discriminatory terms (CNMC, 2023). In a similar case, pay-tv operator TIM and DAZN were fined by the Italian competition authority AGCM after entering an exclusive sub-licensing agreement following the acquisition of Serie A rights. The exclusive partnership hindered other pay-tv operators such as Sky Italia from accessing DAZN and its subsequent sports rights portfolio consisting of, among others, cycling, tennis, and the Summer Olympics. Following the regulatory decision, TIM signed a non-exclusive distribution agreement with DAZN (AGCM, 2023).

To conclude, it is fair to say that despite the emergence of internet-distributed television as a popular avenue for watching live sports, the fundamental characteristics of the sports media rights market remain largely unchanged. While streaming technology increases potential for new entrants in both the sports rights and sports programming markets, premium sports content continues to be relatively scarce and thus control of premium sports rights remains a key source of market power within contemporary pay-tv and wider communications and entertainment markets. As a result, competition authorities are likely to face a constant challenge to prevent a handful of global media platforms, such as Disney/ESPN, Amazon, Comcast/Sky, and DAZN, from using control of premium sports rights to dominate national pay-tv markets. Yet, at the same time, the regulatory solutions employed to date, such as the unbundled sale of rights or NSB rule, seem increasingly inappropriate and ineffective, at least from the perspective of consumers, who are often forced to pay more and/or face the inconvenience of subscribing to a number of different service providers. The impact of current remedies has, so far, remained rather limited. As we have argued in this chapter, a potential way forward for competition regulators is to focus as much on the (downstream) sports programming market as on the (upstream) sports rights market. However, an important challenge lies in finding a precarious balance between preserving the interests of sports organisations, sports broadcasters, and sports consumers. All too often, however, it seems the regulatory approach works in favour of the commercial interests of sports and media organisations, rather than consumers.

References

AGCM (2023). I857 - Italian Competition Authority: TIM fined 760,000 euro and DAZN more than 7 million euro for the TV rights agreement for the 2021–2024 Serie A football championship. Available at: https://en.agcm.it/en/media/press-releases/2023/7/I857 (Accessed: 20 May 2023).

Ahmed, M. and Massoudi, A. (2021). 'Leaked Super League plans reveal goal of US-style football finances', *Financial Times*, 20 April. Available at: https://www.ft.com/content/e80299a4-8012-447a-8512-c24e149304b1 (Accessed: 21 April 2023).

Budzinski, O., Gaenssle, S., and Kunz-Kaltenhäuser, P. (2019). How Does Online Streaming Affect Antitrust Remedies to Centralized Marketing? The Case of European Football Broadcasting Rights. *International Journal of Sport Finance*, 14 (3), pp. 147–157.

Butler, R. and Massey, P. (2019). Has Competition in the Market for Subscription Sports Broadcasting Benefited Consumers? The Case of the English Premier League. *Journal of Sports Economics*, 20 (4), pp. 603–624.

Carp, S. (2021). 'Primeira Liga TV rights to be centralised from 2027/28 season', *SportsProMedia*, 28 January. Available at: https://www.sportspromedia.com/broadcast-ott/media-rights/primeira-liga-tv-rights-centralised-2027-28-benfica-sport-tv/ (Accessed: 15 May 2023).

Cave, M. and Crandall, R. (2001). Sports Rights and the Broadcast Industry. *Economic Journal*, 111 (469), pp. 4–26.

CMA (2022). Anticipated joint venture between Warner Bros. Discovery, Inc and BT Group plc. Decision on relevant merger situation and substantial lessening of competition. Available at: https://assets.publishing.service.gov.uk/media/633413ced3bf7f34f3359655/Warner_Bros_Discovery_BT_-_Decision.pdf (Accessed: 25 July 2023).

CNMC (2023). The CNMC initiates disciplinary proceedings against Telefónica for the agreement with Dazn regarding the exclusive rights to Formula 1. Available at: https://www.cnmc.es/sites/default/files/editor_contenidos/Notas%20de%20prensa/2023/20230504_NP_Incoaci%C3%B3n_TFCA_DAZN_en_GB.pdf (Accessed: 10 May 2023).

Collins, R. (1998). Back to the Future: Digital Television and Convergence in the United Kingdom. *Telecommunications Policy*, 22 (4/5), pp. 383–396.

Cowie, C. and Williams, M. (1997). The Economics of Sports Rights. *Telecommunications Policy*, 21 (7), pp. 619–634.

Dziadul, C. (2023). 'Sports rights ownership fragments', *Broadband TV News*, 2 October. Available at: https://www.broadbandtvnews.com/2023/10/02/sports-rights-ownership-fragments (Accessed: 2 October 2023).

European Commission (1991). Commission Decision 91/130/EEC of 19 February Screensport/Members of the EBU. *OJ* L 63 of 9 March. Available at: https://eur-lex.europa.eu/legal-content/en/TXT/?uri=CELEX:31991D0130 (Accessed: 3 October 2023).

European Commission (1993). Commission Decision 93/403/EEC of 11 June EBU/Eurovision System. *OJ* L 179 of 11 June. Available at: https://eur-lex.europa.eu/legal-content/EN/TXT/?uri=CELEX%3A31993D0403 (Accessed: 3 October 2023).

European Commission (2003). 2003/778/EC: European Commission decision of 23 July 2003 relating to a proceeding pursuant to Article 81 of the EC Treaty and Article 53 of the EEA Agreement, COMP/C.2–37.398 — Joint selling of the commercial rights of the UEFA Champions League. *OJ* L 291/25. Available at: https://eur-lex.europa.eu/legal-content/EN/TXT/?uri=CELEX%3A32003D0778 (Accessed: 3 October 2023).

European Commission (2004). Council Regulation 139/2004/EC of 20 January 2004 on the control of concentrations between undertakings (the EC merger regulation). *OJ* L24/1, Art. 2(3). Available at: https://eur-lex.europa.eu/legal-content/en/ALL/?uri=CELEX%3A32004R0139 (Accessed: 3 October 2023).

European Commission (2005a). *Case COMP/C.2/37.214 – Joint selling of the media rights to the German Bundesliga*. Brussels: European Commission. Available at: https://eur-lex.europa.eu/legal-content/EN/ALL/?uri=CELEX%3A52004XC0914%2803%29 (Accessed: 3 October 2023).

European Commission (2005b). *Case COMP/C-2/38.173 – Joint selling of the media rights to the FA Premier League*. Brussels: European Commission. Available at: https://eur-lex.europa.eu/legal-content/EN/ALL/?uri=CELEX%3A52008XC0112%2803%29 (Accessed: 3 October 2023).

European Commission (2007). White Paper on Sport, Annex I: Sport and EU Competition Rules. Available at: https://eur-lex.europa.eu/legal-content/EN/TXT/PDF/?uri=CELEX:52007DC0391 (Accessed: 5 October 2023).

Evens, T. and Donders, K. (2018). *Platform Power and Policy in Transforming Television Markets*. London: Palgrave Macmillan.

Evens, T. and Lefever, K. (2011). Watching the Football Game: Broadcasting Rights for the European Digital Television Market. *Journal of Sport & Social Issues*, 35 (1), pp. 33–49.

Evens, T., Lefever, K., Valcke, P., Schuurman, D., and De Marez, L. (2011). Access to Premium Content on Mobile Television Platforms: The Case of Mobile Sports. *Telematics and Informatics*, 28 (1), pp. 32–39.

Evens, T. and Smith, P. (2022). Regulating the Digital Sports Broadcasting Market: New Players; Old Problems. In: H. Fujak and S. Frawley (eds.), *Sport Broadcasting for Managers* (pp. 55–75). London: Routledge.

Gardner, J. (2020). 'Project Big Picture rejected by Premier League clubs', *SportsProMedia*, 14 October. Available at: https://www.sportspromedia.com/news/project-big-picture-rejected-premier-league-clubs (Accessed: 25 September 2023).

Gerrard, B. (2006). Competitive Balance and the Sports Media Rights Market: What are the Real Issues? In: C. Jeanrenaud and S. Kesenne (eds.), *The Economics of Sport and the Media* (pp. 22–36). Cheltenham: Edward Elgar.

Harbord, D. and Szymanski, S. (2004). Football Trials. *European Competition Law Review*, 25 (2), pp. 117–121.

Hatton, C., Wagner, C., and Armengod, H. (2007). Fair Play: How Competition Authorities Have Regulated the Sale of Football Media Rights in Europe. *European Competition Law Review*, 28 (6), pp. 346–354.

Heller, C.-P., Sudaric, S., and Winkler, A.-C. (2023). The Centralised Sale of Football Media Rights in Europe. *European Competition Journal*, 19 (3), pp. 449–480.

James, S. (2021). The NFL's Anti-Trust Problem in the Streaming Era. *Journal of Corporation Law*, 46 (3). Available at: https://jcl.law.uiowa.edu/sites/jcl.law.uiowa.edu/files/2021-08/James_Final_Web.pdf (Accessed: 10 March 2023).

Kaushik, M. (2024). 'Reliance-Disney deal may need major tweaks for CCI nod', *Financial Express*, 11 March. Available at: https://www.financialexpress.com/business/brandwagon reliance-disney-deal-may-need-major-tweaks-for-cci-nod-3420737/ (Accessed: 3 June 2024).

Krieger, J. (2024). 'Bundesliga TV rights: German Cartel Office drops no-single-buyer rule', *Broadband TV News*, 30 January. Available at: https://www.broadbandtvnews.com/2024/01/30/bundesliga-tv-rights-german-cartel-office-drops-no-single-buyer-rule (Accessed: 30 January 2024).

Levy, D. (1999). *Europe's Digital Revolution: Broadcasting Regulation, the EU and the Nation State*. London: Routledge.

McCaskill, S. (2023a). 'Real Madrid launch in-house RM Play OTT platform', *SportsProMedia*, 9 June. Available at: https://www.sportspromedia.com/broadcast-ott/ott-and-digital/rm-play-real-madrid-ott-streaming/ (Accessed: 25 March 2024).

McCaskill, S. (2023b). 'Reports: Premier League will offer four-year UK broadcast deals and nears UK£130m EFL settlement', *SportsProMedia*, 15 September. Available at: https://www.sportspromedia.com/news/premier-league-tv-efl-broadcast-deal-sky-tnt/ (Accessed: 15 October 2023).

McCaskill, S. (2024). 'Fubo CEO: Fox, ESPN and WBD joint venture latest desperate move by "streaming cartel"', *SportsProMedia*, 26 March. Available at: https://

www.sportspromedia.com/news/fubo-ceo-fox-espn-and-wbd-joint-venture-latest-desperate-move-by-streaming-cartel/ (Accessed: 15 May 2024).

Nathanson, D. (2023). The NFL-Amazon Agreement vs. Antitrust Legislation: The Future of the National Football League in OTT Services. *Entertainment and Sports Lawyer*, 39 (1). Available at: https://www.americanbar.org/groups/entertainment_sports/publications/entertainment-sports-lawyer/esl-39-01-spring-23/the-nflamazon-agreement-vs-antitrust-legislation-future-the-national-football-league-ott-services/ (Accessed: 12 April 2023).

Noll, R. G. (2007). Broadcasting and Team Sports. *Scottish Journal of Political Economy*, 54 (3), pp. 400–421.

Ofcom (2023). *Pricing Trends for Communications Services in the UK*. Available at: https://www.ofcom.org.uk/__data/assets/pdf_file/0024/273138/pricingtrendsreport2023.pdf (Accessed: 14 May 2023).

Papadopoulos, A. (2010). *The International Dimension of EU Competition Law and Policy*. Cambridge: Cambridge University Press.

Rodger, B. and MacCulloch, A. (2009). *Competition Law and Policy in the EC and UK*. London: Routledge.

Sandvoss, C. (2003). *A Game of Two Halves: Football, Television and Globalization*. London: Routledge.

Sim, J. (2023). 'Serie A gets renewal option for DAZN's domestic rights deal with Senate approval', *SportsProMedia*, 14 February. Available at: https://www.sportspromedia.com/news/serie-a-italy-senate-domestic-tv-rights-deal-extension-dazn-sky/ (Accessed: 15 October 2023).

Smith, P. (2007). *The Politics of Television Policy: The Introduction of Digital Television in the UK*. Lewiston: Edwin Mellen Press.

Smith, P. (2010). The Politics of Sports Rights. The Regulation of Television Sports Rights in the UK. *Convergence: The International Journal of Research into New Media Technologies*, 16 (3), pp. 316–333.

Smith, P., Evens, T., and Iosifidis, P. (2015). The Regulation of Television Sports Broadcasting: A Comparative Analysis. *Media, Culture & Society*, 37 (5), pp. 720–736.

Smith, P., Evens, T., and Iosifidis, P. (2016). The Next Big Match: Convergence, Competition and Sports Media Rights. *European Journal of Communication*, 31 (5), pp. 536–550.

Spangler, T. (2024). 'U.S. reps raise concerns that Disney, Fox, WBD sports streaming venture will be anticompetitive', *Variety*, 16 April. Available at: https://variety.com/2024/tv/news/us-reps-anticompetitive-letter-disney-fox-wbd-sports-streaming-venture-1235972866/ (Accessed: 5 May 2024).

Sweeting, G. (2024). 'Telefonica reclaims La Liga rights for €1.2 billion', *Total Telecom*, 22 January. Available at: https://totaltele.com/telefonica-reclaims-la-liga-rights-for-e1-2-billion/ (Accessed: 22 January 2024).

Szymanski, S. (2002). Collective Selling of Broadcast Rights to Sporting Events. *International Sports Law Review*, 2 (1), pp. 1–6.

Szymanski, S. and Kesenne, S. (2004). Competitive Balance and the Revenue Sharing in Team Sports. *Journal of Industrial Economics*, 52 (1), pp. 165–177.

Szymanski, S. and Zimbalist, A. (2006). *National Pastime: How Americans Play Baseball and the Rest of the World Plays Soccer*. Washington, D.C.: Brookings Institution Press.

Toft, T. (2003). Football: Joint Selling of Media Rights. *Competition Policy Newsletter*, 3, pp. 47–52.

Tonazzi, A. (2003). Competition Policy and the Commercialization of Sport Broadcasting Rights: The Decision of the Italian Competition Authority. *International Journal of the Economics of Business*, 10 (1), pp. 17–34.

8

MAJOR EVENTS LEGISLATION

Since around the 1990s, the growth of pay-tv has prompted policy makers in numerous different countries to introduce legislation designed to preserve coverage of major sporting events and competitions, such as the Olympic Games and the FIFA World Cup, on free-to-air television, commonly known as major/listed events or anti-siphoning legislation. According to a recent survey undertaken by the European Broadcasting Union (EBU), an alliance of mainly, but not only, European-based public service media organisations (see Chapter 4), 24 out of the 31 European countries surveyed operated a form of major events legislation (Oxford Economics, 2024, p.38). For many of these countries, including some of the largest, such as Germany, France, and Italy, major events legislation is coordinated by the European Union (EU), while for others, such as the UK (since its departure from the EU in 2020), it resides at the national level (European Commission, 2022; Woodhouse, 2022). Beyond Europe, a number of other countries, including some of the largest national sports rights markets, namely, Australia, India, and South Africa, have also adopted a form of major events legislation (Evens et al., 2013). While there are national variations in how major events legislation operates, typically the relevant government department in each country maintains a list of sporting events considered of national interest, and the rights to broadcast these events must be offered to free-to-air broadcasters on fair and reasonable terms (Smith et al., 2015). A small number of high-profile international events, such as the FIFA men's football World Cup and the Summer Olympic Games, are included on the lists of virtually all countries, but, for the most part, the sports/events listed reflect particular national/regional preferences and traditions. For example, in Europe, national lists are dominated by football, most notably: the UEFA men's football European Championships (18 countries); football matches played by the national team

DOI: 10.4324/9781003401988-12

(11); the UEFA Champions League for club football teams (10); the UEFA Europa League for club football teams (10); and the final of the major domestic football cup competition (10) (Oxford Economics, 2024, p.38). Reflecting more specific national interests, a wide array of other sports also have events listed in different European countries, including cycling (Belgium, France, Italy), tennis (France, the UK), handball (France, Hungary), rugby (Italy, France, Ireland), and winter sports (Finland, Poland) (European Commission, 2022). Outside Europe, the same pattern is discernible, with, for example, cricket dominating India's list of 'sporting events of national importance' and Australia's listing a host of sports/competitions played almost exclusively in Australia (e.g. Australian Rules football and National Rugby League) (MIB, 2022; Australian Government, 2022, pp.48–9).

From its inception, in various different countries, major events legislation has been subject to regular public and political debate (see, e.g. Evens et al., 2013; Rowe et al., 2023; Scherer and Rowe, 2014; Scherer and Sam, 2012; Smith, 2010). This chapter focuses on the latest issue in this ongoing debate, namely the relevance and application of major events legislation in the age of streaming and platformisation. To this end, the first part of the chapter details why major events legislation remains just as important as ever, if not more important, as a means to protect free-to-air television coverage of national sporting events and enhance cultural citizenship. With particular reference to recent reviews of major events legislation in the UK (2022–24) and Australia (2022–24), the second part of the chapter examines the evolution of major events legislation. This section highlights how major events legislation in the UK and Australia has been reformed in two key ways: first, the scope of existing legislation has been extended to prevent (national- or international-based) streaming services, such as Amazon or Stan Sports (Australia), securing the exclusive live rights to listed events; and second, the range of events covered by major events legislation has also been widened to, at least in part, redress the long-standing under-representation of women's sports events and para-sports. However, with digital, including on-demand (i.e. online highlight/clips), rights remaining outside the scope of major events legislation, debate on its effectiveness in the age of streaming and platformisation has, in all likelihood, only just begun.

The Continued Relevance of Major Events Legislation

From Free-to-Air to Pay-tv and Subscription Video-on-Demand

The introduction (and continued existence) of major events legislation has long been justified on the grounds that coverage of high-profile sporting events will otherwise tend to migrate from free-to-air broadcasting to pay-tv. There is certainly considerable evidence to support this point of view. Perhaps most notably, during the mid-1990s, in Europe, live coverage of top-level domestic football largely shifted from free-to-air television to pay-tv. At around the same time, in New Zealand, live coverage of the matches of the national rugby team, the iconic All Blacks, also moved from free-to-air (TVNZ) to pay-tv (Sky TV) (Scherer and Sam, 2012). And similarly, in Canada, during the early 2000s, the live broadcast rights for a number of popular sports, including curling and Canadian football, were acquired by pay-tv, when historically these sports had been available free-to-air via the public broadcaster, CBC (Scherer and Whitson, 2009).

Since around the mid-2010s, the emergence of subscription video-on-demand (SVoD) services has witnessed a new wave in the migration of live sport away from free-to-air television. For example, in Japan, the dedicated sports SVoD streaming service, DAZN, has been credited with 'converting a population that was sceptical of pay-tv into paying customers', with a host of premium rights deals, including the exclusive live rights for the J-League (football) and almost all NPB (baseball) teams (Bassam, 2021a). In countries with more mature pay-tv markets, SVoD providers have also looked to secure the rights to high-profile events traditionally offered on free-to-air television. For example, in France, in 2019, Amazon agreed a landmark three-year deal with the French Tennis Federation (FFT) for the exclusive (domestic) live rights to ten night sessions at the French Open (Carp, 2019a). Consequently, while most of the tournament remained available on free-to-air television via France's public service broadcaster (PSB), France Télévisions, since 2020, the 'headline match' scheduled for each day's night session has been available exclusively to Amazon Prime subscribers (Bassam, 2020). In 2023, the FFT renewed its deal with Amazon for a further four years (until 2027), including the addition of a further night session and the exclusive coverage of two quarter-final matches (Jones, 2023). A similar pattern, whereby SVoDs carve out supplementary rights deals for events traditionally provided on free-to-air television, is also evident in the US. During the 1990s and 2000s, the size (and wealth) of the US television advertising market helped ensure major sports competitions (e.g. NFL American football, NBA basketball, and MLB baseball) maintained a significant free-to-air presence, albeit increasingly supplemented by pay-tv (Szymanski, 2006). As recently as 2020, it was also possible to conclude 'without equivocation' that major events 'had not migrated [from free-to-air television] to streaming platforms' (Kunz, 2020, p.143). However, with the growing focus of US streaming platforms on using exclusive sports rights to boost their subscriber numbers, this may be beginning to change. Following a reported $110 million deal with the NFL, in January 2024, NBC offered exclusive coverage of the wild card play-off game (between the Kansas City Chiefs and the Miami Dolphins). In Miami and Kansas the game was available on NBC (free-to-air), but outside these 'home television markets' the game was only available via NBC's streaming SVoD service, Peacock (Deitsch and Kaplan, 2023). This was only the second time in over 50 years that an NFL play-off game was not available in every part of the country for free and its migration behind a paywall prompted an 'outcry' from NFL fans (Enten, 2024). Just as significantly, if not more, the game was also 'the single largest live streamed event in US broadcasting history', attracting 2.8 million new subscribers to Peacock (McCaskill, 2024). No doubt keen to replicate NBC/Peacock's success, shortly afterwards Amazon secured the exclusive rights to an NFL play-off game for the 2024–25 season (Spangler, 2024).

Over the last decade, migration of live sports coverage from free-to-air to pay-tv/SVoD has even been evident in relation to some events protected by major events legislation, namely the (Summer and Winter) Olympic Games. In 2015, the International Olympic Committee (IOC) agreed a pan-European €1.3 billion deal with Discovery (now Warner Bros. Discovery (WBD)), the owner of the pay-tv broadcaster, Eurosport, for the exclusive rights to the Olympic Games, between 2018 and 2024 (although only for 2022 onwards in the UK) (Mance, 2015). This meant that Europe's leading PSBs, including the BBC (UK), France Télévisions (France), RTVE (Spain), and Rai (Italy), each lost control of the rights to broadcast the Olympic Games. Although EU (and UK) major/listed events legislation guaranteed the sub-licensing of rights for national free-to-air coverage, this should not obscure the fact that the primacy of the Olympics coverage traditionally offered by European PSBs has been significantly diluted. Under the terms of a series of individual deals with Discovery (e.g. BBC, 2016), Europe's leading PSBs can only offer non-exclusive (exclusive on free-to-air only) coverage, with more extensive coverage available via Eurosport's pay-tv channels and its SVoD services, Discovery+ and (HBO) Max. Clear limitations have also been imposed on the online coverage able to be offered by PSBs, which is restricted to content previously (or currently) broadcast via linear television services. Consequently, in 2021, during its coverage of the Tokyo Olympics, the BBC, for example, was only able to show two events at any one time, which led to complaints from viewers when live coverage of medal-winning performances was missed (Waterson, 2021). In 2023, the IOC agreed a new joint deal with WBD and the EBU for 'all media rights' across 49 territories in Europe, excluding Russia and Belarus, for the four Olympic Games between 2026 and 2032 (Mann, 2023). Under the terms of the deal, WBD will continue to proclaim itself as the 'home of Olympics', with Discovery+ the only place for viewers to experience 'every moment' of the Games (Dixon, 2023). Rather than having to negotiate individual sub-licensing deals with WBD, EBU members will be able to broadcast more than 200 hours of coverage of the Summer Olympics and at least 100 hours of the Winter Olympics on television, as well as 'a broad range' of livestreaming and reporting across digital media platforms. However, at least until after 2032, European public service media organisations will not be able to replicate the BBC's much-lauded 2012 'digital Olympics', when 'live coverage of every Olympic sport from every venue' was offered by the Corporation for all UK citizens to enjoy (BBC, 2013, p.50).

Nevertheless, it should also be acknowledged that the vast majority of the sports coverage provided by pay-tv and/or SVoD services does not consist of programming previously available via free-to-air broadcasters, but rather coverage of sports and sporting events that previously received little, if any, airtime on free-to-air television. In the UK, for example, before the launch of Sky's (then BSkyB) pay-tv service during the 1990s, there was no live coverage of the England cricket team's overseas Test matches. Since 1994, all matches have received live coverage from either Sky, or its pay-tv rival, BT Sport (now TNT Sports). In the same vein, the rise of streaming services has provided sports fans with the opportunity to view even more live sport. For example, in 2023, the WTA and ATP (women's and men's tennis, respectively) tennis tours announced a five-year exclusive rights deal with Sky Sports, covering the UK, Ireland, Germany, Austria, Switzerland, and Italy. From 2024, Sky will cover more than 80 tournaments and offer viewers the option to view over 4,000 matches via its pay-tv services, as well as multiple streams via its digital platforms, including SVoD services, NOW, and WOW (McCaskill, 2023a). All of which is a far cry from the 1980s when the coverage of tennis from Europe's PSBs was limited to individual matches from a handful of the Grand Slam tournaments, or even the 1990s, when pay-tv services offered coverage of more tournaments, but little, if any, choice for viewers over the match to watch. Similarly, in the UK, in 2023, the Football League (representing the three divisions of teams below the Premier League in England) agreed a new £935 million five-year (2024/25 to season 2028/29) deal with Sky for the exclusive domestic live rights to over 1,000 matches each season (Sky Group, 2023). Compared to its existing deal with the League, this represented a 335 per cent increase in the number of matches to be shown, with matches to be made available on either a Sky main channel, or a streaming platform (SportsProMedia, 2023).

Cultural Citizenship in the Age of Streaming and Platformisation

The case for major events legislation is also based on its potential to promote (and/or preserve) 'cultural citizenship' in two key ways (Miller, 2014). First, major events legislation may be justified on grounds of equity. Low-income groups should not be excluded from access to major sporting events by their inability to pay. In the age of streaming and platformisation, the increasing cost of watching live sport is an increasingly salient issue. For example, in the UK, in 2019, the House of Lords Communications Committee highlighted that viewers would need to pay as much as £900 to access all Premier League games across Amazon Prime, Sky Sports, and BT Sport, and argued that this underlined the importance of the protection offered by 'the listed events regime' for the 'availability of major sports events' (House of Lords (Communications Committee), 2019, pp.27–8). Similarly, in Australia, in 2022, against the backdrop of the government's review of anti-siphoning laws (see below), a study commissioned by Free TV, a group representing commercial free-to-air broadcasters, found that 58 per cent of Australians were concerned about the cost of having multiple subscriptions (Deloitte, 2022, p.29). The same report also noted that, despite the rise of SVoDs, Australians were still reluctant to pay for sport, with more than half (56 per cent) 'not willing to pay for sport at all' (Deloitte, 2022, p.47). Furthermore, while relevant to all countries, the cost barrier to watching live sport is a particularly important issue in countries characterised by wide disparities of income between social classes. For example, the Independent Communications Authority of South Africa (ICASA) justified its recent (2021) reform of major events legislation (see also below) by citing that only around 8 million of South Africa's 14 million television households have access to pay-tv (Business Tech, 2021). With this in mind, the ICASA declared that its new regulations were intended to 'redress inequalities in how television is accessed in South Africa' (Business Tech, 2021).

The second significant benefit of ensuring that major sporting events are broadcast on free-to-air television is the generation of what economists refer to as positive network externalities, whereby the shared benefits that can result from the coverage of major sporting events on universally available free-to-air television are more significant than the benefits for any individual viewer, such as the 'feel-good' factor experienced in South Africa following its 2019 Rugby World Cup victory, led by the team's first black captain, Siya Kolisi (BBC, 2019). Against the backdrop of an increasingly fragmented media landscape, it is worth emphasising that live free-to-air television (broadcast and/or streaming) coverage of major sporting events remains one of the few forms of television still able to bring nations together for such shared viewing experiences. For example, in the UK, the final of the 2020 (held in 2021) UEFA European football championships between England and Italy was watched by an average audience of 29.85 million people, an 82 per cent share of the available television audience, and the most watched broadcast in the UK since the funeral of Princess Diana, in 1997 (Carp, 2021). Similarly, in France, in 2022, the FIFA World Cup final between France and Argentina was watched by 24 million, an 81 per cent audience share, and an 'all-time' viewing record in France (FIFA, 2022). In India, the 2023 ICC World Cup Cricket final (between India and Australia) was watched by a record audience of 300 million across all platforms (Sim, 2023). And finally, in the US, the 2024 Super Bowl was watched by just over 123 million viewers (across all platforms), making it the most watched US television broadcast since the (1969) Apollo moon landing (Nicolaou, 2024). Furthermore, the relative importance of live coverage of major sports events on television has markedly increased during the era of streaming. For example, in the UK, during the 1990s, sport featured only twice in the top ten list of most watched programmes, whereas, of the top ten most watched shows in the 2010s, eight out of ten were major sports events (Rogan and Potter,

2021, p.4). Similarly, in Australia, in 2021, sport accounted for all but one of the ten most popular programmes on free-to-air television (metro areas) (Australian Government, 2022, p.18). As put by Rogan and Potter (2021), 'major sports fixtures are the one thing we all still watch together, cheering, or groaning in unison' (p.166).

Opposition to major events legislation stems from an underlying commitment to free market principles. This line of argument is often voiced by pay-tv broadcasters. For example, in Australia, during the 2010s, the leading pay-tv operator, Foxtel, repeatedly called for changes to the country's anti-siphoning law on the grounds that the existing legislation prevented it from competing with (commercial and public service) free-to-air broadcasters (Mann, 2013). At least partly as a result, with support from a politically sympathetic government, in 2017, the number of sporting events and/or competitions covered by Australia's anti-siphoning legislation was significantly reduced, including the removal of international events involving Australian teams playing overseas in rugby league, football, rugby union, cricket, and netball, as well as a host of other major international sporting tournaments, such as Wimbledon and the US Open tennis (Australian Government, 2017a, 2017b). A free market approach to the sale of rights is also often advocated by sports organisations. Many sports organisations resent legal restrictions being imposed on the sale of their rights and argue that they are best placed to judge how to further the interests of their own sport, including how to balance the potential for increased revenue to be gained via pay-tv with the benefits of greater exposure through free-to-air television. For example, in South Africa, the ICASA's initial (2018) proposals for the reform of major events legislation included an increase in the number of events listed, as well as stronger protection for a number of key 'national sporting events', most notably the Summer Olympic Games, the FIFA World Cup, and the Rugby World Cup. These events would be guaranteed 'full live' coverage, rather than the 'live, delayed live, or delayed' coverage provided under the existing rules (ICASA, 2018). The ICASA's proposals were vehemently opposed by some of South Africa's leading sports organisations. In 2019, in public hearings on the draft proposals, numerous sports organisations, including Cricket South Africa, the Premier Soccer League, and South African Rugby Union, argued that the proposed regulations would 'kill' sport in the country as they relied on funds from the sale of their television rights to pay-tv (Mphahlele, 2020). For instance, in its written submission to the ICASA, Cricket South Africa (CSA) highlighted that, in 2018, 69 per cent of its total revenue was derived from broadcast revenue (CSA, 2019, para. 73). At least partly as a result of such opposition, by the time, in early 2021, the ICASA published its final Sports Broadcasting Regulations the plan for guaranteed live free-to-air television coverage of 'national events' had been abandoned (ICASA, 2021). As pointed out by Gary Rathbone, general manager of South Africa's PSB, the SABC, speaking following the publication of the ICASA's new regulations: 'nothing has changed' (Ray, 2021). South Africa's leading pay-tv broadcaster, DStv (MultiChoice), remains free therefore to continue to acquire rights for listed events, with the SABC (experiencing an ongoing financial crisis) then forced to negotiate with the pay-tv broadcaster for secondary rights. This system has often proved ineffective, most notably when, during the 2019 Rugby World Cup, the inability and/or unwillingness of the SABC and DStv to agree a sub-licensing deal meant that, despite being listed, there was no free-to-air television coverage of South Africa's matches, until a public outcry led to a last-ditch deal for live coverage of the final on SABC (Impey, 2019). With South Africa's main sports organisations wedded to the financial support provided by DStv, there is little to suggest the country's major events legislation will be any more effective in future.

The determination of pay-tv broadcasters and (at least some) sports organisations to oppose major events legislation has been similarly evident in India. In 2017, after several years of legal challenges from the country's leading pay-tv broadcaster, Star India, and Indian cricket's main governing body, the BCCI, the Supreme Court ruled that India's major events legislation (the Sports Broadcasting Signals (Mandatory Sharing with Prasar Bharati) Act, 2007) entitled the PSB, Doordarshan, to retransmit listed events on its own terrestrial and (direct-to-home) satellite network, FreeDish, but did not permit (pay) cable operators to retransmit Doordarshan's coverage (Laghate, 2017). The impact of this ruling on public access to major sports events in India has been 'staggering', with, out of 155 million households with television connections, only 4.6 million households having access to Doordarshan terrestrial networks, and the rest connected through either (pay) cable or satellite networks (Vaidialingam, 2017). In 2018, the Indian government's Ministry of Broadcasting (MIB) responded to the Supreme Court's ruling by proposing to extend Doordarshan's authority to retransmit listed events to include 'any cable and/or Direct-to-Home network and/or IPTV' (MIB, 2018). Predictably, India's leading pay-tv broadcasters and sports organisations were far from impressed, with one executive of a sports broadcaster claiming that the MIB's proposal would 'ruin the entire sports industry' because broadcasters will no longer 'bid top dollar to pick up rights' (Laghate, 2018). At least partly as a result, the MIB's plan to update major events legislation in India was not implemented and it seems increasingly unlikely that it ever will be.

Nevertheless, the free market–led arguments of some media and sports organisations do not undermine the underlying case for major events legislation. The key argument in support of major events legislation is not that policy makers and regulators know better than individual sports organisations, but rather that the wider public interest in the form of cultural citizenship is best served by the availability of particular sporting events on free-to-air television. It is not particularly unusual in democratic societies for certain property rights to be subject to state regulation in the public interest. Planning laws, for instance, mean that those who live in heritage properties cannot do with them exactly what they want. To promote cultural citizenship, the same is true for sports organisations and listed events and this continues to be the case in the age of streaming.

The Evolution of Major Events Legislation

During the early 2020s, major events legislation was subject to formal review in the two countries that have arguably been its leading proponents, namely the UK and Australia. In both countries, the continued value of and need for major events legislation were reiterated at an early stage. In the UK, in 2022, the government formally launched its 'digital rights review' by proclaiming that 'certain sporting events of national interest should be shown on free-to-air television so that they can be enjoyed by as wide an audience as possible' (DCMS, 2022a). In Australia, the opposition Labor Party committed to reviewing the country's anti-siphoning legislation during the 2022 Federal Election campaign and initiated the promised review soon after its election victory (Australian Government, 2022). While the new government's initial consultation document posed the question of whether 'the objective' of the anti-siphoning scheme was 'still relevant and appropriate' (p.29), its description of sport as 'an integral part of Australian life and culture' (p.8) and emphasis on the 'relationship between telecast arrangements and sports participation' (p.9) left little doubt about the government's view (Australian Government, 2022). In 2023, the Australian government confirmed its belief that the anti-siphoning scheme remained 'relevant and appropriate in the contemporary media environment' on the basis that 'the risk of nationally important and culturally significant events migrating behind paywalls [...] evident in an analogue media environment [is] also present in a digital environment' (Australian Government, 2023a, p.22). However, the challenge identified by both governments was how to update their respective major events legislation to ensure it 'remain[s] fit for purpose' in the age of streaming and platformisation (DCMS, 2022b, p.25).

Closing the Streaming Loophole

The UK and Australian reviews of major events legislation focused on three key issues. The first of these was how to prevent a (domestic or international) streaming service from acquiring the exclusive rights to cover a listed event, i.e. the so-called streaming loophole. In Australia, under the existing anti-siphoning scheme, a licence condition is imposed on subscription television broadcasting licensees, like Foxtel, preventing them from acquiring the rights to listed events before a free-to-air television broadcaster has had the opportunity to do so. However, as noted by the Australian government, the existing scheme 'did not apply to online services', including: subscription streaming services, such as Netflix and Amazon Prime Video; dedicated (subscription) sports streaming services, like Kayo Sports and Optus Sport; (free) Broadcast Video On Demand (BVOD) services, such as 9Now and 7plus; and digital platforms, including YouTube (Australian Government, 2023a, p.4). To remove this 'regulatory gap' and prevent 'iconic events slipping behind an online paywall', the Australian government proposed new legislation (the *Communications Legislation Amendment (Prominence and Anti-siphoning) Bill 2023*) that would establish a 'broadcasting safety net' (Australian Government, 2023b). Specifically, the new legislation would expand the anti-siphoning scheme to prevent 'media content services (including, but not limited to, streaming services)' from acquiring the rights to listed events, until a free-to-air broadcaster has had the opportunity to secure the rights for its broadcasting service (Australian Government, 2023a, p.36). Just days after the Bill was introduced into Parliament, there was a timely reminder of why the new legislation was required. In 'the most significant streaming only deal in the history of Australian sports broadcasting', Amazon announced that it had secured the exclusive live rights, in Australia, for ICC cricket tournaments, including the men's and women's Cricket World Cups, until the end of 2027 (McCaskill, 2023b). With the changes to the anti-siphoning list introduced in 2017 (see above) and the ICC tournaments scheduled to take place outside Australia, this deal did not breach the existing anti-siphoning law, but it did highlight (again) how, if given the opportunity to do so, SVoDs will in all likelihood hasten the migration of free-to-air sport behind a paywall.

In the UK, concern over the impact of the growth of streaming on the effectiveness of listed events legislation initially focused on the possibility that the UK's main PSBs – the BBC, ITV, Channel 4, and Channel 5 – could lose the protection afforded to them under the scheme. This was because for a broadcaster to 'qualify' to provide exclusive coverage of a listed event its service had to be both 'free-to-view' and able to be received by 95 per cent of the population (via a 'broadcast platform' and on a 'TV set') (Ofcom, 2018, p.3). However, by 2018, with viewers increasingly watching online, the 95 per cent threshold was, as noted by the BBC, 'becoming increasingly difficult to meet' (BBC, 2018, pp.2–3). In response, Ofcom proposed and subsequently adopted two changes to its methodology for determining qualifying services: first, it would take into account viewing via 'all TV platforms, including IPTV', rather than just 'broadcast platforms'; and, second, it would measure reception on a household's 'main screen', rather than only via the 'television set' (Ofcom, 2018, p.1). With these changes, Ofcom ensured that the UK's main PSBs continued to be able to reach the qualifying threshold (Ofcom, 2019, p.1). At the same time, whether by design or not, the requirement that IPTV services need to be received via the 'main screen' established a barrier to, at least in the short term, prevent online streaming services and/or platforms, such as YouTube, from reaching the 95 per cent qualifying threshold (Ofcom, 2019, p.17).

Within just a couple of years, the increasing availability of streaming services via the 'main screen' in UK households prompted a more significant change to the UK's listed events legislation. In 2021, as part of a wider review of the future of public service media (PSM), Ofcom recommended the government 'consider whether to update the criteria that determine which services should carry listed events' and declared that 'there would be merit in assessing whether to change the regime in a way that would strengthen PSM benefits' (Ofcom, 2021, p.25). In 2022, the UK government set out its plans for new broadcasting legislation and, accepting Ofcom's recommendation, declared that 'in recognition of the key role that our public service broadcasters play in distributing content which is both distinctively British and of interest to British audiences [...] we will look at making qualification for the listed events regime a PSB-specific benefit' (DCMS, 2022b, p.25). Soon after, the UK government's Media Bill confirmed the replacement of the 95 per cent threshold with the requirement that qualifying services 'would have to be a PSB service and received free of charge' (Woodhouse, 2023, p.30). More specifically, the 2023 Media Bill defines the services that fall within the scope of the listed events regime as 'relevant services' and then divides 'relevant services' into two categories: first, those 'television and internet programme services' that satisfy the qualifying condition (i.e. PSBs); and second, 'all other relevant services', including (UK or international) streaming services (Woodhouse, 2023, p.30). In response to concerns raised by PSBs and the House of Commons Culture Committee, this all-encompassing definition of 'relevant services' was deliberately constructed to 'close the loophole' that might otherwise allow an 'unregulated streaming service' (i.e. not licensed by Ofcom) to buy the rights for a listed event and put them behind a paywall (House of Commons, 2023a, p.4). With the Media Bill 2023, the UK's new listed events legislation will therefore both close the streaming loophole and also preserve the support offered by the scheme to PSBs in the sports rights market.

Digital (Live and on-Demand) Rights

Albeit in different ways, in both the UK and Australia much of the debate on the future of major events legislation centred on the implications of the growing importance of digital (live and on-demand highlight/clip) rights in the sports media rights market. Yet, beyond closing the streaming loophole, neither government was prepared to shift the focus of their respective forms of major events legislation away from traditional, free-to-air, television broadcasters. In each country, this approach prompted particular criticism from pay-tv broadcasters. In the UK, in response to the government's plan to make qualification for the listed events regime 'a PSB-specific benefit', COBA (the Commercial Broadcasters and On-Demand Services Association), representing pay-tv broadcasters, such as Sky and WBD, complained that the government was 'misguided to exclude all other parties from showing listed events even if they meet the criteria of being widely available and free at point of use' (House of Commons, 2023b). According to COBA, 'the knock-on effect will be to make BBC licence-fee payers foot the bill for these events even if commercial players are willing to show them [online] for free' (Ziegler, 2023). Even more starkly, in Australia, Foxtel proclaimed: '"free access" should no longer be equated with "free-to-air television"' (Foxtel, 2022, p.16). On this basis, Foxtel advocated the adoption of a 'technology-neutral' 'free-to-view' model that would not seek to restrict the acquisition of rights to listed events, but would instead require the relevant 'content service' to ensure that (live and in full) coverage is made available for free and on a broadly available technology (Australian Government, 2023a, p.27). Furthermore, Foxtel had itself recently provided a demonstration of how this model would work in practice. In 2021, Foxtel agreed a 'landmark deal' with Netball Australia, which controversially ended the sport's long-term partnership with the free-to-air broadcaster, Nine Network (Sports Business, 2021). Under the terms of the deal, all Australia's national netball team games and two other games a week were to be broadcast on Kayo Freebies, the free tier of Foxtel's SVoD, Kayo Sports. Following the 2017 reforms (see above), the deal did not breach Australia's anti-siphoning rules, but it did offer a blueprint for how pay-tv operators, like Foxtel, might secure rights for premium sports, including the AFL (Australian rules football) and NRL (rugby league), while complying with a 'free-to-view' model of anti-siphoning legislation (i.e. by offering listed events for free online, but keeping other events behind a paywall).

In the UK, the government's framing of its listed events reforms as a means to support PSBs meant the inevitable rejection of arguments to widen the range of services able to offer listed events. By contrast, in Australia, the rejection of the 'free-to-view' model owed more to practical concerns. The Australian government concluded that the free-to-view model is likely to be 'suitable and appropriate [...] for the anti-siphoning scheme in the longer-term', but that 'technology and market conditions' prevent its adoption 'in the near-to-medium term' (Australian Government, 2023a, p.36). Perhaps most notably, the government pointed out that 11.71 per cent of Australians over 75 had no internet connection at home (Australian Government, 2023a, p.34). On this basis, the Australian government maintained that 'free-to-air broadcasting services' continued to provide the most suitable 'safety net' for free access to listed events (Australian Government, 2023a, p.6).

Despite offering support for free-to-air broadcasters (Australia) and PSBs (UK), the Australian and UK governments still faced criticism from these broadcasters for not extending the scope of their respective forms of major events legislation to directly cover online, including on-demand, rights. In Australia, Free TV Australia highlighted how 'in the modern media environment' Australians are increasingly expecting to be able to access content from free-to-air broadcasts 'on the device of their choice and wherever they are' (Free TV Australia, 2022, p.15). On this basis, Australia's free-to-air broadcasters advocated the adoption of a 'free-to-air first' model of anti-siphoning legislation that would guarantee free-to-air broadcasters the opportunity to acquire broadcast and online rights to listed events ahead of other service providers (including, but not limited to, streaming services) (Australian Government, 2023a, p.41). However, this approach was rejected by the Australian government on the grounds that it would 'substantially broaden' the restrictions faced by sports organisations when selling their rights and 'significantly extend the commercial advantages' given to free-to-air broadcasters by the existing anti-siphoning scheme (Australian Government, 2023a, p.45). In fact, to avoid any such outcomes, the government's 'broadcasting safety net' was deliberately constructed so as not to 'provide free-to-air broadcasters with preferential treatment in terms of their [non-broadcasting] content services (i.e. BVOD or other online services)' (Australian Government, 2023a, p.36).

In the UK, PSBs, and in particular the BBC, focused on the need to include digital, on-demand rights within the listed events regime in order to ensure that 'sporting events continue to reach the widest possible audience' (BBC, 2023). In evidence to the House of Commons Culture Committee, the BBC highlighted the (growing) importance of on-demand digital rights by citing its coverage of the Tokyo Olympic Games (in 2021). According to the BBC, the availability of on-demand short-form clips on the BBC Sport website meant that, in some instances where a British success happened overnight, there was a ten-fold increase in audience on the live TV transmission (BBC, 2023). With this in mind, the BBC argued that, without extending the listed events regime to cover digital, on-demand, rights, access to 'national moments' would 'very likely be restricted, contrary to the objectives of the listed events regime' (BBC, 2023). In 2022, when launching its 'digital rights review' the UK government acknowledged how 'digital rights [...] have become an important element in the sale of sports rights', but are 'not covered by the listed events regime' (DCMS, 2022a). However, the 2023 Media Bill did not address digital rights. Instead, in 2023, the government declared that it was still 'considering this [...] complex issue' and was concerned to maintain the right balance between 'access for audiences' and 'commercial freedoms' for sports organisations (House of Commons, 2023a, p.2). As a result, while the UK government's reforms to listed events legislation prevent a streaming service from acquiring the exclusive rights to cover listed events, they do not necessarily guarantee PSBs access to digital, including on-demand, rights for listed events.

What Events Should be Listed?

In both the UK and Australia, the early 2020s witnessed renewed debate over what events should be included in the list of events to be safeguarded for free-to-air television coverage. This issue has always been a controversial one. Pay-tv broadcasters have long criticised the lack of any clear criteria from governments when determining what events to list (see Smith et al., 2015). While, on the other side of the debate, PSBs and their supporters have repeatedly argued for additional events to be listed, particularly when high-profile sporting occasions are at risk of being available exclusively on pay-tv. Largely as a result, in the UK, pay-tv operators have even on occasion opted to sub-license their rights to certain high-profile events so as to avoid negative publicity and reopening debate on listed events. Most notably, in 2019, Sky decided to sub-license live coverage of the (England v. Australia) 2019 ICC cricket World Cup final to a PSB, Channel Four (Carp, 2019b). Similarly, when the young English tennis player, Emma Raducanu, reached the final of the 2021 US Open tennis tournament, Amazon shared its live coverage with Channel Four (BBC, 2021).

In both Australia and the UK, much of the recent debate on what events should be listed has amounted to little more than the restating of well-established positions. In Australia, Foxtel took the opportunity to restate the argument that anti-siphoning legislation is 'inherently anti-competitive' and called for the list to be 'reduced in scope' so as to only include those events that are 'truly' of national importance and cultural significance (Foxtel, 2022, p.2). Similarly, COMPPS (the Coalition of Major Professional and Participation Sports), representing most of Australia's major sports organisations, argued for a 'narrowing' of the list on the grounds that it imposed an unfair limitation on their ability to maximise revenue from the sale of their rights (COMPPS, 2022, pp.2–3). Alternatively, Free TV Australia (2022, p.19) maintained that the list ensured 'iconic sporting events [are] broadcast for free to all Australians' and, alongside Australia's leading PSBs, the ABC and SBS, advocated an 'expanded list' (Australian Government, 2023a, p.57). In the UK, debate on what events to list was deliberately stifled by the government. Keen to avoid reopening the polarised debate on listed events, when, in 2022, the government announced its intention to reform the listed events legislation, it stressed that the current list provided an 'appropriate balance' between 'retaining free-to-air sports for the public' and allowing 'rights holders to negotiate agreements in the best interests of their sport' (DCMS, 2022b, p.24). Even more clearly, a few months later, when launching its 'digital rights review' the government stated that the review 'would not consider changes to the list of events' (DCMS, 2022a). Despite periodic calls from various Parliamentary Committees for sports events, including Ashes cricket and Six Nations rugby, to be listed (or moved from the 'Group B' list to the 'Group A' list, see Table 8.1), the UK government showed no inclination to amend its position ahead of the publication of its 2023 Media Bill (House of Lords (Communications Committee), 2019, p.28; House of Commons, 2022, p.19).

Nevertheless, there was one issue that both the UK and Australian governments were keen to address in relation to the composition of their respective lists, namely the historic under-representation of women's sport

TABLE 8.1 UK Listed Events

Group A: full live coverage protected	*Group B: secondary (i.e. highlights) coverage protected*
The Olympic Games	Cricket Test Matches played in England
The Paralympic Games	Non-Finals play in the Wimbledon tournament
The FIFA World Cup Finals tournament	All other matches in the Rugby World Cup Finals tournament
The FIFA Women's World Cup Finals tournament	Six Nations Rugby tournament matches involving Home Countries
The European Football Championship Finals tournament	The Commonwealth Games
The European Women's Football Championship Finals tournament	The World Athletics Championship
The FA Cup Final	The Cricket World Cup – the Final, Semi-finals, and matches involving Home Nations teams
The Scottish FA Cup Final (in Scotland)	The Ryder Cup
The Grand National	The Open Golf Championship
The Wimbledon Tennis Finals	
The Rugby World Cup Final	
The Derby	
The Rugby League Challenge Cup Final	

Source: Woodhouse (2022, pp.6–7).

and para-sports. Over the last decade or so, there has been a tremendous growth in the popularity of a host of women's sports, including football, rugby, and cricket. At least in part, this growth has been fuelled by the active promotion and coverage of women's sport by (public and commercial) free-to-air broadcasters across the world, not least in the UK and Australia (see Chapter 4). Furthermore, the popularity and commercial value of women's sport are only likely to gather pace. In the UK, for example, revenue generated by women's sport, including from television rights sales, is predicted to grow to £1 billion a year by 2030 – up from £350m a year in 2020 (Women's Sport Trust, 2021). With its growing popular appeal, women's sport has inevitably attracted increased attention from pay-tv operators. For example, in 2021, DAZN agreed a four-year deal for the global rights to broadcast the UEFA Women's Champions League. As part of this ground-breaking deal, DAZN agreed for many matches to be made available live and for free via its YouTube channel, but these reduce in number over the term of the deal (Bassam, 2021b). It seems likely that DAZN's long-term plan is to build the popularity of the competition via free access, before gradually moving access behind a paywall. Against this backdrop, the UK and

TABLE 8.2 Australia's 'Modernised List' of Events Covered by Anti-Siphoning Legislation

Sport	*Events*
Olympic Games	Each event that is held as part of the Summer Olympic Games, including the Opening and Closing Ceremonies.
	Each event that is held as part of the Summer Paralympic Games, including the Opening and Closing Ceremonies.
	Each event that is held as part of the Winter Olympic Games, including the Opening and Closing Ceremonies.
Commonwealth Games	Each event held as part of the Commonwealth Games, including the Opening Ceremony and the Closing Ceremony.
Horse racing	Each running of the Melbourne Cup organised by the Victoria Racing Club.
Australian Football League (AFL)	Each match in the Australian Football League Premiership competition, including the Finals Series.
	Each match in the Australian Football League Women's Premiership Finals Series.
Rugby league	Each match in the National Rugby League Premiership competition, including the Finals Series.
	Each match in the National Rugby League Women's Premiership Finals Series.
	Each match in the National Rugby League State of Origin Series.
	Each match in the National Rugby League Women's State of Origin Series.
	Each international rugby league test match that: involves the senior Australian representative team; and is played in Australia or New Zealand.
	Each match of the Rugby League World Cup that: involves the senior Australian representative team; and is played in Australia, New Zealand, or Papua New Guinea.
Cricket	Each test match that: involves the senior Australian representative team; and is played in Australia.
	Each match of an 'Ashes' series that involves the senior Australian representative team and the senior English representative team; and is played in the United Kingdom or in Australia.
	Each one-day cricket match that: involves the (senior) Australian representative team; and is played in Australia.
	Each Twenty20 (T20) cricket match that: involves the senior Australian representative team; and is played in Australia.
	Each match of the International Cricket Council Men's Cricket World Cup that: involves the senior Australian representative team; and is played in Australia or New Zealand.
	Each match of the International Cricket Council Women's Cricket World Cup that: involves the senior Australian representative team; and is played in Australia or New Zealand.

Sport	*Events*
	The final of the International Cricket Council Men's Cricket World Cup if the final is played in Australia or New Zealand.
	The final of the International Cricket Council Women's Cricket World Cup if the final is played in Australia or New Zealand.
	Each match of the International Cricket Council Men's T20 World Cup that: involves the senior Australian representative team; and is played in Australia or New Zealand.
	Each match of the International Cricket Council Women's T20 World Cup that: involves the senior Australian representative team; and is played in Australia or New Zealand.
	The final of the International Cricket Council Men's T20 World Cup if the final is played in Australia or New Zealand.
	The final of the International Cricket Council Women's T20 World Cup if the final is played in Australia or New Zealand.
Soccer	Each match of the FIFA Men's World Cup tournament that involves the senior Australian representative team.
	Each match of the FIFA Women's World Cup tournament that involves the senior Australian representative team.
	The final of the FIFA Men's World Cup tournament.
	The final of the FIFA Women's World Cup tournament.
	Each match in the FIFA Men's World Cup Qualification tournament that: involves the senior Australian representative team; and is played in Australia.
	Each match in the FIFA Women's World Cup Qualification tournament that: involves the senior Australian representative team; and is played in Australia.
Tennis	Each match in the Australian Open tennis tournament.
	Each match in each tie of the International Tennis Federation Davis Cup World Group tennis tournament that: involves an Australian representative team; and is played in Australia.
	The final of the International Tennis Federation Davis Cup World Group tennis tournament if the final involves an Australian representative team.
Netball	A semi-final of the Netball World Cup if the semi-final involves the senior Australian representative team.
	The final of the Netball World Cup if the final involves the senior Australian representative team.
Motorsports	Each race in the Formula One World Championship (Grand Prix) held in Australia.
	Each race in the MotoGP World Championship held in Australia.
	Each Bathurst 1000 race in the Supercars Championship.

Source: Australian Government (2023a, pp.64–7).

Australian governments have each moved to incorporate more women's sport under the auspices of major events legislation. In Australia, the government used its review of anti-siphoning legislation as an opportunity to adopt a 'modernised list', adding several women's events to the list, including: the finals matches of the AFL Women's Premiership and the NRL Women's Premiership; the NRL Women's State of Origin Series; and also the Paralympic Games (see Table 8.2). Similarly, in 2022, in the UK, following separate consultations, the Paralympic Games and then the FIFA Women's World Cup Finals and the Women's European Football Championship Finals were added to the (Group A) list (Woodhouse, 2022, p.7). With these changes, as well as the others already detailed, the UK and Australian cases highlight how major events legislation can (and should) be updated to promote cultural citizenship in the age of streaming and platformisation. At the same time, however, by focusing on closing 'the streaming loophole' and not extending the scope of their respective forms of major events legislation to cover digital, including on-demand, rights both governments have, to date at least, focused on preventing the possible negative consequences of streaming, rather than exploiting the potential opportunities offered by digital delivery for enhancing cultural citizenship. At least partly as a result, it seems likely that debate over the need to update major events legislation for the age of streaming is far from over.

References

Australian Government (2017a). Amending the anti-siphoning scheme. Available at: https://www.infrastructure.gov.au/sites/default/files/amending-the-anti-siphoning-scheme_0.pdf (Accessed: 7 April 2024).

Australian Government (2017b). Reform of the anti-siphoning scheme: Regulation impact statement. Available at: https://obpr.pmc.gov.au/sites/default/files/posts/2017/11/anti-siphoning_ris.pdf (Accessed: 10 April 2024).

Australian Government (2022). *Review of the Anti-Siphoning Scheme: Consultation Paper*. Available at: https://www.infrastructure.gov.au/sites/default/files/documents/anti-siphoning-consultation-paper-oct-2022.pdf (Accessed: 3 April 2024).

Australian Government (2023a). *Anti-Siphoning Review: Proposals Paper*. Available at: https://www.infrastructure.gov.au/sites/default/files/documents/anti-siphoning-review-proposals-paper.pdf (Accessed: 2 April 2024).

Australian Government (2023b). 'Modernising Australia's media laws - for all Australians', 29 November. Available at: https://minister.infrastructure.gov.au/rowland/media-release/modernising-australias-media-laws-all-australians (Accessed: 4 April 2024).

Bassam, T. (2020). 'Amazon gets ten French Open night sessions for domestic broadcast', *SportsProMedia*, 13 October. Available at: https://www.sportspromedia.com/news/amazon-french-open-tv-rights-night-sessions-2020-ratings/ (Accessed: 6 April 2024).

Bassam, T. (2021a). 'DAZN Japan "doesn't see FTA networks as competitors", says SVP of subscription growth', *SportsProMedia*, 8 July. Available at: https://www.sp

ortspromedia.com/news/dazn-japan-subscribers-growth-basso-2021 (Accessed: 4 April 2024).
Bassam, T. (2021b). 'DAZN and YouTube partner for global Women's Champions League rights deal', *SportsProMedia*, 30 June. Available at: https://www.sportspromedia.com/news/dazn-uefa-womens-champions-league-tv-rights-youtube-2021-streaming/ (Accessed: 3 April 2024).
BBC (2013). *Annual Report and Accounts 2012/13.* Available at: http://downloads.bbc.co.uk/annualreport/pdf/2012-13/bbc-bbcexecutive-annualreport-review-and-assessment-2012-13.pdf (Accessed: 7 April 2024).
BBC (2016). 'BBC and Discovery Communications sign long-term Olympic Games partnership', 2 February. Available at: https://www.bbc.co.uk/mediacentre/latestnews/2016/olympics-rights (Accessed: 7 April 2024).
BBC (2018). Listed Events: Identifying television services that are free-to-view and widely available, 11 February. Available at: https://www.ofcom.org.uk/siteassets/resources/documents/consultations/category-1-10-weeks/124438-listed-events/responses/bbc/?v=196906 (Accessed: 1 August 2024).
BBC (2019). 'South Africa celebrates rugby world cup win over England', 2 November. Available at: https://www.bbc.co.uk/news/world-africa-50273318 (Accessed: 7 April 2024).
BBC (2021). 'Emma Raducanu: Channel 4 to show US Open final against Leylah Fernandez live', 11 September. Available at: https://www.bbc.co.uk/sport/tennis/58514875 (Accessed: 4 April 2024).
BBC (2023). DCMS committee inquiry on the draft media bill: Written evidence submitted by the BBC. Available at: https://committees.parliament.uk/writtenevidence/121444/html/ (Accessed: 6 April 2024).
Business Tech (2021). 'Updated rules for DStv and sports broadcasts in South Africa', 1 April. Available at: https://businesstech.co.za/news/media/480381/updated-rules-for-dstv-and-sports-broadcasts-in-south-africa/ (Accessed: 8 April 2024).
Carp, S. (2019a). 'Amazon adds French Open domestic rights to tennis portfolio', *SportsProMedia*, 25 July. Available at: https://www.sportspromedia.com/news/amazon-french-open-broadcast-rights-tennis-france-televisions/ (Accessed: 9 April 2024).
Carp, S. (2019b). 'England's Cricket World Cup final goes FTA on Channel 4', *SportsProMedia*, 12 July. Available at https://www.sportspromedia.com/news/cricket-world-cup-final-channel-4-england-new-zealand/ (Accessed: 2 August 2024).
Carp, S. (2021). 'Euro 2020 final delivers mammoth TV figures in UK and Italy', *SportsProMedia*, 13 July. Available at: https://www.sportspromedia.com/news/euro-2020-final-tv-figures-bbc-itv-rai-england-italy (Accessed: 6 April 2024).
COMPPS (the Coalition of Major Professional and Participation Sports) (2022). Submission of COMPPS to the review of the anti-siphoning scheme. Available at: https://www.infrastructure.gov.au/sites/default/files/documents/assr–coalition-of-major-professional-and-participation-sports-compps.pdf (Accessed: 7 April 2024).
CSA (Cricket South Africa) (2019). CSA submission on the Draft Sports Broadcasting Services Amendment Regulations. Available at: https://www.icasa.org.za/legislation-and-regulations/csa-submission-on-the-draft-sports-broadcasting-services-amendment-regulations (Accessed: 6 April 2024).
DCMS (2022a). Listed Events: Digital Rights Review terms of reference. Available at: https://www.gov.uk/government/publications/listed-events-digital-rights-review/listed-events-digital-rights-review-terms-of-reference (Accessed: 6 April 2024).
DCMS (2022b). *Up Next: The Government's Vision for the Broadcasting Sector.* Available at: https://assets.publishing.service.gov.uk/government/uploads/

system/uploads/attachment_data/file/1071939/E02740713_CP_671_Broadcasting_White_Paper_Accessible__1_.pdf (Accessed: 9 April 2024).

Deitsch, R. and Kaplan, D. (2023). 'Peacock to exclusively stream NFL wild-card playoff game in 2024: What this means for viewers', *The Athletic*, 15 May. Available at: https://theathletic.com/4522142/2023/05/15/peacock-nfl-playoff-game/ (Accessed: 8 April 2024).

Deloitte (2022). *Everybody Gets it: Revaluing the Economic and Social Benefits of Commercial Television.* Available at: https://www.freetv.com.au/wp-content/uploads/2022/09/Everybody-gets-it-2022.pdf (Accessed: 2 April 2024).

Dixon, E. (2023). 'Olympics rights shared by EBU and Warner Bros Discovery in Europe until 2032', *SportsProMedia*, 16 January. Available at: https://www.sportspromedia.com/news/olympic-games-warner-bros-discovery-ebu-tv-broadcast-rights-europe-ioc-2026-2032/ (Accessed: 6 April 2024).

Enten, H. (2024). 'Forget Taylor Swift: Peacock's NFL game is the real talking point of America's favorite sport', *CNN*, 13 January. Available at: https://edition.cnn.com/2024/01/13/sport/peacocks-nfl-game-analysis-spt-intl/index.html (Accessed: 10 April 2024).

European Commission (2022). Application and implementation of AVMSD. Available at: https://digital-strategy.ec.europa.eu/en/policies/application-and-implementation-avmsd (Accessed: 6 April 2024).

Evens, T., Iosifidis, P., and Smith, P. (2013). *The Political Economy of Television Sports Rights.* Basingstoke: Palgrave Macmillan.

FIFA (2022). FIFA World Cup Qatar 2022™ in numbers. Available at: https://publications.fifa.com/en/annual-report-2022/tournaments-and-events/fifa-world-cup-quatar-2022/fifa-world-cup-qatar-2022-in-numbers/ (Accessed: 5 April 2024).

Foxtel (2022). *Foxtel Group: Submission in Response to the Review of the Anti-Siphoning Scheme – Consultation Paper.* Available at: https://www.infrastructure.gov.au/sites/default/files/documents/assr–foxtel-group.pdf (Accessed: 4 April 2024).

Free TV Australia (2022). *Submission by Free TV Australia: Review of the Anti-Siphoning Scheme: Response to the Consultation Paper.* Available at: https://www.infrastructure.gov.au/sites/default/files/documents/assr–free-tv-australia.pdf (Accessed: 7 April 2024).

House of Commons (Digital, Culture, Media and Sport Committee) (2022). *Major Cultural and Sporting Events.* Available at: https://committees.parliament.uk/publications/9285/documents/160442/default/ (Accessed: 8 April 2024).

House of Commons (Culture, Media and Sport Committee) (2023a). *Draft Media Bill: Government Responses to the Committee's Twelfth and Thirteenth Reports of Session 2022–23.* Available at: https://committees.parliament.uk/publications/42125/documents/209447/default/ (Accessed: 8 April 2024).

House of Commons (2023b). Pre-legislative scrutiny of Draft Media Bill: Response from COBA to DCMS Select Committee. Available at: https://committees.parliament.uk/writtenevidence/121336/html/ (Accessed: 7 April 2024).

House of Lords (Communications Committee) (2019). *Public Service Broadcasting: As Vital as Ever.* Available at: https://publications.parliament.uk/pa/ld201919/ldselect/ldcomuni/16/16.pdf (Accessed: 4 April 2024).

ICASA (Independent Communications Authority of South Africa) (2018). Draft Sports Broadcasting Services Amendment Regulations 2018. Available at: https://www.icasa.org.za/legislation-and-regulations/draft-sports-broadcasting-services-amendment-regulations-2018 (Accessed: 6 April 2024).

ICASA (Independent Communications Authority of South Africa) (2021). *Sports Broadcasting Services Amendment Regulations 2021.* Available at: https://www.ica

sa.org.za/legislation-and-regulations/sports-broadcasting-services-amendment-regulations-2021 (Accessed: 3 April 2024).
Impey, S. (2019). 'SABC lands deal to air Rugby World Cup final', *SportsProMedia*, 29 October. Available at: https://www.sportspromedia.com/news/sabc-supersport-2019-rugby-world-cup-final-tv-rights-south-africa (Accessed: 7 April 2024).
Jones, R. (2023). 'French Open expands Amazon's night session coverage with new four-year domestic deal', *SportsProMedia*, 31 March. Available at: https://www.sportspromedia.com/news/french-open-roland-garros-amazon-prime-video-streaming-rights-2024/ (Accessed: 7 April 2024).
Kunz, W. (2020). *The Political Economy of Sports Television*. London: Routledge.
Laghate, G. (2017). 'Prasar Bharti cannot air "national importance games" on private cable, DTH: Supreme Court', *The Economic Times*, 22 August. Available at: https://economictimes.indiatimes.com/news/politics-and-nation/prasar-bharti-cannot-air-national-importance-games-on-private-cable-dth-supreme-court/articleshow/60177486.cms (Accessed: 2 August 2024).
Laghate, G. (2018). 'It's not cricket! I&B plan for DD spooks sports broadcasters', *The Economic Times*, 20 October. Available at: https://economictimes.indiatimes.com/industry/media/entertainment/media/its-not-cricket-ib-plan-for-dd-spooks-sports-broadcasters/articleshow/66289576.cms (Accessed: 2 August 2024).
Mance, H. (2015). 'Discovery pays €1.3bn for rights to Olympics in Europe', *Financial Times*, 29 June. Available at: https://www.ft.com/content/8e6c4798-1e57-11e5-ab0f-6bb9974f25d0 (Accessed: 8 April 2024).
Mann, C. (2013). 'Foxtel seeks sports "anti-siphoning" shake-up', *Advanced Television*, 25 November. Available at: https://advanced-television.com/2013/11/25/foxtel-seeks-sports-anti-siphoning-shake-up/ (Accessed: 7 April 2024).
Mann, C. (2023). 'EBU, WBD secure 2026-32 Olympic rights', *Advanced Television*, 16 January. Available at: https://advanced-television.com/2023/01/16/ebu-wbd-secure-2026-32-olympic-rights/ (Accessed: 9 April 2024).
McCaskill, S. (2023a). 'Sky Sports secures ATP and WTA tennis rights until 2029 in UK, Germany and Italy', *SportsProMedia*, 24 November. Available at: https://www.sportspromedia.com/broadcast-ott/media-rights/sky-sports-atp-wta-tennis-tv/ (Accessed: 8 April 2024).
McCaskill, S. (2023b). 'Amazon scores live rights to Cricket World Cup and ICC tournaments in Australia', *SportsProMedia*, 4 December. Available at: https://www.sportspromedia.com/broadcast-ott/media-rights/amazon-prime-icc-cricket-world-cup-streaming-australia/ (Accessed: 8 April 2024).
McCaskill, S. (2024). 'Live sport helps Peacock hit 31m subscribers and narrow losses', *SportsProMedia*, 26 January. Available at: https://www.sportspromedia.com/news/live-sport-helps-peacock-hit-31m-subscribers-and-narrow-losses/ (Accessed: 9 April 2024).
MIB (Ministry of Information and Broadcasting) (2018). Feedback/comments on Draft Sports Broadcasting Signals (Mandatory Sharing with Prasar Bharati) (Amendment) Bill, 2018. Available at: https://mib.gov.in/sites/default/files/Noticedated17october2018onwebsite.pdf (Accessed: 7 April 2024).
MIB (Ministry of Information and Broadcasting) (2022). Notification: Sporting events of national importance. Available at: https://mib.gov.in/sites/default/files/Notification%20of%20sporting%20events%20of%20national%20importance%20.PDF (Accessed: 9 April 2024).
Miller, T. (2014). Before, During, and After the Neoliberal Moment: Media, Sports, Policy, Citizenship. In: J. Scherer and D. Rowe (eds.), *Sport, Public Broadcasting, and Cultural Citizenship: Signal Lost?* (pp. 30–47). London: Routledge.

Mphahlele, M. (2020). 'Icasa sets target for news sports broadcast regulations', *Times Live*, 16 March. Available at: https://www.timeslive.co.za/sport/2020-03-16-icasa-sets-target-for-news-sports-broadcast-regulations/ (Accessed: 7 April 2024).

Nicolaou, A. (2024). 'Super Bowl most watched US broadcast since Apollo moon landing', *Financial Times*, 13 February. Available at: https://www.ft.com/content/c3e2585c-db0f-4649-b618-df08fbe38682 (Accessed: 10 April 2024).

Ofcom (2018). Listed Events: Identifying television services that are free-to-view and widely available: Consultation. Available at: https://www.ofcom.org.uk/__data/assets/pdf_file/0022/124447/consulation-listed-events.pdf (Accessed: 8 April 2024).

Ofcom (2019). Listed events: Identifying services that are free-to-view and widely available: Statement. Available at: https://www.ofcom.org.uk/__data/assets/pdf_file/0020/155090/listed-events-statement.pdf (Accessed: 7 April 2024).

Ofcom (2021). *Small Screen: Big Debate. Recommendations to Government on the Future of Public Service Media*. Available at: https://www.smallscreenbigdebate.co.uk/__data/assets/pdf_file/0023/221954/statement-future-of-public-service-media.pdf (Accessed: 9 April 2024).

Oxford Economics (2024). *The Economic Impact of the Sports Activities of Public Service Media*. Available at: https://www.oxfordeconomics.com/resource/the-economic-impact-of-the-sports-activities-of-public-service-media/ (Accessed: 9 April 2024).

Ray, C. (2021). 'Icasa's superficial regulation amendments for sports broadcasting changes nothing', *Daily Maverick*, 16 April. Available at: https://www.dailymaverick.co.za/article/2021-04-16-icasas-superficial-regulation-amendments-for-sports-broadcasting-changes-nothing/ (Accessed: 4 April 2024).

Rogan, M. and Potter, K. (2021). *All to Play for: How Sport Can Reboot our Future*. London: Ebury Press.

Rowe, D., Tiffen, R., and Hutchins, B. (2023). Keeping it Free: Sport Television and Public Policy in Australia. *Journal of Digital Media and Policy*, 14 (1), pp. 103–123.

Scherer, J. and Rowe, D. (eds.) (2014). *Sport, Public Broadcasting, and Cultural Citizenship: Signal Lost?*London: Routledge.

Scherer, J. and Sam, M. P. (2012). Public Broadcasting, Sport and Cultural Citizenship: Sky's the Limit in New Zealand? *Media, Culture and Society*, 34 (1), pp. 101–111.

Scherer, J. and Whitson, D. (2009). Public Broadcasting, Sport and Cultural Citizenship: The Future of Sport on the Canadian Broadcasting Corporation. *International Review for the Sociology of Sport*, 44 (2/3), pp. 213–229.

Sim, J. (2023). 'Cricket World Cup: Disney Star sets Indian cricket TV audience record', *SportsProMedia*, 27 November. Available at: https://www.sportspromedia.com/news/cricket-world-cup-2023-disney-star-tv-record-viewership/ (Accessed: 5 April 2024).

Sky Group (2023). 'EFL announces landmark broadcasting deal with Sky Sports', 5 May. Available at: https://www.skygroup.sky/en-gb/article/efl-announces-landmark-broadcasting-deal-with-sky-sports (Accessed: 7 April 2024).

Smith, P. (2010). The Politics of Sports Rights: The Regulation of Television Sports Rights in the UK. *Convergence*, 16 (3), pp. 316–333.

Smith, P., Evens, T., and Iosifidis, P. (2015). The Regulation of Television Sports Broadcasting: A Comparative Analysis. *Media, Culture & Society*, 37 (5), pp. 720–736.

Spangler, T. (2024). 'Amazon snags exclusive rights to NFL playoff game for 2024–25 season', *Variety*, 9 February. Available at: https://variety.com/2024/digital/news/amazon-nfl-playoff-game-exclusive-rights-1235906385/ (Accessed: 1 April 2024).

Sports Business (2021). 'Foxtel's five-year netball rights deal prompts fiery response from incumbent Nine', *SportBusiness*, 3 February. Available at: https://www.sport

business.com/news/foxtels-five-year-netball-rights-deal-prompts-fiery-response-from-incumbent-nine/ (Accessed: 9 July 2021).

SportsProMedia (2023). 'EFL agrees record UK£935m Sky Sports rights deal that keeps Saturday blackout in place', *SportsProMedia*, 9 May. Available at: https://www.sportspromedia.com/news/efl-championship-l1-l2-carabao-cup-tv-rights-deal-sky-sports-2024-29-saturday-blackout/ (Accessed: 7 April 2024).

Szymanski, S. (2006). Why Have Premium Sports Rights Migrated to Pay-tv in Europe but Not in the US? In: C. Jeanrenaud and S. Késenne (eds.), *The Economics of Sport and the Media* (pp. 148–159). Northampton: Edward Elgar.

Vaidialingam, A. (2017). 'Part II: Union of India v. BCCI – "Doosra" from the Supreme Court on Broadcast of Cricket Matches by Prasar Bharti', *SpicyIP: Decoding Indian Intellectual Property Law*, 10 October. Available at: https://spicyip.com/2017/10/part-ii-union-of-india-v-bcci-doosra-from-the-supreme-court-on-broadcast-of-cricket-matches-by-prasar-bharti.html (Accessed: 24 April 2024).

Waterson, J. (2021). 'BBC Olympics coverage misses events after loss of TV rights', *The Guardian*, 25 July. Available at: https://www.theguardian.com/media/2021/jul/25/bbc-olympics-coverage-misses-events-after-selling-tv-rights (Accessed: 8 April 2024).

Women's Sport Trust (2021). *Closing the Visibility Gap: Growing the Value of Women's Sport through the Impact of Visibility*. Available at: https://www.womenssporttrust.com/closing-the-visibility-gap/ (Accessed: 8 April 2024).

Woodhouse, J. (2022). Broadcasting: Listed sporting events. Available at: https://researchbriefings.files.parliament.uk/documents/SN00802/SN00802.pdf (Accessed: 7 April 2024).

Woodhouse, J. (2023). *Media Bill*. Available at: https://researchbriefings.files.parliament.uk/documents/CBP-9885/CBP-9885.pdf (Accessed: 5 April 2024).

Ziegler, M. (2023). 'Rival broadcasters want same access as BBC and ITV to "listed events"', *The Times*, 7 September. Available at: https://www.thetimes.co.uk/sport/football/article/rival-broadcasters-want-same-access-as-bbc-and-itv-to-listed-events-dr9hz9tx7 (Accessed: 6 April 2024).

CONCLUSION

Using a range of national and regional examples, this book has analysed how the rise of sports streaming has shaped (and is shaping) the contemporary sports media rights market. It has highlighted how the sports rights market is in the midst of a period of change, with online delivery offering new market entrants, such as DAZN, Amazon, and Apple, as well as established pay-tv broadcasters and public service media (PSM) organisations, a new means to deliver content to sports fans. At the same time, however, the underlying argument made throughout this book is that this period of change is best understood as a process of evolution, rather than revolution. With this in mind, it is worth emphasising several key points, which, taken together, amount to defining characteristics of the sports media rights market. First, the contemporary sports media rights market is still largely defined by traditional national/regional exclusive live rights deals. Chapter 2 detailed how the global sports rights market is, in fact, a host of different nationally, or regionally, focused markets, reflecting particular national/regional sporting traditions and preferences. With one or two notable exceptions this remains the case. Despite the market entry of global digital players, such as Amazon, there has been no discernible move towards large-scale regional, or even global, rights deals.

A second defining feature of the sports media rights market in the age of streaming and platformisation is that exclusive live rights to premium content (e.g. top-tier domestic football leagues in Europe; IPL cricket in India; NFL and NBA in the US, etc.) remain a key source of market power within national pay-tv and wider communications/entertainment markets. If anything, in the age of streaming the particular characteristics of sports content (i.e. unpredictability, the importance of live viewing, and the intense commitment of sports fans) (see Chapter 2) make it more valuable than ever.

DOI: 10.4324/9781003401988-13

This is reflected in the enormous sums media organisations continue to pay to acquire premium sports rights in national markets across the world. Furthermore, as discussed in Chapters 1 and 3, the fact that new entrants, such as DAZN and Amazon, have been willing to invest so heavily in acquiring premium (and other) sports rights is testament to the strategic value attached to live sports coverage within an increasingly competitive media environment. At least partly as a result, to date at least, the sports media rights market has not witnessed a shift away from high-value (temporal) deals for exclusive live rights to the revenue-sharing approach commonly employed within other online media markets (e.g. online advertising) by major players, such as YouTube, Facebook, and Amazon. On the contrary, as ever, the main challenge faced by commercial media organisations who invest in sports rights is how to generate sufficient revenue to cover the high cost of rights acquisition and achieve profitability. Traditionally, pay-tv broadcasters (e.g. ESPN, Canal +, Sky, etc.) have done this by bundling sports content with other entertainment channels. As detailed in Chapter 3, particularly in the US, but in other national markets too, 'cord-cutting' has begun to undermine the profitability of this approach, with many consumers opting to subscribe to one or more, often (at least individually) cheaper, subscription video-on-demand (SVoD) services, rather than a traditional pay-tv bundle. However, there is little, if any, evidence to suggest that media organisations are able to profit from the 'unbundled' sale of sports content in isolation. Most notably, to date, DAZN has made significant losses attempting to pursue this approach, while other new entrants, such as Amazon and Apple, have looked to bundle sports content with other entertainment and/or related services (e.g. home shopping). At the same time, established pay-tv operators are increasingly seeking to reinvent the conventional sport plus entertainment bundle by bundling together their content with access to their own and other online platforms, such as Amazon and Netflix. In this sense, over the last decade or so, the sports media rights market has witnessed the unbundling of sports content followed by attempts (with varying degrees of success) to establish a new (profitable) bundle. At least partly as a result, the distinction between new (digital) entrants and established pay-tv broadcasters is becoming increasingly blurred. For example, in Italy and the UK, as well as other national markets, DAZN has agreed distribution deals with the established pay-tv broadcaster, Sky (Vivarelli, 2022), while Sky has launched a comprehensive online sports streaming platform, Sky Sports+, akin to DAZN (McCaskill, 2024). In the sports media rights market, as well as the wider television industry, the process of platformisation seems set to continue unabated.

A third area where the sports media rights market has seen evolution, rather than revolution, is in the way that sports organisations distribute (and monetise) their rights. Chapter 5 detailed how, despite seemingly endless speculation, major sports events/competitions (e.g. the Premier League) have not abandoned conventional rights deals with media organisations in preference for selling content direct-to-fans (D2F) via an online platform. For most sports organisations, the advantage of guaranteed income from a rights deal with an established media organisation is far more attractive and less costly/risky than attempting to launch a D2F platform. The D2F platforms that have been launched have been largely used to supplement conventional rights deals by providing additional content (e.g. archive and behind-the-scenes footage) for committed fans and/or to serve fans in international markets without an existing national media deal. In this way, D2F platforms have proved most valuable for minority sports, such as rally car racing. For larger sports organisations, the potential to use a D2F platform to distribute live (premium) content has proved most useful as a means to deter commercial media organisations from reducing the value of their bids for rights.

A fourth area of continuity in the contemporary sports media rights market is the continued need for competition regulation (see Chapter 7). Given the high cost and strategic value of premium rights, national sports media rights markets are likely to continue to be dominated by a handful of major media organisations. As a result, intervention from competition regulators is still likely to be required to ensure fair and effective competition in the sports media rights market and wider related pay-tv/communications markets. However, as discussed in Chapter 7, the application of competition law to the sports media rights market has long been problematic, with remedies focused on increasing competition in the (upstream) sports rights market leading to a fragmentation of rights across numerous broadcasters in the (downstream) programming market, and thus increased costs/inconvenience for viewers. If anything, the fragmentation of rights has been accentuated by the rise of sports streaming, highlighting the fact that regulators need to do more to ensure that consumers benefit from competition for sports rights, as well as sports organisations.

With the development of the internet into an increasingly reliable medium for the distribution of live audio-visual content, piracy has become a defining feature of the contemporary sports media rights market. As discussed in Chapter 6, online sports piracy is ubiquitous in most, if not all, national markets. However, despite the frequent warnings of media/sports organisations, there is no evidence to suggest that online sports piracy will lead to a collapse in the value of the sports media rights market. To at least some degree, this is a result of the legal and technical measures employed by media/sports organisations to tackle online piracy, in a 'never-ending game of whack-a-mole' with online sports pirates (see Chapter 6). As argued in Chapter 6, providing easily accessible and affordable legal routes to view sports content is arguably the best long-term solution to online sports piracy. Nevertheless, this should not obscure the fact that the relatively limited impact of online sports piracy on the value of rights is another (the fifth) area where the sports media rights market has seen continuity, as much as change.

Much of this book has focused on the commercial value of the sports media rights market. In fact, it is worth stressing that the rise of sports streaming has for the most part furthered the commercial interests of both media and sports organisations. In this sense, the rise of sports streaming can be seen as the latest stage in the long-established symbiotic relationship between media and sports organisations – an overarching example of continuity in the age of streaming and platformisation (Boyle and Haynes, 2009; Rowe, 2004). Just as significantly, however, coverage of sport on free-to-air television and via the online platforms of PSM continues to be a valuable source of cultural citizenship, and a sixth key defining feature of the sports media rights market. Chapter 4 details how PSM in Europe and beyond continue to play an important role in the contemporary sports media rights market. While PSM account for only a relatively small fraction of total expenditure on sports rights, in many countries, most notably the BBC in the UK, they account for a far larger proportion of the total viewing of sport on television. Perhaps most notably, by providing live free-to-air coverage of major sporting events and/or competitions, such as the FIFA football World Cup (men and women), PSM are able to bring communities and/or the nation together for a shared viewing experience. More generally, PSM coverage of sport (live and recorded) ensures access to a range of different sports for all, including lower-income groups. Faced with the escalating cost of sports rights and a squeeze on their own finances, from around the 2010s, PSM have adopted a number of different rights strategies, most notably increased coverage and promotion of women's sport via both traditional broadcast services and online platforms. At least partly as a result, the last decade has witnessed a significant increase in the popularity of women's sport. In no small part, this is testament to the ability of PSM to promote cultural citizenship and underlines the value that public exposure via PSM continues to offer for sports organisations, particularly minority and/or traditionally under-represented sports, like women's sport.

For PSM to be able to continue to enhance cultural citizenship in such ways requires increased political support from national governments. To begin with, following a decade or so of budget reductions (see Chapter 4), PSM organisations require much greater financial support in order to be able to continue to offer a range of popular and minority sports (as well as to fulfil their wider public service remits). Just as importantly, the continued ability of PSM to enhance cultural citizenship is also dependent on the existence of major events legislation. In numerous European countries, as well as some beyond Europe (e.g. Australia, South Africa, and India), major events legislation effectively ensures that certain major national/international sporting events, such as the Olympic Games, remain available on free-to-air television. In these countries, this is another (the seventh) defining feature of the sports media rights market. Chapter 8 details the continued importance of major events legislation as a way to prevent major sports events migrating from free-to-air television to pay-tv and/or SVoD services. Focusing on recent government-led reviews in the UK and Australia, Chapter 8 details how in both countries the scope of major events legislation has been extended to prevent international or national-based streaming services from securing the exclusive live rights to listed events. However, these reviews were both characterised by a reluctance to extend major events legislation to incorporate digital (including on-demand) rights. As a result, the changes introduced are likely to prove only a short-term solution to ensuring the effectiveness of major events legislation in the age of streaming and platformisation. A future challenge for policy makers will no doubt be to resist pressure from (at least some) media and sports organisations to remove, or at least water down, existing major events legislation.

Overall then, the rise of sports streaming has certainly heralded plenty of eye-catching examples of change in the sports media rights market, including the emergence of new players, like Amazon and DAZN, and the launch of D2F platforms by sports organisations, such as Formula One and La Liga (Spain). However, in this book we have detailed how the established patterns of economic and political organisation that shape the contours of the sports media rights market remain remarkably persistent. On this basis, the last decade or so is best understood as a period of evolution for the sports media rights market, rather than revolution.

References

Boyle, R. and Haynes, R. (2009). *PowerPlay: Sport, the Media and Popular Culture.* Edinburgh: Edinburgh University Press.

McCaskill, S. (2024). 'Sky Sports+ promises up to 100 simultaneous live streams ahead of August launch for EFL season', *SportsProMedia*, 8 May. Available at: https://www.sportspromedia.com/news/sky-sports-plus-efl-sport-streaming/ (Accessed: 5 June 2024).

Rowe, D. (2004). *Sport, Culture and the Media: The Unruly Trinity.* Maidenhead, UK: Open University Press.

Vivarelli, N. (2022). 'Sky seals key Serie A soccer deal with DAZN in Italy', *Variety*, 4 August. Available at: https://variety.com/2022/tv/global/sky-soccer-dazn-serie-a-1235333629/ (Accessed: 5 June 2024).

INDEX

Page numbers in **bold** indicate Tables.